Breeding Latin American Tigers

Breeding Latin American Tigers

OPERATIONAL PRINCIPLES FOR REHABILITATING INDUSTRIAL POLICIES

Robert Devlin
Graciela Moguillansky

A COPUBLICATION OF THE UNITED NATIONS
ECONOMIC COMMISSION FOR LATIN AMERICA
AND THE CARIBBEAN AND THE WORLD BANK

ISBN: 978-0-8213-8688-0
eISBN: 978-0-8213-8744-3
DOI: 10.1596/978-0-8213-8688-0

Library of Congress Cataloging-in-Publication Data has been applied for.

Cover design by Drew Fasick.

Latin American Development Forum Series

This series was created in 2003 to promote debate, disseminate information and analysis, and convey the excitement and complexity of the most topical issues in economic and social development in Latin America and the Caribbean. It is sponsored by the Inter-American Development Bank, the United Nations Economic Commission for Latin America and the Caribbean, the Brookings Institution, and the World Bank. The manuscripts chosen for publication represent the highest quality in each institution's research and activity output and have been selected for their relevance to the academic community, policy makers, researchers, and interested readers.

Advisory Committee Members

Titles in the Latin American Development Forum Series

Breeding Latin American Tigers: Operational Principles for Rehabilitating Industrial Policies (2011) by Robert Devlin and Graciela Moguillansky

New Policies for Mandatory Defined Contribution Pensions: Industrial Organization Models and Investment Products (2010) by Gregorio Impavido, Esperanza Lasagabaster, and Manuel García-Huitrón

The Quality of Life in Latin American Cities: Markets and Perception (2010) by Eduardo Lora, Andrew Powell, Bernard M. S. van Praag, and Pablo Sanguinetti, editors

Discrimination in Latin America: An Economic Perspective (2010) by Hugo Ñopo, Alberto Chong, and Andrea Moro, editors

The Promise of Early Childhood Development in Latin America and the Caribbean (2010) by Emiliana Vegas and Lucrecia Santibáñez

Job Creation in Latin America and the Caribbean: Trends and Policy Challenges (2009) by Carmen Pagés, Gaëlle Pierre, and Stefano Scarpetta

China's and India's Challenge to Latin America: Opportunity or Threat? (2009) by Daniel Lederman, Marcelo Olarreaga, and Guillermo E. Perry, editors

Does the Investment Climate Matter? Microeconomic Foundations of Growth in Latin America (2009) by Pablo Fajnzylber, José Luis Guasch, and J. Humberto López, editors

Measuring Inequality of Opportunities in Latin America and the Caribbean (2009) by Ricardo de Paes Barros, Francisco H. G. Ferreira, José R. Molinas Vega, and Jaime Saavedra Chanduvi

Globalization and Development: A Latin American and Caribbean Perspective (2003) by José Antonio Ocampo and Juan Martin, editors

Is Geography Destiny? Lessons from Latin America (2003) by John Luke Gallup, Alejandro Gaviria, and Eduardo Lora

About the Authors

The research and writing for this book was done while Robert Devlin was a Senior Economist and Regional Advisor at ECLAC (he is currently Director of the Department for Effective Public Management at the Organization of American States) and while Graciela Moguillansky was a Senior Economist in ECLAC's International Trade and Integration Division (she is currently an international consultant).

Contents

Foreword

The magnitude of the global economic and financial crisis, erupting in the second half of 2008, shook experts and public opinion across the world. Unsurprisingly, the economic debate has focused on the international financial crisis and its impact on the real economy. This debate revolved around the short-term mechanisms for confronting the crisis and the best ways to overcome it.

This publication is distinct in that it invites the reader to take a long-term view from the outset and insists on the need to develop a strategic vision of the future for Latin America and the Caribbean. There is a growing consensus in the region that in an era of globalization, the foundations for macroeconomic stability, while necessary, are insufficient for the development of the countries of the region and their economic convergence with the richer countries of the world.

With this in mind, the authors of the book, like Fernando Fajnzylber in his time, turn their attention to a group of successful countries outside the region and the impact that medium- and long-term strategies supported by industrial policies have had on their productive transformation and development.

The importance of this research, which is at the heart of this book, is found not only in the analysis of the strategies themselves, which relate to the economic, political, and cultural context and are impossible to recreate, but also in the common operational principles guiding the public sector's organization for effective formulation and implementation of these strategies.

One of the first points highlighted is the extent and nature of the collaboration between government and the private sector and the influences of this collaboration on the development of long-term strategies and the manner of their implementation through programs and incentives within the framework of a public good. Called "public-private alliances" by the authors, these collaborations are a fundamental topic developed in this publication. The selected case studies show that formulating consensus-based, intelligent strategies, and the institutionally well-governed public-private collaboration that accompanies them, has a close relationship to the effectiveness of the policies and supporting programs.

How is this relevant to Latin America and the Caribbean?

The region has made progress in achieving macroeconomic stability and, given the previous period of debt crisis, in certain aspects of export growth. However, the countries of the region have remained behind their nonregional competitors in productivity growth, export diversification, and the incorporation of added value and knowledge to exports and related activities. This lack of progress introduces a source of vulnerability in the face of unexpected changes in the price of primary commodities and the threat of low-wage competition from emerging countries in Asia, Eastern Europe, and other regions that could reposition themselves in the future. It also explains why countries in Latin America and the Caribbean have been unable to sustain a process of closing the income gap with richer countries of the world.

Although countries outside the region have prioritized the foundations for macroeconomic stability, they have also constantly been using and readjusting strategies and industrial policies designed to climb the hierarchy of world production and exports. Furthermore, following the international crisis, this proactive attitude allowed many country economies to recover quickly and reposition themselves more competitively in the medium and long term.

Regarding Latin America and the Caribbean, the authors point out that, beside the recent economic stimulus to combat the global recession, public programs that aim to promote economic activity and exports frequently constitute "archeological structures" passed down from one government to another, rather than a coherent collection of incentives arising from a strategic vision of the future for productive transformation. Moreover, these programs often do not have the resources available for their implementation, their technical teams lack consolidation, they are beset by excessive politicization, and they are not the outcome of a consistent dialogue with the participation of the private sector. Although many factors can explain the shortcomings in the pace of economic transformation, competitiveness, and export development in Latin America and the Caribbean in relation to competitors, there is a need to pay close attention to the lack of a strategic focus and the transient characteristic of public-private alliances, as well as to the inconsistent efforts to develop the capacity of the state to effectively design and deploy industrial policies that promote economic transformation.

The research findings manifest a concerted effort to examine in depth the "how" of public sector institutional organization for developing and implementing strategies and support programs that address the microeconomic dimensions of productive transformation. The authors observe that these operational details for public sector action are as important as the strategies and policies themselves. Indeed, the uniqueness of the study is its focus on the "how," an area often overlooked in the policy debate.

Last, the relevance of the inductive method used by the authors should be noted. It is through this method and analysis of real experiences that they have been able to identify "operational principles" for public sector organization that can effectively support transformation strategies.

It is undeniable that this publication is a valuable contribution to the debate on industrial policies and public-private alliances as strategic elements necessary to drive Latin America and the Caribbean toward development.

Alicia Bárcena
Executive Secretary
Economic Commission for Latin America and the Caribbean (ECLAC)

Acknowledgments

This book would not have been possible without generous funding from the Economic Commission for Latin America and the Caribbean (ECLAC), the Ibero-American General Secretariat (SEGIB), the Productive Development Corporation (CORFO) of Chile, and the Government of the Republic of Korea. The Leadership Program for Governance and Development (PROLIDER) financed by the Organization of American States (OAS), the Spanish Agency for International Development Cooperation (AECID) and the ECLAC gave us the opportunity to share the findings of our project with various countries.

We would also like to warmly thank the authors of the nonregional case studies who supplied us with their many drafts, answering our many questions: Annette Hester, Antonio Bonet, David O'Donovan, Heikki Kotilainen, Leah Lawrence, Nigel Haworth, Piero Formica, Shankaran Nambiar, Sharon Siddique, Sree Kumar, Terry Cutler, Thomas Andersson, Vladimir Benàček, and Yoo Soo Hong.

We also extend our thanks to the authors of Latin American cases studies: Gustavo Baruj, Ilan Bizberg, María Alejandra Botiva, Luis Chang, Hugo Chávez, José Gómez, Ana María Guerra, Carlos Américo Pacheco, Juan José Palacios, Joseph Ramos, José Segura, and Basil Springer.

We are extremely grateful for the critical and unwavering support shown by a number of individuals: José Luis Machinea, Alicia Bárcena, Enrique Iglesias, Osvaldo Rosales, and Inés Bustillo and Carlos Álvarez from CORFO, the departmental directors and staff at the ECLAC, as well as the ambassadors from the Ministry of Foreign Affairs of Chile, who in one form or another gave us generous words of encouragement and logistical support during the field research and write up process. We received proficient technical assistance from Agustín Cornejo, Alfonso Finot, and Raúl Holz. And finally, the editorial team for the book was patient and professional, feeding us with suggestions that clearly enhanced the final product.

Abbreviations

A*STAR	Agency for Science, Technology and Research (Singapore)
AOSTRA	Alberta Oil Sands Technology and Research Authority
APEC	Asia-Pacific Economic Cooperation
ASEAN	Association of Southeast Asian Nations
DETE	Department of Enterprise, Trade and Employment (Ireland)
ECLAC	Economic Commission for Latin American and the Caribbean, United Nations (CEPAL, in Spanish)
EU	European Union
FDI	foreign direct investment
GDP	gross domestic product
ICT	information and communications technology
IP	industrial policy
ISI	import substitution industrialization
NAFTA	North American Free Trade Agreement
NGO	nongovernmental organization
OECD	Organisation for Economic Co-operation and Development
PDP	Productive Development Policy (Brazil)
PNDII	Second National Development Plan (Brazil)
R&D	research and development
SAR	special administrative region
SMEs	small and medium enterprises
STPC	Science and Technology Policy Council (Finland)
TEKES	Finnish Funding Agency for Technology and Innovation (Finland)
TFP	total factor productivity
UNESCO	United Nations Educational, Scientific, and Cultural Organization
WTO	World Trade Organization

Introduction

As a region Latin America and the Caribbean (hereon Latin America) has not performed well economically. Since the colonial era, notwithstanding episodic growth spurts by some countries, the region has watched as successive countries in other parts of the world have raised their gross domestic product (GDP) per capita, leapfrogging past Latin America on the world economic stage. Several of these countries moved out of dire poverty to reach the upper echelons of world income. The one Latin American country to stand above this trend, Argentina, had the distinction of rising to the ranks of the richest countries in the world at the beginning of the 1900s, only to slip steadily to an undistinguished middle-income status in subsequent decades.

Beginning in the last half of the 20th century, the primary means by which countries successfully engaged in a process of catch-up with rich countries was by strengthening and improving the quality of their integration into the international economy. In this context, export development was a major tool to stimulate investment, innovation, and growth. The role of exports was boosted by the unprecedented growth of international trade and finance. These countries each approached international integration and export development in a different way, however. To generalize, some gave priority to developing industrial capacities in the domestic market and then, after achieving some threshold of competitive strength, ventured more aggressively into international export markets. This approach was more feasible for countries with large domestic markets. Other catch-up countries, with very small domestic markets, proactively upgraded their economies, exports, and growth, all while being very integrated with international markets from the start. Still others mixed the two approaches, exporting existing comparative advantages but also at the same time proactively working to provide conditions for the birth of new sectors and activities in the domestic market that were eventually encouraged (often quite quickly) to become internationally competitive and contribute to export development.

Today private markets and firms dominate world economic activity. If firms are to have the necessary capacities to be agents of economic transformation and growth, many requirements and conditions must be met. In addition to an enabling macroeconomic environment, firms need, among other things, access to information about markets and probable future trends; incentives to search for and invest in new, sophisticated, and risky activities; the ability to innovate through imitation or creative adaptation of technologies for commercial application; access to credit; an educational system that generates a supply of appropriately skilled labor; availability of essential public goods; a facilitating business environment; sectoral coordination and development of networks and clusters; and techniques of marketing and product differentiation.

Market forces do not necessarily spontaneously generate effective responses to all these challenges, especially in developing countries where markets and institutions are seriously incomplete. In Latin America in particular, all these ingredients, coupled with government failures, have been binding constraints on growth to one degree or another, depending on the country and circumstances.

The last 25 years of public policy in Latin America have been dominated by Washington Consensus–type adjustments focused on consolidation of macroeconomic balances and market-oriented institutional reforms that strongly discouraged state interventions in productive activities. Now, however, given disillusionment with the consensus (where government became a kind of inferior good), Latin America is showing an emerging interest in more systemic, proactive public interventions that can assist the private sector in overcoming structural constraints on innovation, productive transformation, and export development. In principle, the shift toward acceptance of a more proactive state— augmented by the response to the great world economic recession of 2008–09—is a useful step toward pragmatism in public policy. Indeed, a more proactive public policy would seem to be a reasonable objective for Latin America, because the "visible hand" of public interventions can be seen in many success stories in Asia, Oceania, Europe, and even North America. So modern precedents exist for more proactive public policy in Latin America aimed at supporting economic transformation and growth. The question now is what type of government intervention will be successful and how will it be achieved effectively.

In the interwar years and again in the early post–World War II period, governments in Latin America actively intervened in the economy. That intervention involved a top-down, government-dominated approach geared toward inward-looking import substitution industrialization with public enterprises playing a big role. Efficiency and growth-effective international integration were not primary objectives in the region as they are today. This era of import substitution industrialization has been unfairly demonized; important advances were made in development, some of which were unfortunately dismantled by the Washington Consensus reforms (Ocampo 2006). Nevertheless, comparatively speaking, the region's post-1950 economic growth performance was undistinguished. We think that this traditional approach to state intervention must not be resurrected in the current era of renewed interest in a proactive state.

An extensive theoretical and case-based literature supports state interventions that promote productive transformation and export development. In recent years thinking by those receptive to this type of selective state intervention has evolved into what some term a "modern" industrial policy. This approach stresses that the most successful strategies and interventions emerge out of a social *process* of close alliance between the public and private sectors (the scope of the latter varying depending on the relevance of different categories of stakeholders to the objectives to be met). In the fast-changing and competitive world of globalization, each party has (or potentially could generate) some of the information necessary to identify market, institutional, and attitudinal constraints that should be addressed by support strategies but also less insight than can be generated by joining forces and undertaking a coordinated effort. Moreover, the governance of the alliance must function to preserve the public welfare, meaning that while the state should closely collaborate with the private sector, it must be subject to procedures and mechanisms to avoid being captured by special interests.

Ideas abound about what constitutes sound industrial policies and so-called best-practice support programs. But the literature has not yet developed the more detailed picture of the "how" of industrial polices—the organization of the social process of an alliance and the internal organization of the government for leading that process and formulating and implementing public strategies to support productive transformation. That "how" is critical. Yes, attention to good policy is important. But attention to the social process and organization necessary for arriving at a strategy and making it effectively operational—as well as being alert to the need for midstream corrections—is equally or more important to produce successful outcomes.

This book will examine the "how" of 10 countries outside Latin America that have experienced contemporary processes of sustained catch-up or that have done better than Latin America countries with a similar endowment of resources.[1] Although they differ in many ways in their history, culture, political system, economic structure, level of development, and geographic location, these 10 countries share a common element: the authorities have actively applied a medium- to long-term development strategy (either with an economy-wide focus or with a more limited focus on specific sectors or activities). These strategies, although differing in scope, specificity, and depth of content, have increasingly been based on a vision that goes well beyond the macroeconomic adjustment and liberalization issues that were the focus of much of the Washington Consensus era. Most of these countries have been working proactively to forge a forward-looking vision that can guide medium- and long-term strategies with specific goals supported by public microeconomic incentives that directly stimulate structural change and productivity growth.

These strategies are generally not a creation of the central government alone but instead arise out of public-private alliances involving elements of political leadership, civil society participation, and consensus building or, at the least, public understanding. This process has taken different forms from one country to another with different degrees of effectiveness. While the success of these strategies hinges on politics and technical design, no less important is the existence of an appropriate public institutional framework capable of execution. Rather than emphasizing efficiency in all aspects, such a framework focuses on coherence and effectiveness in achieving established goals, the possibility of experimenting with incentives, flexibility, error correction, and the strategy's ability to transcend the bounds of political cycles.

This book does not aim to demonstrate a causal relationship between the strategies and their content, on the one hand, and, on the other, the outcomes in these countries as they affect structural change and economic growth. We do think, however, that the association between the two that is evident in our success cases (and in others), coupled with the awkwardness of negative critiques, is a persuasive argument for Latin America to experiment more systematically with medium- to long-term development strategies supported by modern industrial policy. In any event, our fundamental aim is simply to report on and gain insights from our extraregional success cases concerning the "what" and, most of all, the "how" of formulating and implementing successful strategies and the associated public institutional structures supporting them. The focus on the illustration of the "how" is one of the novelties of our study.

Methodologically speaking, we are fully aware that Latin America should not try to replicate the strategies, institutions, or processes of our extraregional success cases. Clearly, there are too many cultural, political, economic, and historical specificities for that to be possible or wise. Nonetheless, when reduced to its bare substance, the organizational operation of the public sector and the alliances, albeit quite different in form, is quite similar in the most successful countries. Hence, raising the specific experiences of institutional organization and operational processes—particularly in terms of the "how"—to a perspective with more abstract dimensions allows us to detect generic operational principles on organizational issues. Part 1 presents 11 principles inductively developed from our extraregional case studies. Moreover, we concretely illustrate the principles by drawing on the different ways that our success cases followed them.

Our analysis was supported by 10 background case studies of our successful countries that we commissioned in 2007. Although the principles hold through time, these studies are largely a snapshot of the "how" in countries where the "how" is in continous institutional evolution.[2] The major methodological stress was on digging deep into the institutionally driven "how" of effectively organizing the public sector for formulating development strategies, better governing alliances, and executing related support policies and programs. To maintain a manageable focus, we limited the analysis of strategies and organization primarily to those dealing with export development and the associated public agents and processes for attracting foreign direct investment, making small and medium enterprises competitive in world markets and supporting export promotion and innovation. While circumscribed, our focus on export development nevertheless has the benefit of aiming at a central dimension of the countries' strategy for economic transformation.[3]

After examining the "how" of the extraregional success cases through the prisim of our 11 principles, we then examine, in part 2 of the book, how well nine Latin American and Caribbean countries fare measured against these principles.

As for the specific structure of the book, chapter 1 reviews the current situation of Latin America, which historically has been a laggard in economic performance. Chapter 2 introduces the first principle: the urgency of developing a medium- to long-term strategy for productive transformation based on industrial policies. The chapter examines the debate about industrial policies and outlines why we think that modern arguments for industrial policies are compelling for Latin America. With this motivation in mind, the chapter then examines the nature of the strategies deployed over the decades by our 10 extraregional success cases.

Chapter 3 focuses on the principle that strategies for productive transformation with modern industrial policies should rest on effective, locally grown public-private alliances. The chapter creates a typology of the alliances in our success cases, analyzing and illustrating them in some detail. Chapter 4 introduces and illustrates principles 3–6, which focus on the "how" of public sector leadership in the public-private alliance and the fomulation and execution of strategies. Chapter 5 presents and illustrates principles 7–11, which are concerned with the public sector management of support programs and incentives.

Chapter 6 shifts the focus to Latin America. It reviews the past and current nature of development strategies in the region, pointing to their strengths and weaknesses as tools for guiding productive transformation. Using concepts developed in part 1, the chapter then critically examines the role and nature of emerging public-private alliances that support the contemporary strategies. In chapter 7 we follow the path of principles 3–11 to critically evaluate the nature of public sector leadership in strategy execution and the modes for managing programs and incentives. Finally, chapter 8 presents our central conclusions, which suggest that while some countries in Latin America have been planting the seeds of these 11 principles gleaned from our extraregional success cases, they still have considerable work to do.

Notes

1. Seven of our country cases—Finland, Ireland, the Republic of Korea, Malaysia, Singapore, Spain, and the Czech Republic (the last as a recent market economy)—achieved catch-up after 1960. Sweden caught up with the richer countries well before 1950. Australia and New Zealand also became relatively rich early on, but in recent decades these two countries have lagged significantly behind other advanced countries, although they have generally done better than South American countries also rich in natural resources. We also examined two subnational cases, one of an alliance in one of Spain's autonomous communities and another of innovation in hydrocarbon sector in Alberta, Canada (see annexes 4A and 4B).

2. Hence the illustrations of the organizational principles in the book, including those for Latin America, are time bound at 2007–08, with only selective updates.

3. Digging into the "how" was not easy because the authors of our background papers were more accustomed, as is usually the case in social sciences, to analyzing the "what."

Reference

Ocampo, José Antonio. 2006. "Latin America and the World Economy in the Long Twentieth Century." In *The Long Twentieth Century, The Great Divergence: Hegemony, Uneven Development and Global Inequality,* ed. K. S. Jomo. New Delhi: Oxford University Press.

Part I

Operational Principles for Effective Public Management of Industrial Policies

1

The Latin American Laggards

Development is often described as a process by which a country's per capita income grows to "catch up" with that of "leading" rich countries. A corollary is that over any long period of time the more backward a country is when it starts the development process, the greater the potential for rapid advance that can close the income gap with lead countries.[1] History has exhibited many instances of catch-up, one of the most notable being the United States, which caught up with and then overtook Britain in the income ranks during the 19th century. Modern examples of catch-up also exist—but not in Latin America, where falling further behind lead countries in per capita income, and even being leapfrogged by poorer countries, has almost become a way of life.

The Elusive Path to Convergence

Economic development in Latin America began more than 500 years ago. By the early 16th century Spanish and Portuguese colonization of Mexico, Central and South America, and parts of the Caribbean was well under way. The British colonization of North America started 100 years later. Notwithstanding the late start, over the next 300 years the British colonies and later their successor, the United States, would catch up with Latin American in income and then surpass it. By 1900 per capita income in the United States (in purchasing power parity) was some four times the mean of the eight largest Latin America economies. As Coatsworth (1998, 26) observed, "Latin America became an underdeveloped region between the early eighteenth and late nineteenth centuries." He attributed much of this lag to the inferior institutional setting and the slowness of Latin American governments to adopt reforms after winning independence in the early 19th century.[2]

More broadly, according to per capita gross domestic product (GDP) data collected by Maddison (2006), since 1500 Latin America has been falling behind what today constitutes the world's developed economies (defined as those that belong to the Organisation for Economic Co-operation and Development (OECD), with only a partial recovery in the export-led-growth era of 1870–1913 and during the Great Depression of the 1930s. The region has done somewhat better when measured against the GDP per capita of the world—especially in the interwar period[3]—but at the end of the 20th century the region was not better positioned than it was in the early 19th century (table 1.1) Even during the great commodity boom of the early 2000s, Latin America, while growing at its fastest rate in at least 40 years (ECLAC 2008a), ranked last in the growth tables of developing-country regions (Devlin and Moguillansky 2009).

Perhaps the greatest contemporary embarrassment has been with regard to the countries of Asia. Beginning in the early decades of the 20th century Latin America engaged in import substitution industrialization (ISI) behind external protective barriers, a process that intensified during the Great Depression.[4] In the 1950s East Asian countries were much poorer than Latin America. Observing Latin America's relative success in the interwar period, and the emergence of major development theories suggesting that state promotion of import substitution industrialization could lead to growth,[5] they too pursued forms of state-led ISI. However, in the 1960s, in the face of liberalization of interwar restrictions in the industrial countries and expansion of globalization and world trade at an unprecedented pace (Crafts 2000), a number of these countries pragmatically combined ISI with an export-led strategy for growth.[6] Latin America, in contrast, perhaps a victim of path dependency derived from its own earlier success, pursued a relatively more doctrinaire deepening of classic ISI. Only in the second half of the 1980s, during the era of the historic debt crisis and adoption of liberalizing structural reforms under the watchful eye of the World Bank, International Monetary Fund, and U.S. Treasury, did Latin America begin a deliberate foray into the internationalization of its economies.[7]

In any event, between the 1960s and the 1990s one Asian economy after another leapfrogged Latin America in the growth rankings. This happened in waves, with the early economies being the Republic of Korea; Singapore; Taiwan, China; Malaysia; Thailand; and Indonesia. The latest round included China, India, and Vietnam (figure 1.1).[8] If performance involved only growth rankings, the issue would be one of relative positions. But those Asian economies that leapfrogged Latin America have been able to sharply reduce poverty in a sustained fashion, while Latin America has not (Devlin, Estevadeordal, and Rodríguez-Clare 2006).

Table 1.1 Latin America in the World Economy

Region	1820	1870	1913	1929	1950	1965	1973	1980	1990	2000
Per capita GDP by region (dollars)										
Western Europe	1,232	1,974	3,473	4,111	4,579	8,441	11,416	13,197	15,966	19,002
United States, Australia, New Zealand, and Canada	1,202	2,419	5,223	6,673	9,268	12,967	16,179	18,060	22,345	27,065
Japan	669	737	1,387	2,026	1,921	5,934	11,434	13,428	18,789	21,069
Asia (excluding Japan)	577	550	658	—	634	936	1,226	1,494	2,117	3,189
Latin America	692	681	1,481	2,034	2,506	3,439	4,504	5,412	5,053	5,838
Eastern Europe and former USSR	688	941	1,558	1,570	2,602	4,333	5,731	6,231	6,455	4,778
Africa	420	500	637	—	894	1,164	1,410	1,536	1,444	1,464
World	667	875	1,525	—	2,111	3,233	4,091	4,520	5,157	6,012
Interregional disparities (percentages)										
Latin America/United States	55.1	27.9	27.9	29.5	26.2	25.6	27	29.1	21.8	20.8
Latin America/World	103.7	77.8	97.1	—	118.7	106.4	110.1	119.7	98.0	97.1
Latin America/Africa	164.8	136.2	232.5	—	280.3	295.4	319.4	352.3	349.9	398.8
Latin America/Asia (excluding Japan)	119.9	123.8	225.1	—	395.3	367.4	367.4	362.2	238.7	183.1
Latin America's share in world production	2.2	2.5	4.4	—	7.8	8	8.7	9.8	8.3	8.4

Source: Ocampo 2006.
Note: — = Not available.

Figure 1.1 GDP per Capita Growth Rates: LAC vs. Selected Asian Countries

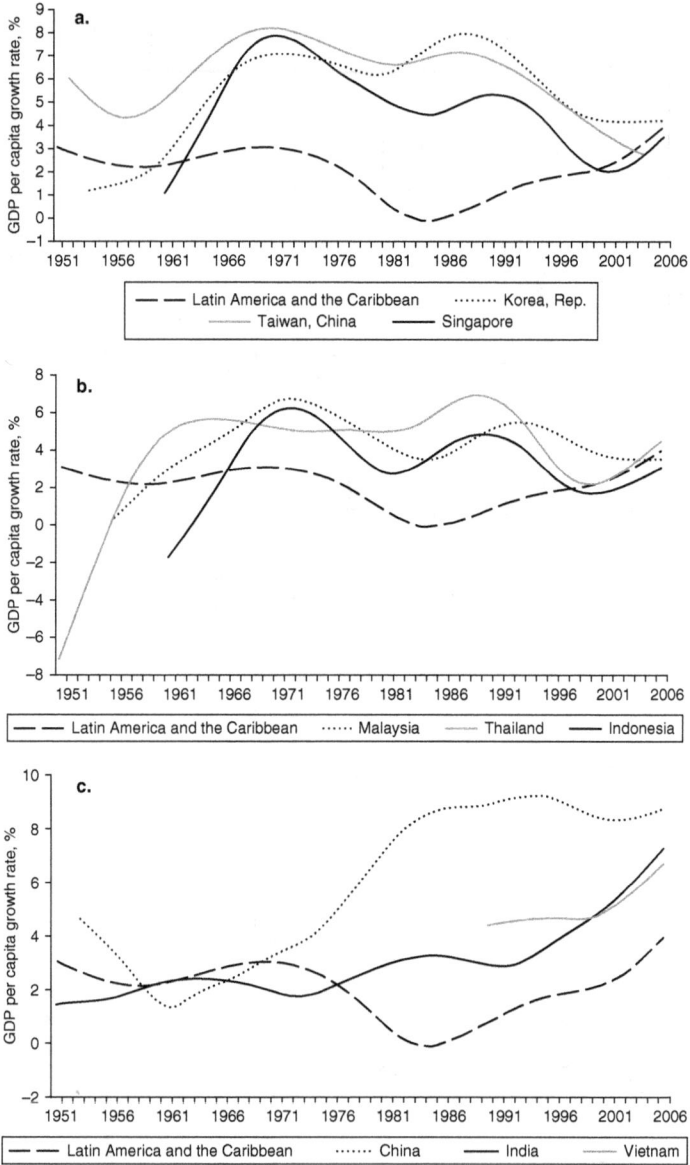

a.

Latin America and the Caribbean ⋯⋯ Korea, Rep.
Taiwan, China   Singapore

b.

Latin America and the Caribbean ⋯⋯ Malaysia   Thailand   Indonesia

c.

Latin America and the Caribbean ⋯⋯ China   India   Vietnam

Source: Penn World Tables (http://pwt.econ.upenn.edu/php_site/pwt_index.
php); World Bank Development Indicators; and Hodrick-Prescott Filtered
(http://en.wikipedia.org/wiki/Hodrick-Prescott_Filter).

With very few exceptions, individual Latin American countries have been laggards in convergence since 1960. A decade-by-decade comparison of GDP per capita as a percentage of the average GDP per capita of the rich OECD countries (not including Mexico and Korea) shows a lackluster performance. Bar graphs for GDP per capita for most of the region's countries fail to image "a stairway to heaven"; on the contrary, while maybe not "a stairway to hell," the image is one of stepping further down from the upper reaches of the world economy (figure 1.2).

The pattern is quite remarkable. Only Chile has shown a steady closing of the gap since the late 1980s, and even then, its income per capita compared with the OECD average income per capita was only marginally higher than it was in 1960. Costa Rica, Panama, and Peru managed to halt the widening of the gap in income in the initial years of the 21st century.[9]

In the years preceding the world crisis of 2008, an exceptionally favorable external environment, especially record levels of commodity prices, contributed importantly to strong growth in the region (IDB 2008).[10] As the world economy recovered in 2010–11, commodity-producing countries in Latin America are outperforming many of their richer OECD counterparts, which are troubled by debt overhangs. But this better performance, while partly related to prudent macroeconomic management, again is related more to an exogenous factor—China's successful stimulus package and Asian demand for South America's commodities—than dynamic productive transformations at home (ECLAC 2010).

The Latin American Reformers: Did the Washington Consensus Help or Hamper Growth?

When viewed in a contemporary setting, the lagging growth performance and sluggish endogenous dynamics may be perplexing to some. After all, Latin America countries were some of the best students of the Washington Consensus—the gold standard, for many in the 1990s, on which to judge policy reform and prospects for achieving and sustaining growth.[11] The reforms focused first on fiscal discipline and liberalization and then on institutional strengthening (Rodrik 2006). As Rodrik (1996, 10, 18) points out: "The reforms were strongest and most sustained in Latin America. . . . It is striking how many Latin American countries have come within reaching distance of completing the items on the Washington Consensus." Indeed, the initial systematic evaluation of the performance under the consensus reflected that effort (Williamson 1990), and Latin America's reforms continued for some time. Most indexes of the reform process are suggestive of considerable effort from the mid-1980s to 2000 (Morley, Madrazo, and Pettinato 1999; Lora 2001).

Figure 1.2 GDP per Capita as a Percent of OECD Average: Selected Latin American Countries

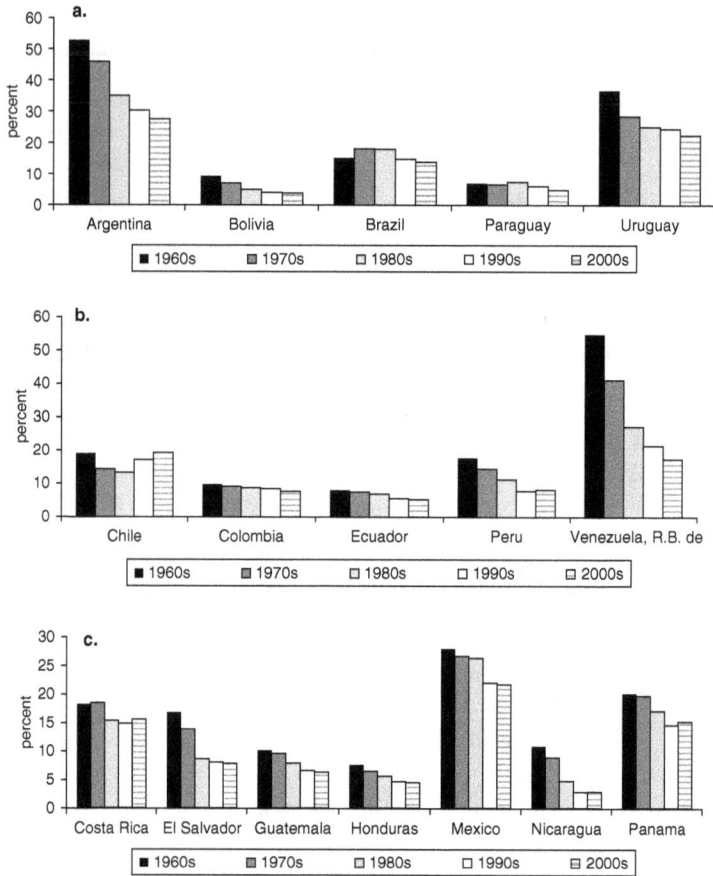

Source: World Bank World Development Indicators.
Note: Mexico and the Republic of Korea are not included in the OECD averages.

Nevertheless, standards are elastic. One could argue, as some have done (Krueger 2004; Singh and others 2005), that the disappointing contemporary growth experience in Latin America came about because the countries just did not go far enough with the reforms. The reform effort did indeed slacken after 2000. An alternative reason, however, has been raised by others who suggest that the concept underlying the reforms was seriously flawed.[12] We share that perspective.

On the one hand, the initial reform push lumped essential macroeconomic stabilization policy concerns with doctrinaire liberalization to the
exclusion of "illiberal tools," such as a proactive state with market interventions, which other countries, such as those in East Asia, have used to
overcome market and nonmarket constraints on structural change and
promote microeconomic industrial transformation and sustained high
rates of growth (Rodrik 1996). On the other hand, a second wave of
reforms pushed from Washington focused on a long list of best-practice
institutions colored by what Rodrik (2006, 979) and others called "institutional fundamentalism," which improperly confused institutional form
with function. In essence there was little tolerance of the historical reality
that a multiplicity of institutional forms can serve a market objective, even
in advanced capitalist economies (Jung-en Woo 1999; Hall and Soskice
2001). In sum, the Washington Consensus leaned on an expectation that
a set of "correct prices" and "correct institutions" alone would spontaneously drive stabilization, economic transformation, and growth.

Rodrik (2006, 974) also has observed that "nobody believes in the
Washington Consensus anymore." British prime minister Gordon Brown
in the April 2009 meeting of the Group of 20 declared that "the old Washington Consensus is over."[13] That is only partially true, however.

In Latin America the legacy of the Washington Consensus, a moniker that for better or worse defined the high period of reforms, has had
some positive dimensions in instilling a critical awareness of the role of
macroeconomic stability in growth—a traditional vulnerability in Latin
American policy making. The region has progressively strengthened its fiscal balances, raised care for public indebtedness, warded off its traditional
bouts with hyperinflation, guarded against negative real interest rates, and
progressively strengthened systemic public regulation. The region has also
paid a great deal more attention to international integration, export development, and the wisdom of creating an adequate cushion of international
reserves to face external contingencies. Human capital development and
social protection also have taken a higher place on the policy agenda of
many countries (ECLAC 2006). As a result most Latin American economies are now more resilient. Indeed, the region's economies weathered the
great world recession of 2008–09 better than they would have in the past.
Moreover, even with the emergence in recent years of governments that
typically would be classified as "on the left" of the political spectrum, the
primacy of macroeconomic balance and international integration has not
been seriously questioned. And as long as the world economy avoids an
economic depression, few governments would likely question the basic
tenet that benefits can be derived from internationalization of the economy. So the Washington Consensus is not totally bereft of contributions
to a better Latin America.[14]

However, the legacy of the consensus, at least in popularized interpretations, is less robust in other areas that have also been shown to be critical

for high and sustained rates of growth.[15] On the march toward the consensus policy framework, there was less agreement among advocates on policy design, leading to a critical mass of support for what had already been proven to be highly risky adventures in economics—liberalized, but exorbitantly high, real interest rates; exchange rate anchors without exit strategies; and simultaneous capital- and current-account openings. As Ffrench-Davis (2005) reminds, permissive oversight of these phenomena created "wrong" outlier macro prices that actually promoted "short-termism" and an "unfriendly" market environment for the medium- and long-term drive to achieve development through investment, productive transformation, and sustained growth. The macroeconomic policy design certainly did create vulnerability to crisis, with real manifestations of this in Mexico (1994), Brazil (1999), and Argentina (2002).[16] Meanwhile, the extent of local capacities for developing and managing instruments was underestimated as were the possibilities for eclectic institutional and policy design. In addition, these miscalculations were coupled with an underestimation of the importance of market failures and other restrictions that undercut transformative microeconomic incentives, of the role of building capacity in enabling a proactive state to address and assist in overcoming the restrictions, and of the appropriateness (sometimes inevitability) of selectivity in application of policy instruments. Finally, short shrift was given to the gradualism and intermediate institutional and policy stances that have been used by many catch-up countries, most recently China (Devlin 2008). Hence, while some dimensions of the Washington Consensus may not be completely irrelevant today, as some claim, in Latin America the consensus is in many of its dimensions a mostly distant, and not entirely appreciated, memory.[17]

Characteristics Underpinning Latin American Growth: A Brief Overview of the Stylized Facts

The underperformance of Latin America is not surprising given many of the characteristics of growth that the United Nations Economic Commission for Latin America and the Caribbean (ECLAC; CEPAL in Spanish) has repeatedly noted. Many of these characteristics were not directly addressed by the Washington Consensus, perhaps because of assumptions of automatic market responses to the "right" prices and institutions. Some of the characteristics can be outlined here.[18]

Volatile Growth Rates.   Latin America's growth has been highly volatile (figure 1.3). The volatility was caused by repeated external shocks (demand, financial, terms of trade, and international policy management),[19] but aggravated by endogenous policy decisions such as fixed, overvalued exchange rates; procyclical fiscal and monetary policy; regulatory

Figure 1.3 Standard Deviation of GDP Growth Rates

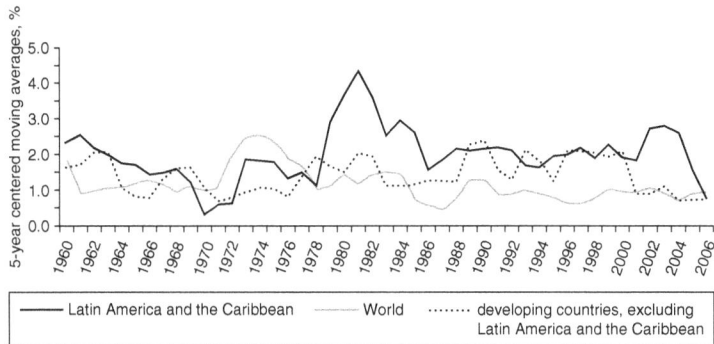

Source: ECLAC 2008b.
Note: Five-year-centered moving averages.

lags; and questionable sequencing of reforms such as between current- and capital-account opening (ECLAC 1995). This high volatility affects future expectations in a way that encourages short-term perspectives and discourages medium- or long-term commitment to risk taking and investment. And of course it also wastes financial and human resources.

Mediocre Investment Levels and Productivity. Meanwhile, over the years savings and investment rates have been mediocre. The best average gross fixed investment ratios have barely exceeded 20 percent (table 1.2). Low investment levels handicap learning and the incorporation of technological progress. Moreover, the investment that took place was concentrated in the export sector; high sustained rates of growth require a more broadly based investment pattern. Not only has investment been less than robust, but the contribution of total factor productivity (TFP) to growth has been modest, especially compared with the East Asian tigers. Over 1960–90, TFP contributed 20–30 percent of growth in the East Asian Tigers, but only 5 percent in Latin America (Crafts 2000). Moreover, the region's poorest postwar performance in TPF was during the reform period (table 1.3). This low contribution likely explains why capital-to-output ratios have tended to rise over a number of decades: the ratio averaged 3.8 percent in 1950–80, but 6.7 percent in 1990–2002.

Declining Share of Manufacturing. Another salient feature is that manufacturing's share of total output has declined in many Latin American countries, perhaps prematurely according to ECLAC (figure 1.4). This is a significant consideration because manufacturing typically is a handmaiden of learning, innovation, and technological development. The phenomenon

Table 1.2 Selected Indicators of the Latin American Economy

Country	Size of territory Thousands of km²	Population Millions 2007	Growth of per capita GDP (annual %), constant 2000US$ᵃ		Per capita GDP (constant 2000US$)ᵃ		Gross domestic savings (% of GDP)ᵇ		Foreign direct investment (% of GDP)		Gross fixed investment (% of GDP)ᶜ	
			1980–89	1990–2007	1980	2007	1980–89	1990–2007	1980–89	1990–2007	1980–89	1990–2007
Mexico	1,943,950	105.3	0.1	1.7	5,114	6,533	25.7	20.5	1.2	2.5	20.2	19.5
Costa Rica	51,060	4.5	−0.5	2.8	3,184	5,022	17.1	14.5	1.5	3.6	20.0	19.1
El Salvador	20,720	6.9	−3.0	2.2	1,898	2,326	6.9	13.0	0.3	1.9	12.8	16.7
Dominican Republic	48,380	9.8	1.6	3.3	1,477	2,881	14.9	20.3	1.0	3.4	22.0	22.1
Panama	74,430	3.3	−1.3	3.6	3,176	5,190	28.6	23.2	0.0	5.9	17.6	18.9
Colombia	1,109,500	46.1	1.3	1.8	1,621	2,461	20.3	16.3	1.3	2.7	17.4	18.5
Peru	1,280,000	27.9	−2.0	2.5	2,256	2,751	25.8	20.8	0.1	3.0	23.6	19.8
Chile	748,800	16.6	2.7	4.0	2,520	6,153	19.0	22.5	2.0	5.4	17.2	22.7
Argentina	2,736,690	39.5	−2.2	2.9	7,551	9,357	22.4	17.5	0.7	2.5		18.5
Uruguay	175,020	3.3	0.1	2.5	5,282	7,497	16.8	13.3	0.5	1.8	14.1	13.3
Brazil	8,459,420	191.6	0.8	0.9	3,557	4,212	23.4	16.3	0.7	2.1	21.0	17.4
Venezuela, R.B. de	882,050	27.5	−2.9	1.5	5,820	5,787	25.0	28.5	0.2	2.3	20.8	20.4
Barbados	430	0.3	1.4	0.0	7,810	8,454	19.8	15.3	0.5	0.8	19.2	16.7
Latin America and the Caribbean	20,156,480	562.8	−0.3	1.6	3,652	4,528	23.0	18.7	0.8	2.5	20.1	18.7

Source: World Bank, World Development Indicators; Comtrade; based on Lall classification.
a. Data for Barbados are for 2002.
b. Data for Barbados up to 2005.
c. Data unavailable for Argentina between 1980 and 1992; data for Colombia up to 1999 and for Barbados up to 2005.

Table 1.2 Selected Indicators of the Latin American Economy (*continued*)

Country	Total R&D expenditure (% of GDP)[d] 1996–2005	Export growth (annual %) constant US$2000[e]		Medium technology exports (% of manufacturing exports)[f]		High technology exports (% of manufacturing exports)[f]		Imports and exports (% of GDP)[g]	
		1980–89	1990–2007	1986–89	1990–2007	1986–89	1990–2007	1986–89	1990–2007
Mexico	0.41	9.7	9.8	25.4	37.1	5.6	22.2	19.5	51.6
Costa Rica	0.33	5.7	9.2	5.5	11.2	3.1	18.1	48.0	85.5
El Salvador	0.08	-6.6	10.2	6.6	13.1	3.5	5.6	32.5	59.9
Dominican Republic	—	-1.6	6.4		18.5	5.1	0.5	77.3	89.8
Panama	0.32	-0.1	5.1	2.0	2.2	1.6	2.2	159.0	156.2
Colombia	0.22	5.3	6.3	6.1	12.1	0.5	1.9	24.8	36.1
Peru	0.11	-0.8	7.9	3.4	2.4	0.4	0.5	21.6	33.6
Chile	0.57	6.9	8.2	2.6	5.1	0.4	0.5	39.1	59.9
Argentina	0.43	3.2	7.6	11.3	16.0	2.2	2.3	10.0	19.9
Uruguay	0.27	3.7	6.6	25.3	9.8	0.7	1.5	23.0	37.3
Brazil	0.87	10.5	7.2	25.3	26.3	4.2	6.6	10.7	20.6
Venezuela, R.B. de	0.37	-0.2	1.0	3.2	6.0	0.1	0.4	38.5	46.5
Barbados	—	—	1.8	20.8	18.9	15.2	9.9	—	105.3
Latin America and the Caribbean	0.56	4.2	7.2	15.8	23.8	3.0	11.4	19.6	37.6

d. Data availability: Costa Rica, no data 2001–02; Brazil, 1996–2005 (no data 1997–99); El Salvador, 1998; Colombia, 1996–2001; Peru, 1997–2004; Chile, 1996–2004; Argentina, 1996–2006; Uruguay, 1996–2002 (no data 2001), and LAC 1996–2005 (no data 1997–99)

e. Data for Barbados up to 2003.

f. Data for República Bolivariana de Venezuela, Uruguay, Argentina, Chile, Colombia, El Salvador, and Costa Rica up to 2006; for Dominican Republic up to 2001.

g. Data for Barbados from 1991 to 2002.

— = Not available.

Table 1.3 Latin America's Growth and Productivity, 1950–2002

percent

Indicator	1950–80	1980–90	1990–2002
GDP growth			
Weighted average	5.5	1.1	2.6
Simple average	4.8	1.0	2.9
GDP per capita			
Weighted average	2.7	–0.9	1.0
Simple average	2.1	–1.2	0.9
GDP per worker			
Weighted average	2.7	–1.7	0.1
Simple average	2.4	–1.9	0
Total factor productivity[a]			
Weighted average	2.0	–1.4	0.2
Simple average	1.9	–1.4	0.6

Source: Ocampo 2006.
a. Argentina, Bolivia, Brazil, Chile, Colombia, Costa Rica, Ecuador, Mexico, Peru, and República Bolivariana de Venezuela.

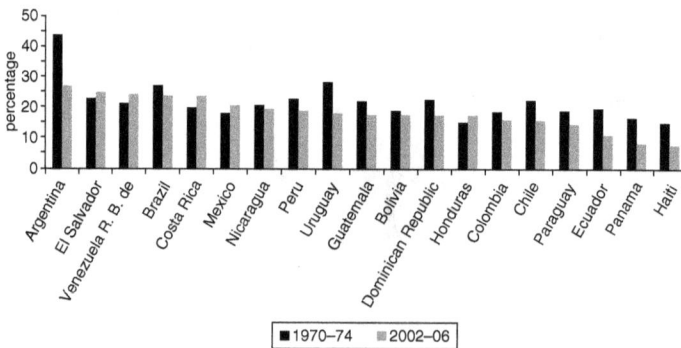

Figure 1.4 Latin America and the Caribbean: Manufacturing Sector Share of Total Value Added

Source: ECLAC 2008b.

undoubtedly partially represents rationalization of the allocation of resources in the face of change in relative prices stemming from liberalization and the intensifying emergence of low-wage exporters in Asia.

However, notwithstanding this rationalization, the phenomenon may have been magnified by the result of the fast and relatively indiscriminate trade liberalization of the late 1980s and early 1990s, coupled with bouts of exchange rate overvaluation, which contributed to destruction of some activities of the ISI era that might have had the potential to compete and survive. As a result, economies were pushed further toward their static comparative advantage in natural resources.

Declining Participation in Engineering-Intensive Industries and Low R&D. Not only did manufacturing lose its position in many economies, but the participation of engineering-intensive manufacturing industries also declined in almost all countries between the early 1970s and the early 2000s. Moreover, engineering-intensive manufacturing is below the world average (figure 1.5). Even compared with other natural-resource-based economies like Australia and New Zealand, Latin America's engineering-based activities fare badly. This finding is troublesome because countries that have diversified from natural resources to higher value-added industries have used returns from the former to strengthen engineering- and scientific-intensive sectors as well as the knowledge content of natural resource sector activities themselves (Stijns 2001). Meanwhile, the extremely low investment in research and development in all Latin American countries (except Brazil) is a proxy for a low level of innovation in the region (see table 1.2).

Figure 1.5 Share of Engineering-Intensive Industries in Manufacturing Output Compared with World Average

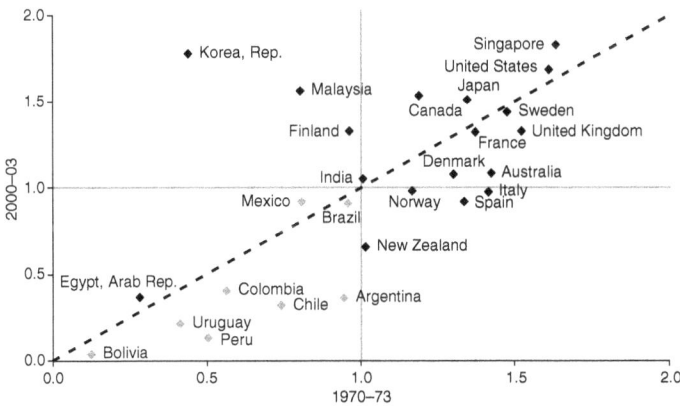

Source: ECLAC 2008b.

Insufficient Export Growth.   In the era of liberalization (mid-1980s–1990s), the region's average growth in volume of exports was strong and rising, running at an average of 7.5–8.0 percent a year (compared with 4.0–5.0 percent in previous decades). In value terms, however, the performance has been less robust, in part because of reliance on commodities in most countries, which until the boom of the early 2000s encountered relatively depressed prices (World Bank 2008). Moreover, imports rose faster than exports, reflecting a high-income demand elasticity and low price elasticity. Hence, the region did not escape its traditional external constraint on growth until the commodity boom. It would appear that most of Latin America needs sustained rates of export expansion closer to those of the Asian tigers if the region is to realize growth sufficient to converge with rich countries (tables 1.2 and 1.4).

The era of liberalization saw Latin America increase its share of world trade to around 5 percent in the mid-2000s, from a little over 4 percent in 1990. This expansion was not enough to recover 1960 levels, however, which closed in on 6 percent. Moreover, the expansion was largely attributable to Mexico, which experienced a great export expansion under the North American Free Trade Agreement (NAFTA). In contrast, the value of exports in East Asia has been on a steady rise, from 1 percent of world trade in 1960 to nearly 6 percent in the mid-2000s.

Table 1.4 Growth of Value of Exports: Selected Latin American and Asian Countries

percent

Country	1960s	1970s	1980s	1990s	2000s
China	..	22.5	6.1	11.9	24.4
Korea, Rep.	30.1	22.8	11.5	14.2	12.2
Malaysia	6.0	8.2	9.2	12.7	7.0
Singapore	..	..	12	9.4	8.4
Thailand	10.3	10.4	13.6	10.4	7.7
Argentina	7.3	6.3	3.2	8.4	6.2
Brazil	6.7	8.6	10.5	5.3	9.3
Chile	3.8	10.0	6.9	9.7	6.2
Colombia	3.5	5.7	5.3	7.1	4.4
Costa Rica	10.1	8.0	5.7	11.9	6.2
Mexico	6.0	10.1	9.7	12.5	6.4
Latin America	5.3	5.0	4.2	7.9	6.3

Source: UN Comtrade.
Note: ·· = Negligible.

Poor Export Market Positioning.   ECLAC has developed a competitive-ness matrix for exports with four categories:

- *Rising Stars*: a country exports dynamic products, where growth in world demand is faster than the average and increases its market share.
- *Lost Opportunity*: a country exports dynamic products but loses market share.
- *Falling Stars*: A country exports products for which demand is grow-ing at less than the world average, but nonetheless increases its market share.
- *Retreat*: a country exports products for which demand is growing at less than the world average, and is losing market share.

The majority of Latin American exports are in products that are los-ing market share. In 1985–95, 60 percent of exports were in this cat-egory. This share fell slightly for the region as a whole in 1995–2004, thanks in part to Brazil, but mostly because of Mexico's strong increase in dynamic exports under NAFTA. Brazil increased its dynamic segment from about 30 percent to over 60 percent, while Mexico increased it from slightly more than 30 percent to over 50 percent. Both countries, but especially Mexico, achieved this growth through "rising stars." The Andean countries (Bolivia, Colombia, Ecuador, Peru, and República de Bolivariana Venezuela) and Chile lost shares in dynamic markets; Chile, however, sharply increased its presence in "falling star" markets. Mean-while in both periods Central America increased its market share in the less dynamic export products.

Lagging in Diversification.   Although results are mixed, empirical work shows a link between trade and productivity growth (Pagés 2010). Recent empirical work also shows that as countries rise in income from low levels they evolve from a concentrated production and export base to greater degrees of diversification. As countries with a relatively high level of in-come approach the technology frontier, specialization takes hold again in the activities in which they excel. This empirical pattern appears in the form of an inverted U (Imbs and Wacziarg 2003; Klinger and Lederman 2006) and suggests that, to develop, countries initially have to diversify their capacities to produce and export through imitation and adaptation behind the technological frontier. In sum, scholarly work strongly suggests that countries at Latin America's level of development need to succeed not only in export growth but also in export diversification if they are to scale the hierarchy of world production and income.

Diversification of production and exports has two major practical advantages for economic growth. On the one hand, a "portfolio effect" reduces vulnerability to swings in external demand and prices. On the other, a dynamic effect of investment and "learning by doing" through pursuit of new activities can have spillover effects for the whole economy (Agosin 2009).

Latin America as a whole has progressed in export diversification (figure 1.6). The most diversified countries are Brazil and Mexico, and the least diversified are in the Andean area, which were further caught up in the commodity boom preceding the global recession in 2008. Nevertheless, diversification of the majority of the countries lags behind emerging Asia and what would be expected given their income levels (CAF 2006).

Figure 1.6 Export Concentration Measured by Herfindhal-Hirshman Index, 1984–85 to 2005–06

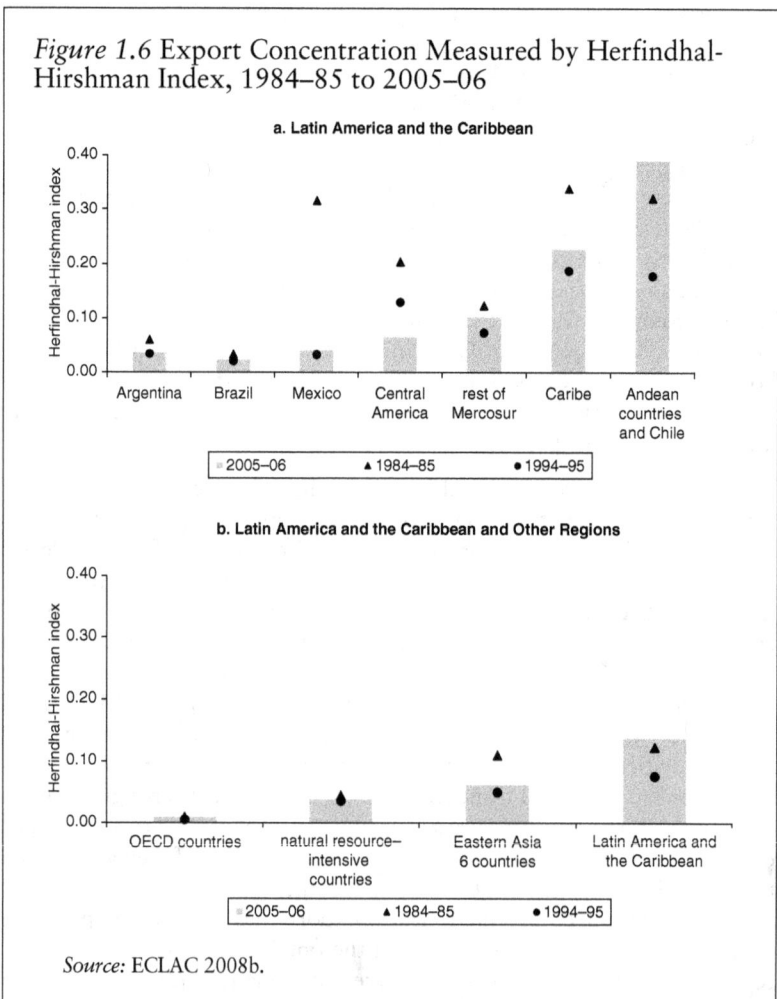

a. Latin America and the Caribbean

2005–06   ▲ 1984–85   ● 1994–95

b. Latin America and the Caribbean and Other Regions

2005–06   ▲ 1984–85   ● 1994–95

Source: ECLAC 2008b.

Technological Content of Exports. As a general proposition one can argue that the export of high- and medium-tech products involves more physical and human capital as well as innovation than do low-tech exports and many natural-resource-based exports.[20] High-tech products also may integrate better into global production networks with opportunities to scale up value chains. These types of products also tend to have relatively more dynamic demand growth. Hence aspiring to diversify into these products can be a way to stimulate economic growth.

Mexico and Central America have shown a very significant diversification in this direction thanks to creation of special export processing zones, efforts to attract foreign direct investment, and the granting of trade preference regimes by the United States. Argentina also has gained in medium-tech manufactured exports (see table 1.2).

However, in Mexico and Central America the value of medium- and high-tech exports as a percentage of total export value is considerably higher than their value added as a percentage of total export value added. Mexico is a good example (figure 1.7). This reflects the reality that exports of many high- and medium-tech products are the end result of processing imported parts and components where the main value added is cheap labor. Manufactures export processing has accounted for 50–60 percent and 70–80 percent of exports for Central America and the Dominican Republic and for Mexico, respectively. While export processing has been an initial platform for progressively adding value in many East Asian countries, that phenomenon has been slower to develop in Latin America.[21]

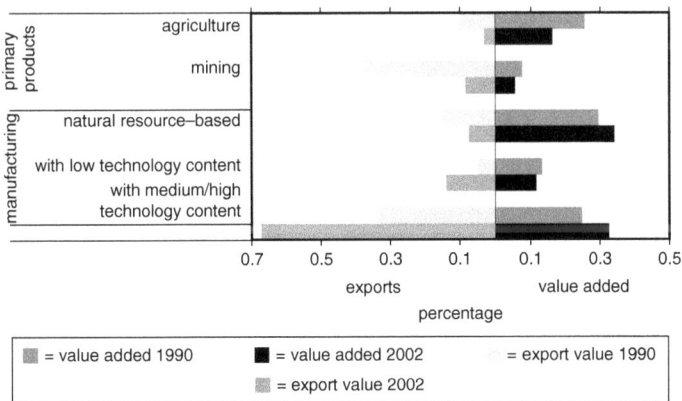

Figure 1.7 Mexico: Participation in Exports and Value Added, by Type of Export, 1990–2002

Source: ECLAC 2008b.

Data suggest that in recent years valued added in export processing in Mexico and Central America and the Dominican Republic has been relatively stable at 22–24 percent of the total value of these exports. The major local component is labor. In the mid-2000s export processing employed nearly 2.5 million people in Mexico and more than 600,000 in Central America and the Dominican Republic.

Inequality. Latin America has suffered from severe inequality since its colonial days (Coatsworth 1998). In the past few years some countries, such as Brazil, Colombia, and Mexico, have made modest progress in addressing the problem, but the countries of the region nonetheless remain among the most inequitable in the world. Aside from normative considerations, inequality certainly undermines the tapping of the full potential of a country's human capital and has been an underlying source of social unrest as well as political uncertainty, both of which can affect investment and risk taking. Indeed, inequality is often viewed as one of the main constraints on Latin American growth, economic transformation, and ability to converge with rich countries (Thorp 1998; Dominguez 2008; Fukuyama 2008).

Competitiveness. While competitiveness indexes always have their shortcomings, the Global Competitiveness Index of the World Economic Forum (2008) is revealing of the region's plight.[22] The only Latin American countries in the top 50, out of 131 countries, are Chile and Barbados.

Table 1.5 Latin America in the Global Competitiveness Index Rankings: 2007–08

		Rankings		
1–25	*26–50*	*51–75*	*75–100*	*100–131*
None	Chile	Mexico	Jamaica	Ecuador
	Barbados	Panama	Honduras	Bolivia
		Costa Rica	Trinidad and Tobago	Nicaragua
		El Salvador	Argentina	Suriname
		Colombia	Peru	Paraguay
		Brazil	Guatemala	Guyana
		Uruguay	Dominican Republic	
			Venezuela, R.B. de	

Source: World Economic Forum, *Global Competitiveness Report 2007–2008.*
   Note: Chile is the one Latin American country that has a higher ranking than China.

Chile is also the only Latin American country that outranked China (table 1.5). Even so Chile performs poorly in key indicators of competitive dynamism such as education and innovation. Major Latin American countries, even the relatively more competitive ones, also score poorly in the OECD's PISA international reading and math tests. This shortcoming indicates that, notwithstanding achievements in expanding school enrollments, the region's educational systems have severe quality deficiencies. And the region's poor infrastructure explains a significant part of its high transport costs compared with the United States and Europe (Mesquita Moreira, Volpe, and Blyde 2008).

In conclusion, it is clear from this brief overview that Latin America's "falling behind" is no accident. The list of shortcomings constructs a tree with dense foliage (figure 1.8). The reforms of the era of the Washington Consensus contributed positively in some dimensions of economic policy, but on the whole the flaws noted here have been decisive.

Figure 1.8 Factors Conditioning Latin American Growth

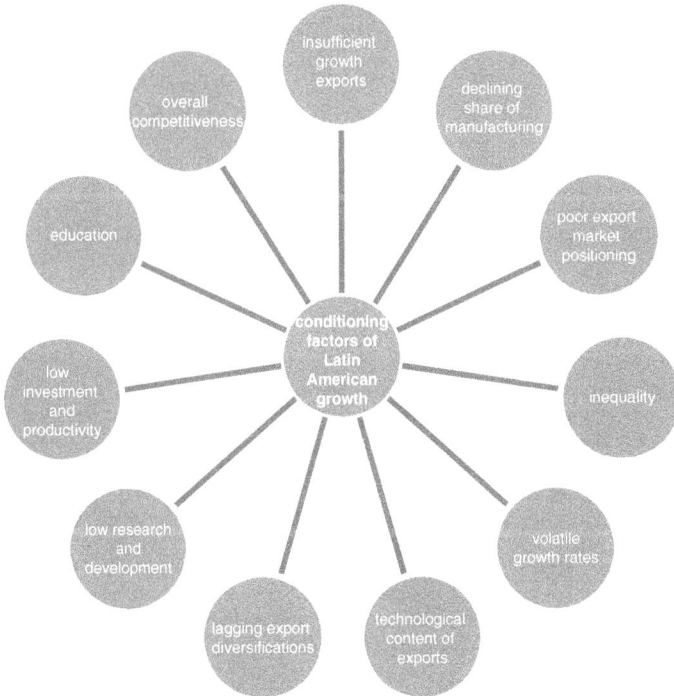

Source: Authors.

Notes

1. The catch-up is possible in principle because the laggard can potentially access new capital on the technological frontier to replace technologically outmoded capital, thereby boosting productivity levels. The leader cannot leverage its economy in a similar way because it is already on the technological frontier (Abramovitz 1986). Very backward countries also can leverage growth through the availability of elastic labor supplies (Lewis 1955), which in conjunction with industrialization allows movement from low productivity subsistence agriculture to higher productivity activities.

2. It is commonly recognized that European colonization had long-term effects on the nature of underdevelopment. Inferior institutions and legal systems are often blamed for the lagging performance of former Spanish, Portuguese, and French colonies. But even within a given set of colonies, the local administrators' choices of types and intensity of investments could have long-term effects (Huillery 2009). In any event, a more complete picture of Latin America's path dependency can be drawn from Furtado (1970) and Thorp (1998), who cite as factors the interaction of initial colonial conditions with the nature of export products and their impact on local markets, access to technological progress, public policies, and external factors including foreign capital and government interventions.

3. During the Great Depression Latin America sharply increased external protection through tariffs, nontariff barriers, and devaluation. It also defaulted on foreign bondholders with little retaliation from the latter because of their difficulties in organizing a coordinated response (Devlin 1989). The protection, coupled with a positive transfer of resources arising from the default, and a proactive expansionary government budget, stimulated one of the best growth performances in this difficult era (Ocampo 2006). Indeed, Diaz-Alejandro (1985) captured the times when he remarked that the doom and gloom on Wall Street was in contrast to mills in São Paulo that were humming.

4. The intensification was a response to the collapse of international markets and a flurry of international protectionism.

5. See, for example, Prebisch (1949), Rodenstein-Rodan (1943), Lewis (1955), Nurske (1967), and Hirschman (1958).

6. For the case of the Republic of Korea, see Hong (2008).

7. Chile was the exception. Internationalization began in the mid-1970s under the Pinochet regime.

8. As can be seen in the figure, the East Asian countries and Latin America began to converge in growth rates toward the end of the 1990s. This convergence resulted largely from the exogenous effects of the financial crisis and contagion in the East Asian countries at the end of the 1990s and the unusually high growth rates for Latin America attributable to high commodity prices in the six years preceding the world economic crisis of 2008.

9. An alternative indicator of well-being, the Human Development Index, shows Latin America faring better. This index shows that the region substantially converged and narrowed the gap with OECD countries between 1950 and the end of the century. This finding is not surprising, because the index discounts income and gives significant weight to mortality rates, which tend to fall secularly as a result of global trends in technology and public health (Crafts 2000).

10. This growth was concentrated in South America, abundant in natural resources.

11. To clarify, the moniker "Washington Consensus" was coined in a study organized by Williamson (1990). The consensus was explained as a consensus among the Washington-based technocrats, policy makers, politicians, and others

working in the U.S. government, multilateral institutions such as the World Bank and International Monetary Fund, think tanks, and the like on what constituted good structural reform policy. Leaving aside whether there was really a true consensus in Washington (there was not, although those close to power generally paid little attention to dissent), the study was an effort to discern how much Latin American governments shared that perspective and followed its guidelines as they navigated the crisis and adjustments of the 1980s. The label "Washington Consensus" was hung on views of those who strongly identified with the liberalizing reform agenda of the era, some of whom were far more ideological in tone and substance than the version originally set out by Williamson.

12. For just a few examples of this enormous literature, see Ffrench-Davis (2005), Rodrik (2006), Stiglitz (2003a; 2003b), Ocampo (1998; 2001), Jung-En Woo (1999), and Ibarra (2004).

13. John Weisman and Alister MacDonald, "Obama, Brown Strike Similar Notes on the Economy," April 3, 2009. http://online.wsj.com/article/SB123871661163384723.html.

14. In a recent work, Birdsall, de la Torre, and Caicedo (2010) distinguish in a very balanced way the pros and cons of the consensus for Latin America.

15. Williamson (2009, 1) recently commented on the many critiques of the Washington Consensus: "First, as originally conceived the Washington Consensus advised not simply the microeconomic liberalization ..., but also macroeconomic discipline and opening up (globalization). . . . Second, according to the alternative version espoused by Joe Stiglitz . . . the Washington Consensus was a neoliberal manifesto. But neoliberalism is normally considered to embrace such doctrines as monetarism, reduction of the progressive thrust of taxation, opposition to state action to redistribute income, and minimization of the role of the state, rather than just the reasonable liberalizing (micro) reforms. . . . These additional doctrines never did commend a consensus in Washington so I do not consider they constitute a Washington Consensus."

16. These adventures were most conspicuously undertaken by the consensus's poster child, Argentina. That is ironic, since there was a certain consensus in the academic literature that the big economic crisis of the Southern Cone countries in the late 1970s was linked to these very types of policy design. For a review of policy problems of that era, see ECLAC (1995).

17. Chile, the best Latin American performer, might be pointed to as the real poster child of the Washington Consensus. However, especially since the democratic transition, it has been more eclectic than has generally been recognized. One example was the extensive and then controversial use of short-term capital controls, much criticized in Washington circles (but now receiving more acceptance). More recently, it has an ambitious strategy to promote innovation in selected real or potential clusters. And some of the Pinochet-era export successes (such as forestry) were built on public programs that preceded the coup d'etat. Ffrench-Davis (2005) probably has one of the most complete analyses of what a more effective reform process would look like. Also see Ocampo (2005).

18. In many cases space limitations force the use of averages. However, in recent decades only Chile systematically breaks out of the pack. Unless otherwise indicated, this overview material is drawn from ECLAC (2008b) with updates and refinements introduced by the authors.

19. An enormously important exogenous policy shock was the cartel of commercial banks, multilateral lenders, and creditor governments that designed rescue packages in the face of the region's inability to service external foreign debt in the 1980s. The rescue was aimed more at the commercial banks than at Latin America. Indeed, the packages "squeezed" a historically unprecedented transfer of resources from Latin America to the banks for most of the 1980s, saving them

from bankruptcies. However, the transfer was a major contributor to the lost decade of growth. Moreover, some of the adjustments pushed by the cartel also weakened rather than strengthened the medium-term prospects for the region's growth. For details, see Devlin (1989) and Ramos (2007).

20. Nevertheless it is possible to add knowledge and value to natural resource exports through innovation. An example is Australia and New Zealand, two countries that have achieved developed-country income status on a natural resource export base.

21. A World Bank (2006) report on China pointed out that China's trade basket continues to rapidly diversify and move up-market. New product varieties are emerging every year, with an expanding private sector leading the drive. Moreover, import substitution is deepening domestic supply chains, with export processing steadily falling as a percent of total exports to 50 percent, according to the Bank. Preeg (2006) reports that high-tech information and telecommunication equipment is a leading driver of exports, and he observes that Chinese valued added for information technology exports will soon reach 70 percent.

22. The index covers 12 "pillars," each with many subindicators: institutions, infrastructure, macroeconomic stability, health and primary education, higher education and training, goods market efficiency, labor market efficiency, financial market sophistication, technological readiness, market size, business sophistication, and innovation.

References

Abramovitz, Moses. 1986. "Catching Up, Forging Ahead, and Falling Behind." *Journal of Economic History* 46, no. 2 (June).

Agosin, Manuel. 2009. "Export Diversification and Growth in Emergent Economies." *CEPAL Review* 97 (LC/G.2400-P), Economic Commission for Latin America and the Caribbean, Santiago, Chile (April).

Birdsall, Nancy, Gustavo de la Torre, and Felipe Valencia Caicedo. 2010. "The Washington Consensus: Assessing a Damaged Brand." Working paper 213, Center for Global Development, Washington, DC (May).

Coatsworth, John. 1998. "Economic and Institutional Trajectories in Nineteenth-Century Latin America." In *Latin America and the World Economy since 1800*, Cambridge, MA: Harvard University, David Rockefeller Center for Latin American Studies.

CAF (Corporación Andina de Fomento). 2006. *Camino a la transformación productiva en América Latina.* Caracas: CAF, Economic and Development Report Series.

Crafts, Nicholas. 2000. "Globalization and Growth in the Twentieth Century." Working paper WP/00/44, International Monetary Fund, Washington, DC (March).

Devlin, Robert. 1989. *Debt and Crisis in Latin America: The Supply Side of the Story.* Princeton, NJ: Princeton University Press.

———. 2008. "China's Economic Rise." In *China's Expansion into the Western Hemisphere,* ed. Riordan Roett and Guadalupe Paz. Washington, DC: Brookings Institution.

Devlin, Robert, Antoni Estevadeordal, and Andrés Rodríguez-Clare. 2006. The *Emergence of China: Opportunities and Challenges for Latin America and the*

Caribbean. Cambridge, MA: Harvard University, David Rockefeller Center for Latin American Studies.

Devlin, Robert, and Graciela Moguillansky. 2009. "Public-Private Alliances for Long-Term National Development Strategies." *CEPAL Review* 97 (LC/G.2400-P), Economic Commission for Latina America and the Caribbean, Santiago, Chile (April).

Diaz-Alejandro, C. 1985. "The Early 1980's in Latin America: The 1930's One More Time?" Paper presented at the expert meeting on crises and development in Latin America and the Caribbean, Economic Commission for Latin America and the Caribbean, Santiago, Chile (May 29–30).

Domínguez, Jorge. 2008. "Explaining Latin America's Lagging Development in the Second Half of the Twentieth Century: Growth, Strategies, Inequality and Economic Crises." In *Falling Behind*, ed. Francis Fukuyuma. New York: Oxford University Press.

ECLAC (Economic Commission for Latin America and the Caribbean). 1995. *Policies to Improve Linkages with the Global Economy.* E.95.II.g.6, Santiago, Chile.

———. 2006. "Shaping the Future of Social Protection: Access, Financing and Solidarity-Summary." ECLAC, Santiago, Chile (March).

———. 2008a. *Economic Survey of Latin America and the Caribbean, 2007–2008.* LC/G.2386-P/E, Santiago, Chile.

———. 2008b. *Structural Change and Productivity Growth Twenty Years Later: Old Problems, New Opportunities.* LC/G.2367 (SES.32/3), Santiago, Chile.

———. 2010. *Latin America in the World Economy 2009–2010. A Crisis Generated in the Centre, and Recovery Driven by the Emerging Economies.* E.10. II.G.5, Santiago, Chile.

Ffrench-Davis, R. 2005. *Reformas para Amércia Latina: después del fundamentalismo neoliberal.* Buenos Aires: Siglo XXI.

Fukuyama, Francis. 2008. "Conclusions." In *Falling Behind*, ed. F. Fukuyama. New York: Oxford University Press.

Furtado, Celso. 1970. *Economic Development of Latin America.* Cambridge, U.K.: Cambridge University Press.

Hall, Peter, and David Soskice. 2001. "An Introduction to the Varieties of Capitalism." In *Varieties of Capitalism,* ed. P. Hall and D. Soskice. Oxford, U.K.: Oxford University Press.

Hirschman, Albert. 1958. *The Strategy of Economic Development.* New Haven, CT: Yale University Press.

Hong, Yoo Soo. 2008. "Public and Private Sector Alliances for Innovation and Economic Development: The Korean Case." Paper presented at the seminar "Public-Private Partnerships for Innovation and Export Development" held by the Economic Commission for Latin America and the Caribbean and the Iberoamerican Secretariat, Seville, September 13–14.

Huillery, Elise. 2009. "History Matters: The Long-Term Impact of Colonial Public Investments in French West Africa." *American Economic Journal of Applied Economics* 1, no 2.

Ibarra, David. 2004. "The Devious Maze of the International Order: The Importation of Reforms." *CEPAL Review* 82 (LC/G.2220-P), Economic Commission for Latin America and the Caribbean, Santiago, Chile (April).

Imbs, Jean, and Romain Wacziarg. 2003. "Stages of Diversification." *American Economic Review* 93, no. 1 (March).

IDB (Inter-American Development Bank). 2008. *All that Glitters May Not Be Gold.* Washington, DC: IDB.

Jung-en Woo, Meredith, ed. 1999. *The Developmental State.* Ithaca, NY: Cornell University Press.

Klinger, Bailey, and Daniel Lederman. 2006. "Diversification, Innovation and Imitation inside the Global Technological Frontier." Policy Research Working Paper 3872, World Bank, Washington, DC.

Krueger, Anne. 2004. "Meant Well, Tried Little, Failed Much: Policy Reform in Emerging Market Economies." Paper presented at a roundtable at the Economics Honor Society, New York University, March 23.

Lewis, W. Arthur. 1955. *Theory of Economic Growth.* London: George Allen and Unwin.

Lora, Eduardo. 2001. "Structural Reforms in Latin America: What Has Been Reformed and How to Measure It." Research Department Working Paper 466, Inter-American Development Bank, Washington, DC.

Maddison, Angus. 2006. *The World Economy: A Millennial Perspective.* Paris: Organisation for Economic Co-operation and Development.

Mesquita Moreira, Mauricio, Christian Volpe, and Juan Blyde. 2008. *Unclogging Arteries: The Impact of Transport Costs on Latin America and Caribbean Trade.* Washington DC: Inter-American Development Bank.

Morley, Samuel, Roberto Madrazo, and Stefano Pettinato. 1999. "Indexes of Structural Reform in Latin America." Economic Reforms Series 12 (LC/L.1166-P/I), Economic Commission for Latin America and the Caribbean, Santiago, Chile.

Nurske, Ragnar. 1967. *Problems of Capital Formation in Underdeveloped Countries and Patterns of Trade and Development.* New York: Oxford University Press.

Ocampo, José Antonio. 1998. "Beyond the Washington Consensus: An ECLAC Perspective." *CEPAL Review* 66 (LC/G.2049-P/E), Economic Commission for Latin America and the Caribbean, Santiago, Chile (December).

———. 2001. "A New Look to Development Agenda." *CEPAL Review* 74 (LC/G.2135-P/E), Economic Commission for Latin America and the Caribbean, Santiago, Chile (August).

———. 2006. "Latin America and the World Economy in the Long Twentieth Century." In *The Long Twentieth Century, The Great Divergence: Hegemony, Uneven Development and Global Inequality,* ed. K. S. Jomo. New Delhi, Oxford University Press.

Ocampo, José Antonio, ed. 2005. *Beyond Reforms.* Stanford, CA: Stanford University Press.

Pagés, Carmen, ed. 2010. *The Age of Productivity.* Washington, DC: Inter-American Development Bank.

Prebisch, Raúl. 1949. "Crecimiento, desequilibrio y disparidades : interpretación del proceso de desarrollo económico." *Economic Survey of Latin America and the Caribbean, 1949.* Santiago, Chile: Economic Commission for Latin America and the Caribbean.

Preeg, Ernest. 2006. *Economic Report.* Arlington, VA: Manufacturers' Alliance.

Ramos, Joseph. 2007. "Alianzas público-privado, estrategias para el desarrollo exportador y la innovación: Chile." Economic Commission for Latin America and the Caribbean. International Trade and Integration Division, Santiago, Chile.

Rosenstein-Rodan, P. 1943. "Problems of Industrialization of Eastern and South-Eastern Europe." *Economic Journal* 53, no. 210/211 (June).

Rodrik, Dani. 1996. "Understanding Economic Policy Reform." *Journal of Economic Literature* 34 (March).

———. 2006. "Goodbye Washington Consensus, Hello Washington Confusion. A Review of the World Bank's Economic Growth in the 1990s: Learning from a Decade of Reform." *Journal of Economic Literature* 44 (December).

Singh, Amoop, and others. 2005. "Stabilization and Reform in Latin America: A Macroeconomic Perspective of the Experience since the 1990s." IMF Occasional Paper 238, International Monetary Fund, Washington, DC.

Stiglitz, Joseph. 2003a. *Globalization and Its Discontents*. New York: Norton.

———. 2003b. "Wither Reform? Towards a New Agenda for Latin America." *CEPAL Review* 80 (LC/G.2204-P/E), Economic Commission for Latin America and the Caribbean, Santiago, Chile (August).

Stijns, Jean Philippe. 2001. "Natural Resource Abundance and Economic Growth Revisited." University of California, Berkeley (March).

Thorp, Rosemary. 1998. *Progress, Poverty and Exclusion: An Economic History of Latin America in the Twentieth Century*. Washington, DC: Inter-American Development Bank.

Williamson, John. 1990. *The Progress of Policy Reform in Latin America*. Washington, DC: Institute for International Economics.

———. 2009. "The Washington Consensus and the Global Crisis." Peterson Institute for International Economics, Washington, DC (April 22).

World Bank. 2006. "Quarterly Update, China." Washington, DC (August).

———. 2008. *Global Economic Prospects 2009*. Washington, DC.

2

The First Principle: Medium-to Long-Term Development Strategies Supported by Industrial Policies Can Foster Economic Catch-Up

Overtly or tacitly, governments usually have a development strategy. A strategy is a template for action, or a formal plan, to attain particular goals. Development strategies can have very different characteristics, however. Simplifying for the purpose of illustration, in market economies strategies may be said to be differentiated chiefly by the assumptions about the pace of economic transformation brought about by natural market forces. These assumptions in turn affect the nature of the primary goals set and the pattern (scope, types, and amount) of public interventions in pursuit of those goals.

The Character of Development Strategies: An Initial Snapshot

On the one hand are the strategies that primarily focus on public sector interventions designed to set free and strengthen the autonomous action of market forces, examples being adjustment and liberalization policies, coupled with regulatory frameworks, oriented toward macroeconomic stability; protection of property rights and the legal institutions underpinning them; liberalization of external trade and investment; and provision of certain basic public goods such as security, education, and basic infrastructure. This "custodian" approach to state intervention, a term used by Evans (1995), bespeaks of confidence that the relatively free play of market forces will promote, on the whole, an adequate pace of economic transformation. Hence the state's role is primarily that of overseeing market-based rules and providing a "sound" macroeconomic enabling environment. That in turn will support market-based price incentives for businesses themselves to lead a process of economic transformation based on the country's international comparative advantage. Moreover, even when recognizing that market prices might diverge from social valuations (so-called market failures), the belief in both the limited nature of the scope of these failures, as well as the limited capacity of government to effectively deal with them (stemming from identification problems, or the political economy risks of rent seeking, for example) counsels against proactive public sector interventions of the type associated with so-called industrial policy (IP) (see, for example, Krueger 1990; Noland and Pack 2002; and Pack and Saggi 2006).[1]

As a consequence, in this perspective, the goals and scope of public interventions should be relatively limited and kept at "arm's length" from the workings of market forces. The bottom line of the "benevolent market forces" school of thought is that an ambitious scheme of public interventions, even in the face of possible market failures, is likely only to create distortions that will inhibit full exploitation of international comparative advantage and handicap growth and development. Pack and Saggi (2006, 293) illustrate this point of view in reference to industrial policies when they suggest that "hewing to the main tenets of the Washington Consensus (while recognizing its weaknesses) might prove a better investment of limited government competence and legitimacy than the extraordinarily complex strategies required by either the new or old industrial policy."

In contrast, proponents of industrial policies are mistrustful of certain market signals. In effect, this approach believes that market price signals may in certain circumstances be very unreliable guides for the allocation of resources in support of economic transformation, because they will encourage underexploitation of opportunities to upgrade economic activity and may even lock economies into a low-wage comparative advantage (Cimoli and others 2006).[2] The grounds for this perspective are, on the one hand, the belief, with some evidence, that market failures exist and are in fact quite significant, especially in developing countries (Harrison and Rodriguez-Clare 2009; Fernandez-Arias 2010).[3] On the other hand, the perspective can be extended beyond market failures, which theoretically have a static general equilibrium point of reference, to a more real world framework that emphasizes medium- to long-term dynamic factors related to learning, capacity building, adaptation, and innovation, and their critical roles in economic transformation. Moreover, some technologically specific platforms in particular sectors or activities push these dynamic factors to their fullest potential better than others, but serious obstacles of both an economic and noneconomic nature mean that access to these platforms is not spontaneous (see, among others, Fajnzylber 1990; Katz and Kosacoff 1998; Lall 2000; Cimoli and others 2006; Hausmann and Klinger 2006; and Peres and Primi 2009).

The bottom line here is that public sector interventions must be proactive and emerge out of a medium- to long-term strategy that identifies and tackles obstacles to economic transformation on an array of fronts (micro, meso, and macro) using intelligent horizontal and vertical policy interventions adapted to the opportunities and risks at play. The public interventions should be directed at rectifying serious market failures or at addressing the broader institutional and cultural obstacles to accessing dynamic production processes and technology, such as the failure of the private sector to spontaneously lead structural change because of aversion to risk and the inertia derived from the comforts of incremental change. Moreover, there is a degree of specificity to these dynamic processes and technological applications with which public interventions must align themselves (Wade 1990; Chang 1994; Peres and Primi 2009; Cimoli and others 2006). Hence, inevitably there is a need to be selective in the design and application of at least part of the policy package; as Hausmann and Rodrik (2006) state in the title of a paper, governments are "doomed to choose." In any event, the goal of industrial policy is to accelerate economic transformation and convergence with rich countries beyond what unfettered market forces would offer.

Proponents of industrial policies fully recognize that they encounter challenges regarding available public sector skills, agency problems, inertia in policy sets, sectoral interests, and corruption (Nelson 1987; Pérez 1992; Kosacoff and Ramos 1999; Lall 2000). However, they believe that effectively identifying and acting on areas for policy interventions is less daunting than often presumed. They also believe that selectivity is less dangerous than typically presumed. Indeed, as Rodrik (2008) points out, even in the context of the Washington Consensus agenda, governments were encouraged to identify interventions for provision of public goods in social areas that were not necessarily less complex than those of industrial policy. Moreover, governments have been selective in their allocation of resources and development of programs for these purposes. Meanwhile, Rodrik (2004) also points out that dysfunctional rent seeking and corruption are risks not only in industrial policy but in any area of public policy. And these problems can be constrained through design of the institutional framework and the modalities of industrial policy (Wade 2004; Todesca, Larghi, and Besmedrisnik 2006; Amsden 2007; Devlin and Moguillansky 2009). Hence, while not underestimating the challenges of pursuing IP effectively, its proponents believe that "yes governments can," to different degrees according to their circumstances, be more strategic in policy formulation than market fundamentalists would likely admit.

There are three potential patterns of state action in this more proactive framework, which Evans (1995) has laid out nicely. One is the pattern of "demiurge," or the state as a producer. Although all states produce things, a pattern of state action in the spirit of a demiurge is underpinned by a broad assumption that the private sector is incapable of undertaking a strategic economic activity. A second pattern is "midwifery," where doubts about the private sector's capacity are balanced by an estimation that the capacity can be built; in this case, the state assists the private sector in acquiring that capacity instead of directly undertaking the new challenging activity. Third is a pattern of "husbandry," where the private sector is quite capable of undertaking new complex activities, but the state. when needed, assists it in navigating the challenging waters of globalization and technological change. These patterns can coexist in the state's policy matrix, but one or more may dominate at any time and stage of development, as we show later in this chapter. As for the instruments of IP, the classic has been tariff protection, but in fact horizontal and vertical instruments are many and varied, with new ones emerging all the time.[4] Some of the instruments actually used for export development are highlighted in later chapters.

Finally, in point of fact, most countries' strategies have not strictly followed either of the two stylized approaches described here but contain elements of both (Evans 1995; Ul Haque 2007). What is at issue, rather, are the mechanisms used and the dominant approach in the orientation of public policies.

A debate still rages over these two stylized approaches to development strategy—one that extends back to the early days of capitalism.[5] In the contemporary era the proponents of the first policy alternative, known as "monetarists" in the 1960s, are today called "neoclassicals" or "neoliberals," while the second were formerly called "structuralist" or "dirigiste" and now are known as advocates of "neostructuralism," "political economy," or "developmentalism." The contemporary debate originated with the famous disagreement in development economics between monetarists and structuralists in the pre-1980 import substitution industrialization period—for which Latin America was a major prop (de Oliviera Campos 1964). In those days the structuralists held sway in the development debate. The emergence of the Reagan-Thatcher antigovernment ideology of the 1980s, coupled with the severe debt crisis in Latin America and other developing countries, delegitimized structuralist proactive public policy and contributed to the pendulum swinging hard to the so-called neoliberal approach, as expressed in the influential Washington Consensus discussed in chapter 1. However, faced with the poor, lagging, or flagging performance of the best students of the consensus, the much better performance in a number of countries with more proactive government policies, and the manifest crisis in the North caused by unreserved faith in the efficiency of markets, industrial policy "is back."[6] Indeed, as we discuss in later chapters, interest is growing in Latin America about development strategies underpinned by industrial policies.[7] Moreover, contemporary proponents of neostructuralism have brought a great deal of "value added" to industrial policy vis-à-vis its earlier formulations, an issue we highlight momentarily.

Opting for the Industrial Policy Approach: The Power of Association

Industrial polices have a long history. Indeed, in recent centuries few countries have become rich without passing through a period in which industrial policy, most notably infant industry protection, among other instruments, has not been deployed before reaching a state of a "liberal" economy (Bairoch 1993; Chang 2003; Fajnzylber 1988, 1990; Reinert 2004, 2009; Lin and Monga 2010).[8] Many studies of the effects on development of industrial policy have been conducted by its advocates and critics. But the studies have not silenced the debate. Wade (2004, 345) nicely captures part of the dynamic:

> The debate about the role of the state in economic development demonstrates the power of infinite repetition as a weapon of modern scholarship. The issue is normally posed in terms of the "amount" of state intervention or the "size" of government. The neoclassical side says that more successful cases show relatively little intervention in the market, while less successful cases show a lot (Brazil and Mexico compared to East Asia; or sub-Saharan Africa at the bottom). It uses this evidence to urge governments to shrink the size of the state and remove many of the interventions from the market. The political economy side says that the neoclassicals have their facts wrong; the most successful cases show "heavy" or "active" intervention. It concludes from this evidence that governments *can* [author's emphasis], in some circumstances, guide the market to better industrial performance than a free market, even in the absence of neoclassical-type market failure. But neither side has been noticeably enthusiastic to specify just what evidence would be consistent with its position and what would not. Both have exercised a selective inattention to data that would upset their way of looking at things. So the debate about the role of the state is less a debate than a case of paradigms ("parrot-times") talking past each other.

Part of the problem here, aside from faith in certain paradigms, is the real difficulty of precise measurement of the impacts of industrial policy. The more rigorous mainstream contemporary analysis has focused primarily on East Asia where most analysts at least do agree that governments have been proactive interventionists in markets. Three issues are usually addressed: whether targeted industries received significant financial support, whether industrial structure differed from that predicted by an economy's income and population, and whether the strategically supported industries' productivity performance proved better than that in nonstrategic sectors (Weiss 2005; Harrison and Rodriguez-Clare 2009).

However, there are many problems in assessing results. The precise dynamic transmission mechanisms of industrial policies can be extremely complex and hard to fully understand, let alone model. Indeed, rigorous evaluation of the impact of a single, sectorally focused incentive program on, say, productivity, is extremely challenging (Hughes 2007), not to mention more aggregated perspectives. Developing robust counterfactuals to determine how performance would have been without industrial policy is very difficult, particularly when examining very robust economic performances. In addition, data problems (such as measuring capital stock) in and between countries can be serious, and in data sets the instrumentation of industrial policy can often be difficult to isolate from other political economy motivations (McClelland 1975). Then there is the troublesome issue of endogeneity in assessing the causality of correlations. Results of statistical modeling are also very sensitive to the time periods selected, for example in growth accounting, as Sarel (1996) demonstrates for the East Asia debate. And some interventions such as administrative guidance and "moral suasion" are not easily quantifiable for purposes of modeling. Finally, there is a large body of comprehensive case studies on the Asian tigers. Many arrive at positive conclusions about the effectiveness of industrial policy on investment incentives, learning, technological adaptation, and industrial and export development. However, some case studies are less favorable in their conclusions. And, of course, for many economists case study work lacks sufficient generality to be persuasive. Hence, examination of the overall results of the many studies undertaken often leads to conclusions like "mixed results," "inconclusiveness," or "agnosticism" regarding the effects of industrial policy (Wade 1986, 1990; Weiss 2005; Rodrik 2008; Harrison and Rodriguez-Clare 2009; Sarle 1996).

The lack of conclusive empirical evidence leaves development economists in the dilemma of having to make a choice in uncertainty about a recommended policy thrust for growth and economic transformation. One could rely on an "association" argument that medium- and long-term strategies with industrial policy have been present in virtually all successful cases of catch-up and thus risk what Wade (2004, 348) calls the "Darwinian fallacy," that is, "the assumption that because something exists it must be vital to the survival of the organism or society in which it exists." Or one could risk Wade's "Ptolemaic fallacy" and assume that only policies consistent with the neoliberal paradigm could have been the factor behind successful growth experiences.

As mentioned, history shows few instances of catch-up without the presence of industrial policies. The contemporary catch-up of developing countries with rich ones involves a relatively select club. Since 1960, 15 countries (out of a universe of 106 with available data) have closed the income gap with the United States by 10 percentage points or more (measured by gross domestic product, or GDP, per capita) (table 2.1). Of these, only Hong Kong SAR, China, would clearly approximate the neoliberal paradigm on government interventions. Conversely, more than half of these countries use, or have used, formal strategic national development plans to guide policy. Other developing countries, such as Malaysia, the Czech Republic, and China,[9] have not met the outlined threshold but have achieved considerable catch-up using strategic industrial policies. Of course, many countries that have used industrial policies of one sort or another have been unsuccessful or had only mediocre economic performance. The source of the problem can usually be readily identified, however, as stemming not from industrial policy per se but from flawed design or implementation or from exogenous shocks. Hence, as development economists, we have decided on these grounds, coupled with the significant number of comprehensive case studies showing a favorable impact of IP on success stories, to risk (with due caution) the Darwinian fallacy and promote in this book the idea that it is a good "bet" for Latin America to deepen a commitment to, and cultivate a capacity for, an explicit medium- to long-term development strategy supported by a modern industrial policy.

More on Why We Think Medium- to Long-Term Development Strategies with Industrial Policies Are Important for Latin America

The literature on industrial polices is vast. We do not review it here; interested readers can consult elsewhere for a review (for example, Peres and Primi 2009; Harrison and Rodriguez-Clare 2009; Noland and Pack 2002). What we do highlight are the areas of the industrial policy defense that we find especially compelling for Latin America and that, in our view, make an intelligent bet on industrial policies well worth the risks involved.

Generally speaking, the mindsets, or intellectual cultures, of the skeptics and advocates of industrial policy are very different, and that difference also influences thinking about development processes.[10] We believe that the proponents of IP promote a thought process that is more relevant for Latin American policy makers if they want to successfully navigate the dynamic and increasingly competitive world of globalization for the purposes of more economic transformation, growth. and catch-up. The dimensions of this mindset that we find especially compelling are:

A Dynamic Industrial Production Bias Based on a Notion of Efficacy. Many skeptics of IP operate in a static, neoclassical Pareto-like efficiency framework that is especially protective of consumer welfare and often looks askance at even temporary consumption losses arising from the "distortions" induced by industrial policy.[11] Aside from the fact that on

Table 2.1 Catch-Up 1960–2007: Countries That Closed the Income Gap with the United States by 10 Percentage Points or More

GDP per capita as % of U.S. GDP per capita

Economy	1960s	1970s	1980s	1990s	2000–07
Austria	55.2	66.6	69.0	70.3	69.6
Finland	54.0	64.4	69.9	65.0	71.1
Hong Kong SAR, China	27.5	40.6	61.0	76.8	78.9
Iceland	74.2	86.8	98.9	88.8	93.8
Ireland	37.0	41.7	44.3	57.1	80.1
Japan	66.0	99.8	108.7	117.1	106.0
Korea, Rep.	8.3	12.3	17.8	28.4	34.9
Luxembourg	93.1	95.2	97.5	122.8	141.0
Malta	7.9	13.8	20.8	26.6	27.9
Norway	78.5	88.5	100.5	105.8	109.8
Oman[a]	9.6	21.5	24.7	25.2	26.0
Portugal	18.9	26.6	27.3	31.0	31.0
Singapore	17.7	31.2	44.4	60.4	69.4
Spain	31.9	40.0	38.0	40.5	42.6
Taiwan, China	12.8	21.0	32.7	49.9	56.4

Source: The authors on the basis of World Bank database.
Note: The amounts shown refer to constant 2000 dollars.
a. Data are available only until 2006.

its own terms Pareto optimality per se does not guarantee maximization of welfare, the more modern interpretations of industrial policy stress that economic transformation is based on the "efficacy" of promoting processes of investment and deepening industrialization that, in a continuous and cumulative way, facilitate access to codified and tacit knowledge that supports new production and technological capacities.[12] In this view, efficacy can trump efficiency in certain circumstances of learning, as noted by Cimoli and others (2006).

A Forward-Looking Medium- to Long-Term Strategy. As Montaigne pointed out long ago, "No wind works for the man who has no port of destination."[13] By its very nature a commitment to IP encourages countries to strategically organize and prioritize medium- and long-term-oriented goals that mobilize a nation's attention and efforts toward building capacities that accelerate the economic transformation of an economy.[14] The scope of IP can vary. Using the language of Hausmann, Rodrik, and Sabel (2008), it can be "in the small," that is, focused on public inputs to improve the productivity of existing activities; or "in the large," that is, focused on efforts to establish new industries. Because the region has largely mastered the art of macroeconomic balance, we think economic growth and development in Latin America would benefit if government strategy moved more decisively and coherently beyond the relatively consolidated short-term macroeconomic management that so heavily weighs on policy, combining this focus with a progressively stronger, goal-driven, medium- and long-term strategy for economic transformation.

Ambition.   As Evans (1995) observes, the IP approach magnifies concern with a country's ranking in the global economic hierarchy, on the assumption that the ranking is not irremediably fixed by the existing structure of static comparative advantages, but that public interventions can assist in scaling up the economy or accelerating the process. In other words, comparative advantages are "man-made" (Fajnzylber 1983, 1990; Adelman 2000). Hence, IP instills a culture that replaces complacency about "god-given" endowments and static comparative advantage, even in the face of respectable economic performance, for another stressing experimentation underpinned by the notion that "we can learn and do better." This ambitious culture is especially important in much of Latin America where natural resource rents, or political economy rents such as rich country trade preferences, can and do instill complacency that ultimately contribute to underperformance and economic vulnerability (ECLAC 2008).

Emulation.   Modern IP thinking is underpinned by attention to activities in the richer, more advanced countries and, as an expression of ambition, aims in different ways over time to strategically emulate them in order to learn and build new and upgraded capacities (Reinert 2009). As mentioned in chapter 1, it has been empirically observed that as countries rise in income, their economies evolve from a high degree of specialization in production and export to a stage of diversification, only to begin again to specialize at relatively high levels of income and closer proximity to technological frontiers (Imbs and Wacziarg 2003; Klinger and Lederman 2006). This suggests that development policy should strongly promote diversification because it enables new activities that generate learning and new capacities that support economic transformation and growth (Fajnzylber 1988; ECLAC 1990; Lall 1997; Rodrik 2004). On this criteria Latin America clearly lags in diversification (CAF 2006; ECLAC 2008; Agosin 2009).

Not all activities are equal, however. On the one hand, certain products entail specific skills and capacities that have some similarities with other production processes and facilitate migration to new activities, while other products are so skill specific that they are isolated, making migration difficult (Hausmann and Rodrik 2006).[15] The more isolated a country's skill set in production, the more critical is industrial policy to push diversification because market forces will not generate easily assessable bridges to new activities. On the other hand, links among production activities are in technological hierarchies where certain core technologies are located that are specific to industries or activities that are exceptionally dynamic in fostering learning, productivity, and the "making" of new and upgraded comparative advantages (Cimoli and others 2006; Lall 1993; Perez 2001). These technologies emerge along the technological frontier and diffuse. Because what a country produces today determines the accumulation of knowledge, skill, and comparative advantage of tomorrow, it is important to focus on progressive development of national capacities that permit, through imitation or innovation, entrance into production and activities that embody these dynamic technologies.[16] This type of development will not necessary happen spontaneously through market forces; indeed, markets that support certain strategic activities may not be complete or exist at all in the local economy.

Strategic Alertness to Interdependence and Spillovers.   Proponents of IP disagree among themselves about the relevance of focusing exclusively on so-called market failures as opposed to focusing on the more comprehensive issue of capabilities and knowledge accumulation through selective promotion of certain production processes and activities.[17] However, if one abstracts from a static equilibrium notion of misalignment of social and market prices, few would probably dispute the potential importance of interdependencies and spillovers arising from actions of market agents. The neoliberal paradigm culturally pays much less attention to this issue because of core assumptions of independence among economic agents.

Many spillovers can be relevant to success in growth and economic transformation of an economy (Chang 1994; Noland and Pack 2002; Harrison and Rodriguez-Clare 2009). Some seem exceptionally important for Latin America. IP is traditionally very alert to "infant industries" with intra- and interindustry scale economies that arise from production links and knowledge spillovers, because scale can raise productivity and lower costs for new activities and hence enhance their competitiveness enough to create a comparative advantage. These spillovers highlight coordination problems that IP should assess and address.

A second relevant type of spillover is informational spillover arising from undertaking new activities. A successful new activity in a local economy generates new information that will spill over and encourage new entrants that will imitate and expand the country's learning process. Recently, Hausmann and Rodrik (2006) cautioned that this type of informational spillover—in principle, good for an economy—may discourage the initial investment in discovery of a profitable new activity. That is because the "first mover" anticipates that if the investment is successful, copycats will erode rents, whereas if it fails, the new entrant bears all the costs. The prescription for this problem is public support policies and programs to encourage discovery. Other economists, however, have shown that the first mover is not necessarily at a disadvantage (Newfarmer, Shaw, and Walkenhorst 2009).[18] Nevertheless, it is safe to say that information itself is a major bottleneck and hence public interventions to intensify access to information that facilitates discovery and investment in new activities is a valuable role for industrial policy.

Evolutionary Thinking. IP is, for the most part, not bound in a static paradigm that is good for all times and places. Rather, thinking is rooted in the real evolution of national and world economies. Hence, one observes a constant progression of thinking in line with real events.

For example, in recent years industrial organization has undergone major changes. Advances in transport, information, and other technologies have led firms and industries in the global marketplace to increasingly decentralize their production systems. While knowledge (often tacitly embodied in organizations and activities) and new capacities are still importantly generated in closed units of firms and industrial sectors, there has been an explosive rise of national and international, relatively mobile, collaborative networks underpinning production and technological activities that provide knowledge, develop capacities, and stimulate innovation in dynamic activities (Cimoli and others 2006). Hence, catch-up strategies must place increasing emphasis on developing more opportunistic institutional and policy instruments to assist the private sector in developing capacities for identifying, accessing, and exploiting opportunities that do not necessarily emerge lineally from current activities. This approach is what Sabel (2009a and b) calls the new "open industrial policy," which leans toward relatively more horizontal interventions that can support multiple potential new activities and thereby minimize risks associated with a focus on one particular sector. While we do not think that the concept of open industrial policy negates the usefulness of more vertical approaches, it certainly should be incorporated into strategic thinking. As another example, the establishment of the World Trade Organization (WTO) under the Uruguay Round has made it more difficult to use certain more traditional forms of IP. However, IP not only encourages pragmatic exploration of real world loopholes in WTO rules, but it also has increasingly stressed investment strategies in supply-side issues and innovation where those rules are much less comprehensive (Bora, Lloyd, and Pangestu 2000; DiCaprio and Gallagher 2006; Weiss 2005).

Finally, perhaps the most important evolution in thinking about IP is the critical role of public-private alliances in strategy development and implementation, a subject discussed in detail in chapter 3.

Integrated Perspective for Policy. The neoliberal culture tends to focus on micro- and macroeconomic polices in separate compartments. IP stresses the need for full alignment of the two in thought and action. Hence, the IP frame of mind would try to ensure that short-term macroeconomic management and adjustments are consistent with the medium- to long-term strategy of productive transformation. IP "red lights" would be very high situations to emerge such as real domestic interest rates, a sharp influx of volatile short-term capital together with overvalued exchange rates, a fiscally starved public sector, or cutbacks in strategic investments that sustain national capacity building. The neoliberal mental paradigm of faith in market forces tends to allow more permissiveness in this regard because "the market knows best."[19] This point is important for Latin America, which has made major macroeconomic adjustments during the reform era and during the great world economic recession of 2008–09 without always fully accounting for the longer-term consequences for economic transformation.

Development Strategies in Practice

As mentioned in the introduction, our analysis in part 1 of the issue of development strategies, coupled with the "how" of their formulation and implementation, involves 10 countries that we term "success cases," either because they have sustained a process of economic convergence with rich countries or because they have performed better than Latin America countries with a similar endowment of resources. Moreover, our focus throughout this chapter and the rest of part 1 is largely on that segment of national strategy that focuses on export development.[20] We use this narrow focus for two reasons. First, it gives us a manageable vehicle to illustrate the "how" of development strategies, which usually encompass many areas. The second is that export development has been a core objective, guiding and stimulating growth and economic transformation in the success cases studied.

Ten Extraregional Success Cases

Before fully entering into the analysis of strategies, we briefly outline some general indicators that describe the countries studied in this chapter. Most of our success cases are small economies, both in terms of population and size of territory (table 2.2). The exceptions are Australia, Malaysia, the Republic of Korea, and Spain, middle-sized countries with between 20 million and 50 million inhabitants. Six of these economies—Finland, Ireland, Korea, Malaysia, Singapore, and Spain—were notably poor in the 1950s. The table also shows that the growth rate of almost all these countries has been higher in the past 25 years than that of the average of high-income members of the Organisation for Economic Co-operation and Development (OECD). In marked contrast with the Latin American region, this growth has led to sustained processes of economic convergence with rich countries (figures 2.1 and 2.2).[21] The major exceptions are Australia and New Zealand, which had a diverging trend; however, they managed to reach and maintain rich country status on an export platform of natural resources. As for Sweden, its income has been one of the highest among OECD members since the mid-20th century.

Table 2.2 General Indicators for 10 Success Cases

Country	Size of territory Thousands of km²	Population Millions (2007)	Growth of per capita GDP (annual %, constant 2000 US$)		Per capita GDP (constant 2000 US$)		Gross domestic savings (% of GDP)a		Foreign direct investment (% of GDP)b		Gross fixed investment (% of GDP)a	
			1980–89	1990–2007	1980	2007	1980–89	1990–2007	1980–89	1990–2007	1980–89	1990–2007
Australia	7,682	21.0	1.8	2.1	14,291	24,142	25.3	23.3	1.8	2.2	26.8	24.2
Czech Republic	78	10.3	—	2.0	—	7,408	—	27.7	—	5.6	—	27.3
Finland	304	5.3	3.1	2.0	15,576	28,755	27.3	25.6	0.3	2.8	26.1	19.2
Ireland	68	4.4	2.7	5.2	9,957	31,636	18.8	33.2	0.6	6.3	20.8	20.6
Korea, Rep.	99	48.5	6.4	5.0	3,221	14,540	30.9	34.4	0.3	0.7	29.6	32.9
Malaysia	330	26.5	3.1	4.0	1,848	4,715	30.2	41.7	3.2	4.6	29.5	30.2
New Zealand	270	4.2	1.1	1.6	10,265	15,033	23.2	22.6	3.1	3.6	23.6	21.0
Singapore	6,9	4.6	5.3	4.2	9,043	28,964	41.8	47.4	10.0	13.2	40.4	31.0
Spain	504	44.9	2.3	2.3	8,826	16,354	21.9	23.1	1.3	2.9	21.9	25.0
Sweden	449.9	9.1	2.0	1.8	19,330	31,764	21.7	23.4	0.4	4.8	20.5	17.3
OECD high-income countries	—	—	2.3	1.8	17,340	29,805	22.2	20.9	0.6	1.9	22.3	20.8

Source: Authors elaboration based on the World Bank, World Development Indicators (online database) and OECD numbers.
a. Data for OECD, Ireland, and New Zealand only to 2006.
b. Data for Czech Republic only from1993.
— = Not available.

Figure 2.1 GDP per Capita as Share of OECD Average for Seven Success Cases, 1960–2007

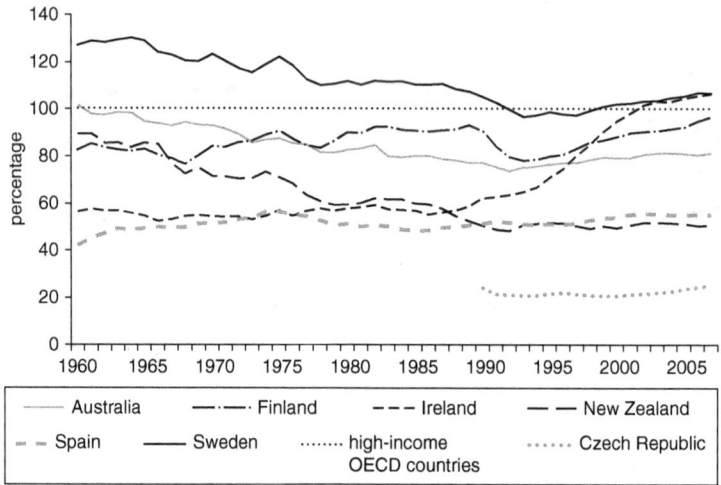

Source: Authors, based on World Bank World Development Indicators database.

Figure 2.2 GDP per Capita as a Share of OECD Average: Three Asian Success Cases

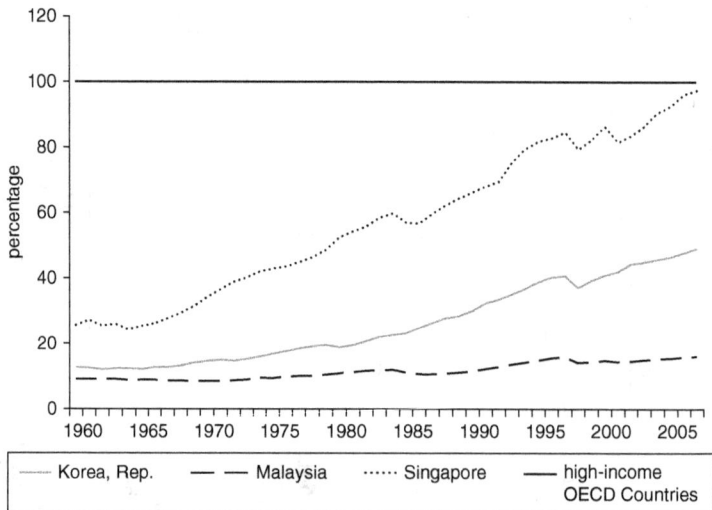

Source: Authors, based on World Bank database.

Table 2.2 also shows that all countries have had very respectable or high rates of saving in relation to GDP, with coefficients above 40 percent in Malaysia and Singapore. The same table also demonstrates the importance of foreign direct investment (FDI) for the learning process of some countries, in terms of both structural change and export development (especially in the Czech Republic, Spain, Ireland, Malaysia, Singapore, and Spain). In Korea and Finland (and Sweden), in contrast, FDI was discouraged until rather late in their development processes when national capacities were well developed.

The last column in table 2.3 shows the proportion of GDP accounted for by trade. Although this percentage differs considerably from country to country, it remains significant for all of them, with trade openness increasing over the past 15 years. These rates of trade as a share of GDP are consistent with the importance of export growth in all these countries, with rates in most of the success cases that are higher than those of the high-income OECD countries and more than twice as high as GDP growth rates. Within the export basket, medium- and high-technology products have increased significantly, except in countries endowed with abundant natural resources.[22]

Research and development (R&D) efforts (which is part of a strategic approach toward a knowledge economy in most of these countries) tend to be much higher in the success cases than in Latin American countries (except in Malaysia), with a positive trend observed in recent years.

Finally, each of these countries has its unique historical story, which we do not elaborate on here. But we do highlight in broad terms their political dynamics in the postwar era. Australia, Ireland, Finland, New Zealand, and Sweden are full-fledged Western democracies. Spain and Korea were under authoritarian strongmen until transitions to democracy in the 1970s and 1980s, respectively. Malaysia and Singapore were granted independence form Britain in the early 1960s and have had de facto one-party rule since then. Meanwhile, the Czech Republic was in the Soviet bloc until the 1990s.

The Strategies: Stylized Facts

Summary characterizations of the strategies applied by the selected countries are shown in annex table 2A, noting landmark events, or major inflection points, over time. (For additional details of the countries' specific experiences, see annex 2A). An analysis of these strategies shows a number of common elements, as well as factors that differ for or are specific to a given country. The following sets out the stylized facts.

First, the strategies generally show increasing emphasis on proactive public policies designed to overcome obstacles (including market failures) that obstruct the creation of new comparative advantages. In all, the economies' industrial policies were supported by fiscal stances that provided space for the proactive public policy.[23]

Table 2.3 Trade Indicators in the 10 Success Cases

Country	Total R&D expenditure (% of GDP)[a]		Export growth (annual %, constant 2000 US$)[b]		Medium-tech exports (% of manufacturing exports)[c]		High-tech exports (% of manufacturing exports)		Imports and exports (% of GDP)[d]	
	1990-1999	2000-06	1980-89	1990-2007	1980-89	1990-2006	1980-89	1990-2006	1980-89	1990-2007
Australia	1.6	1.7	5.3	5.6	6.5	10.7	2.7	6.1	24.5	38.9
Czech Republic	1.1	1.3	—	9.8	—	38.6	—	12.8	—	118.8
Finland	2.8	3.4	3.4	7.5	26.9	26.8	6.0	20.8	43.8	67.6
Ireland	1.3	1.2	8.3	11.4	15.4	12.8	24.2	36.8	79.8	146.7
Korea, Rep.	2.4	2.7	11.5	13.3	30.7	36.1	14.7	29.6	36.9	70.5
Malaysia	0.3	0.6	9.2	10.1	9.3	17.2	19.4	42.5	110.6	195.8
New Zealand	1.1	1.2	3.6	4.9	6.2	9.8	2.2	4.2	45.3	66.5
Singapore[e]	1.7	2.2	—	13.9	21.8	19.3	28.1	50.7		
Spain	0.9	1.0	5.2	7.4	32.8	42.0	6.5	9.8	25.8	52.9
Sweden	3.6	3.9	4.1	6.6	40.9	36.2	13.1	20.6	49.8	76.7
OECD high-income countries	2.3	2.4	4.7	6.0	—	—	—	—	25.7	39.4

Source: Authors' elaboration based on the World Bank, World Development Indicators (WDI) (online database) and OECD numbers.

a. WDI: Finland until 2007; Australia and Malaysia until 2004; New Zealand until 2005.

b. WDI: Ireland, New Zealand, and OECD until 2006.

c. Comtrade on Lall classification. Czech Republic from 1993.

d. OECD, New Zealand, Ireland until 2006.

e. Export average growth for 1990, 1995, 2000, 2004–07 (www.singtat.gov.sg).

— = Not available.

Second, strategies have been flexible and dynamic over time in response to changes in external or internal conditions, or both. Singapore has been one of the best practitioners in this regard, a fact noted by the country's prime minister, Hsien Loong Lee (2003, 5), who has stated: "No system works forever. As the external environment changes, and as economies evolve, institutions and policies that used to work can become outdated or even dysfunctional. Countries will adjust incrementally over time to these changes, but eventually incremental change is not enough. Then it becomes necessary for countries to break the mold and remake themselves—a difficult but essential process."[24]

Third, one general trend in the evolution of strategies reveals a common shift—taking place at a varying speed depending on the country—toward the strengthening of integration with the world economy.[25] The focus on export development also is general. While the domestic market offers more opportunities for structural change within large countries, small and medium-size countries naturally focus their efforts on actions conducive to export development.[26] Although these countries are all open economies now, they have differed considerably in the degree, content, and time line for trade and financial liberalization as well as in their openness to FDI. In response to the great 2008–09 recession, most of the success cases have provided short-term stimulus to their economies and are simultaneously reviewing their longer-term strategies in light of probable changes in the characteristics of the world economy (the so-called new normal).[27] However, none is questioning the commitment to international integration.

Fourth, with the exception of Australia and New Zealand, export development has been synonymous with ambition to progressively diversify and upgrade production to be able to export increasingly more sophisticated product lines. Two paradigmatic success cases, Ireland and Korea, are illustrated below in figure 2.3.

Fifth, in all 10 countries, these export development strategies are medium- or long-term strategies. Significant differences, however, exist in the scope, depth, and coherence of these strategies and in the degree of proactivity and structural orientation of their vision of the future. The scope of public actions to promote export development, as well as the degree of balance between horizontal and focused applications, varies between countries and from one priority area to another. Some countries have relied relatively more on highly specific policies that are clearly focused on particular sectors, branches of activity or clusters, whereas in others a mix of horizontal policies combined with more a limited selective approach to certain branches of activity has dominated. And in some countries intervention focuses on selected stakeholders—specific types of enterprises such as transnationals, whether generic or of a particular type; local small and medium enterprises, or SMEs; centers of excellence, and

Figure 2.3 Two Examples of Export Upgrading

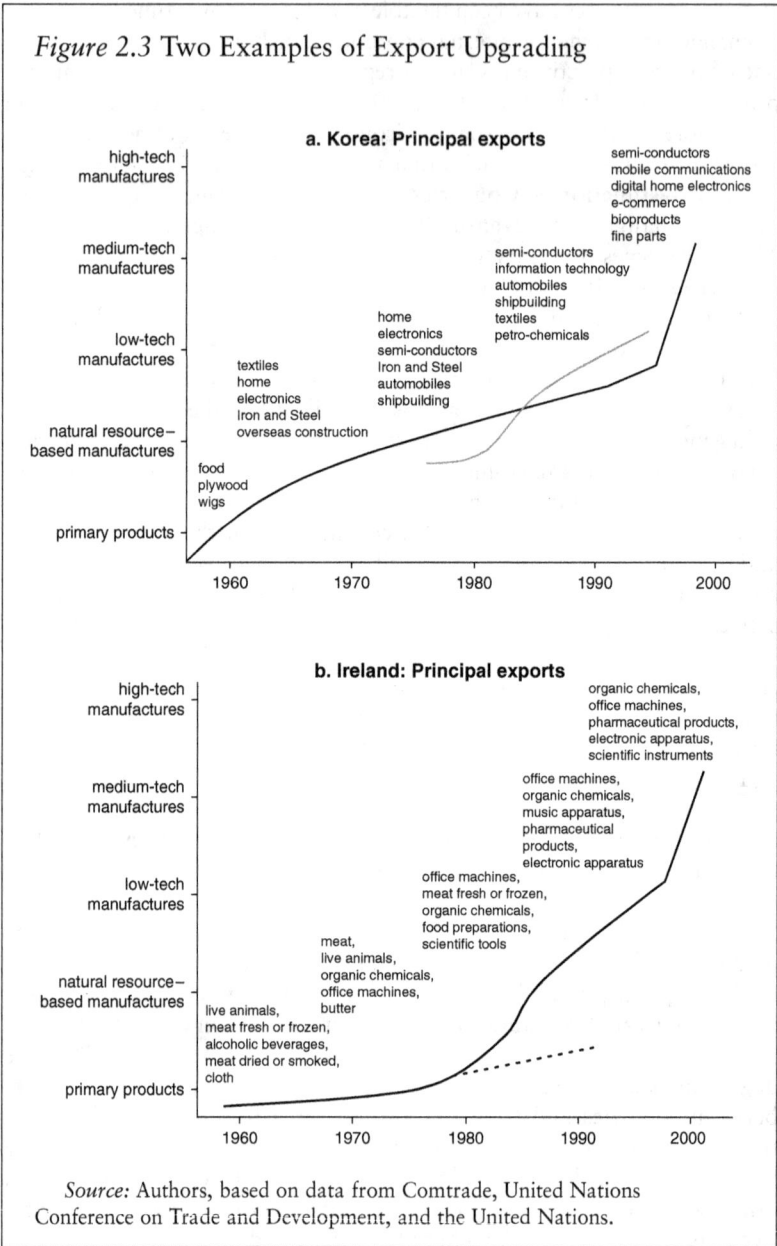

a. Korea: Principal exports

high-tech manufactures

semi-conductors
mobile communications
digital home electronics
e-commerce
bioproducts
fine parts

medium-tech manufactures

semi-conductors
information technology
automobiles
shipbuilding
textiles
petro-chemicals

low-tech manufactures

home electronics
semi-conductors
Iron and Steel
automobiles
shipbuilding

textiles
home electronics
Iron and Steel
overseas construction

natural resource–based manufactures

food
plywood
wigs

primary products

1960   1970   1980   1990   2000

b. Ireland: Principal exports

high-tech manufactures

organic chemicals,
office machines,
pharmaceutical products,
electronic apparatus,
scientific instruments

medium-tech manufactures

office machines,
organic chemicals,
music apparatus,
pharmaceutical products,
electronic apparatus

low-tech manufactures

office machines,
meat fresh or frozen,
organic chemicals,
food preparations,
scientific tools

meat,
live animals,
organic chemicals,
office machines,
butter

natural resource–based manufactures

live animals,
meat fresh or frozen,
alcoholic beverages,
meat dried or smoked,
cloth

primary products

1960   1970   1980   1990   2000

Source: Authors, based on data from Comtrade, United Nations Conference on Trade and Development, and the United Nations.

universities. In other countries, intervention is applied across the board and does not target any one actor in particular.

Sixth, all the strategies are underpinned by macroeconomic policies designed to maintain fundamental balances. The countries with the more ambitious policies for productive transformation have been careful, however, to align the commitment to macroeconomic balances with industrial policy objectives. All the countries have experienced episodes of instability at one time or another, but in recent decades a focus on fundamental macroeconomic balances has been a constant. In our group of success cases, Ireland and Spain are examples of successful industrial policies and prosperity that have led to complacency, in both cases at that macroeconomic level where financial market and real estate property bubbles developed and burst, creating major economic crises.

Seventh, the capacity of an economy is only as good as the quality of the people working in it. In all 10 countries, a fundamental basis for strategy implementation is the strengthening of basic and secondary education, along with higher education, as these countries increasingly focused on moving up the world's production hierarchy.[28] Educational development is a generational issue, and efforts are therefore undertaken from an early stage of development with attention to increasing coverage and quality throughout the various phases involved.

Eighth, some strategies are linked to formal planning processes. In such cases, the structure and composition underlying those plans vary, of course, from country to country. Table 2.4 shows which countries (half

Table 2.4 National Plans in Selected Countries

Czech Republic (before 1990)	Central planning
Czech Republic (after 1990)	Three-year plans
Finland	Three-year plans or guides
Ireland	Seven-year plans
Korea, Rep. (up to 1993)	Five-year plans
Korea, Rep. (1997 onward)	National plans are dropped, but each ministry has indicative plans.
Malaysia	Indicative (complementary and interactive) plans that include a 30-year "vision," a 10-year framework plan, and a budgeted 5-year plan.

Source: Authors, based on official data.

those studied) had national plans. In the Czech Republic, Finland, Ireland and the Republic of Korea (before 1997), plans were created in a framework that reflected not only goals and priorities, but also a multiyear commitment (indicative or hard) for allocation of funding.[29]

We think the existence of formal indicative plans offers some advantages for countries pursuing catch-up, particularly when they are accompanied by indicative resource allocations from finance ministries and reflect a degree of political consensus that provides relative continuity of successful initiatives over political cycles. First, formal plans constitute a systematic national analysis that orders thinking beyond the day-to-day events by establishing forward-looking goals and priorities. Second, plans not only validate and motivate the actions of the public bodies responsible for the strategies (development agencies) and support their authority to implement programs and policies but also can serve as a sort of indirect coordination mechanism. (This institutional area is discussed in a later chapter.) The inclusion of goals for which multiyear funding commitments are in place can help to raise the credibility of the strategy in the mind of the private sector and reinforce executing agencies' mandates. Last, even assuming flexibility, ex post the plan can serve as a public reference point for assessment of the effectiveness of the authorities' converting words into deeds. That is clearly the case in Finland and Ireland.

Ninth, some strategies, such as that of Australia, arise from a government's political platform and are, in essence, very vulnerable to political cycles. The national strategy that was in force until the change of government administration in 2009 was, to a certain extent, simply a grouping, or framework, for government programs already under way. A recent strategy in New Zealand, which reflected the components of the Clark administration's political platform, combined the essence of the strategy implemented by a previous administration with a new, more structured approach for 10 years, starting from 2006. This "economic transformation" initiative reached the stage of defining goals, identifying opportunities and limitations, and formulating indicative plans of action; however, it remains to be seen what a conservative government elected in 2009 will do. On the other hand, the strategies of countries such as Spain and Sweden are not set out in documents; they are informal or tacit in nature, reflected implicitly in government programs.

Tenth, national strategies and their components often overlap with strategies at the subnational level, with varying degrees of linkage. In more politically centralized countries, regional strategies are coordinated with the national strategy. In other cases the links may be weaker, and strategies may even be somewhat independent, as can be seen in the case of Spain. Such a characteristic inevitably has implications for the strategy's effectiveness.

Four Strategic Orientations

Although, national strategies cover a wide range of development topics, two key components have invariably been export development and strategic strengthening of integration with the world economy. In almost all of our case countries, strategies in pursuit of this goal include support for FDI attraction, the internationalization of local enterprises, export promotion, and innovation.[30]

Strategic orientations in this area can be integrated within an overarching national strategy or can constitute relatively independent strategies. In the interest of organizing the analysis, only multiyear, formally documented strategies have been examined.

As may be seen from table 2.5, innovation is currently the most widespread orientation in the selected countries and indeed in most cases is the lead strategy. Moreover, innovation's emergence as a strategic pole of development is relatively recent in most of the countries. The emergence of central interest in innovation is driven in part by the strategic goal of accessing new and dynamic transversal technologies—such as biotech, ICT (information and communications technology), and nanotechnology—but also by the need to raise a country's productivity in goods and services sectors, as well as to upgrade them, in the face of competition from lower-wage countries. Another important

Table 2.5 Four Strategic Orientations for Strengthening Integration with the World Economy

Country	FDI attraction	Internation-alization of SMEs	Export promotion	Innovation
Australia	√			√
Czech Republic	√		√	√
Finland				√
Ireland	√	√	√	√
Korea, Rep.		√	√	√
Malaysia	√	√	√	√
New Zealand		√	√	√
Singapore	√	√	√	√
Spain		√[a]	√	√
Sweden				√

Source: Authors, based on official data.
Note: The √ symbol indicates a formally drawn-up strategy that is in force.
a. Refers to autonomous communities.

characteristic is that these orientations are generally well linked in the more organized strategies.

Attraction of Foreign Direct Investment.   Attracting FDI has been of key importance in the strategies of countries initially exhibiting limited skill sets. In effect, they have sought to make rapid progress in industrialization and in export development by piggybacking on FDI. Such is the case for Ireland, Malaysia, Singapore, Spain, and, more recently, the Czech Republic. As mentioned earlier, active attraction of FDI came late in the stage of development of Finland, Korea, and Sweden because these countries had the basis for relatively more autonomous national learning processes.[31]

In the countries that relied on FDI from the beginning to kick-start their economies, the first aim was usually to generate employment.[32] But as they succeeded in attracting firms and established credibility as an overseas base for foreign firms' exports, policies became more discretionary. Singapore, for example, redirected the incentives from FDI activities in low-wage production processes to sectors of higher value and skill (such as electronics) and more recently to activities at or near the technological frontier. That has required, in addition to monetary rewards to establish or upgrade FDI, a push in higher education and attraction of foreign talent, especially in science and technology. Meanwhile, those countries that began to attract FDI at a late stage of development often were motivated by pressure from trade partners to be more open to FDI, coupled with the desire to avoid restrictions on local firm investment overseas and the need to intensify integration with world production networks.

Internationalization of Businesses.   The internationalization of businesses focuses mostly on encouraging local firms, particularly SMEs, to gain access to external markets. The strategies aim to link local businesses to international value and export chains either indirectly through supplying locally based multinational corporations or directly as coproduction partners in an international value network. This approach generally involves incentives and support programs for local firms in training, development of business plans, and technological upgrading and in search and discovery of investment and export opportunities either in conjunction with local FDI or more independently.

The promotion of domestic supply links with locally based FDI is a common strategy. Singapore was an early mover in this regard. The strategy was seen as a vehicle to add value to local firm activities and encourage FDI to establish deeper roots in the local economy, thus discouraging the "footloose investor" practices that so plague export platforms in parts of Latin America. Also, attention to local firms was often an attempt to reduce growing dualism between dynamic foreign firms and lagging local enterprise. Attention to local SMEs also can assuage domestic political backlash concerning grants and subsidies used to attract FDI.[33] In any event, Ireland started providing incentives to FDI without much attention to domestic linkages, but came, albeit a bit late, to a strategy similar to that of Singapore (Ruane and Ugur 2006). A similar path was followed in Malaysia and the Czech Republic, the latter concentrating especially on developing an automobile cluster.

In some countries, local firms are being encouraged to "go international" on their own. This is the case in Korea, where local conglomerates have begun to transfer part of their production outside the country, thereby making it necessary for local SMEs to look for alternatives, be it in new products or markets. Singapore and Spain also actively promote "reverse FDI" by local businesses, some of which have become multinationals themselves (in Singapore, several of these companies are "government-linked").

Efforts are also focused on promoting start-ups by introducing entrepreneurs to special academic-business liaison programs and business associations as well as by generating seed money and logistical support for them. This strategy is present in all the countries but receives very high priority in Finland and Sweden, which consider that they are lagging in this area given their level of development and wealth.

Export Promotion.   Export promotion has a long history in all 10 countries. Strategies typically focus on assisting consolidation of market share, targeting certain new markets by product and country or region, as well as developing brand or country recognition. To achieve their goal, governments assist in gathering information about potential markets in other countries, promote the exporting country's image, help put suppliers and buyers into contact with one another, and support improvement in the quality of goods and services through training and support for international standards ratings. Since the mid-1990s export promotion strategies have increasingly been linked to strategic initiatives to negotiate free trade areas.

Innovation.   Last, as noted, development strategies are increasingly being led by support for innovation, with all 10 countries aware that the future of their export development and international growth depends on the creation of new goods and services and on improved productivity, especially in the face of competition from low-wage countries such as China, India, and Vietnam.

Innovation policies are largely defining the national development strategies, not to mention export strategies, in advanced countries such as Finland, Korea, and Sweden. Other countries that are relatively less developed in regard to innovation are trying to narrow the R&D and innovation gaps that separate them from the more advanced OECD countries (table 2.6). That is the case for the Czech Republic, Ireland, Malaysia, New Zealand, and Spain, which are seriously lagging behind in their innovation efforts. For its part, Singapore, also lagging, has made huge investments in R&D and innovation, while Ireland's commitment has also risen dramatically in a short period of time. This effort also entails promoting investments in infrastructure for innovation; in human capital; and in closer national and international links between businesses, the academic world, and

Table 2.6 Strategic Orientation: Innovation

Australia	Strengthen the national innovation system for more effective dissemination of new technologies, processes, and ideas; support a culture of collaboration within the research sector and between researchers and industry; increase international collaborations on research and development of entrepreneurs and researchers; improve policy development and service delivery. Diversify and increase value added in natural-resource-based industries. Development of biotechnology and ICT.
Czech Republic	Strengthen R&D as a source of innovation. Establish no more than seven priority areas for public investment. Strengthen public-private partnerships. Human resources training. Increase the competitiveness of the economy by incorporating innovation into industry and services to attain levels close to those of the advanced European Union countries. Improve the public administration of innovation, consolidating sources of R&D funding and the administration of support for innovation.
Finland	Expand the sector-based, technology-oriented strategy through broad-based innovation policy that contributes to creating the preconditions for operating models combining the needs of users, consumers, and citizens, alongside knowledge, creativity, and competence. The main targets are to be pioneering in innovation activity and to assure an innovation-based development of productivity. Finland has already oriented technology development and innovation to the forestry sector, the metals industry, ICT, biotechnology, new software materials, nanotechnology, knowledge-intensive services, and social well-being industries.
Ireland	Invest heavily in R&D, give multinational companies incentives to locate more R&D capacity in Ireland, and retain and commercialize ideas that flow from that investment. Develop a world-class level of research based on investment in research-related infrastructure and human capital at the highest level with international networks. Develop business-sector linkages with research and development activities. Focus research on sectors considered to be of key importance for leading economic and social growth—biosciences, bioengineering, energy, and ICT—as well as selected traditional areas.

Table 2.6 Strategic Orientation: Innovation *(continued)*

Korea, Rep.	Move from a capital-driven industrial strategy to one driven by innovation, emphasizing technology and efficiency. There is also a particular focus on 193 products with established high potential.
Malaysia	Develop a knowledge-based economy, increasing the role of the private sector in research and development and in innovation. Two critical areas in the strategic vision are ICT and the electrical and electronics industry. Strengthen the institutional framework and the efficiency of its services.
New Zealand	Guide investment in innovative ICT, biotechnology activities, and creative industries. Strengthen collaboration between firms and the academic world. Boost the commercialization of innovation. Improve the return on public investment in innovation.
Singapore	Increase R&D spending to 3 percent of GDP by 2010. Focus spending on a small number of areas where it can be competitive: existing clusters (electronics, chemicals, marine engineering, biomedicine) and new areas based on competitive strengths and growth potential: water technology and interactive digital media. Strike a balance between basic and applied research. Further develop private research and establish more R&D links with business and the world's research talent.
Spain	Close the gap in innovation and R&D with the European Union countries in the framework of the Lisbon Strategy and of agreements on the use of European Union funds.
Sweden	Maintain the country's leadership in research and education, with emphasis on science and mathematics. Establish priorities in areas of basic and applied research. Improve links between businesses and the academic world. Strengthen innovation in SMEs.

Sources: Authors based on official data, see Government of Australia (2008), Government of Finland (2009); Government of Ireland (2008); National Research Foundation for Singapore (no date); Government of the Czech Republic (2004); Nambiar (2007) and EPU (2006) for Malasyia; Hee (2006) for Korea; and Ministry of Economic Development (2002) for New Zealand.

government. This type of networking is vitally important for innovation. In most of our 10 case countries, priority support is being given to selected activities or sectors. The table also demonstrates that attention is being given to two core transversal technologies, biotechnology and ICT.

Annex 2A Strategies in Selected Countries

Australia

In Australia the First and Second World Wars gave rise to a strategy of self-sufficient development that lasted for several decades. As a result, industrialization and economic diversification gathered pace, with growth based on domestic demand and exports of raw materials. In the mid-1980s economic instability, a low growth rate, and high inflation led to reforms geared toward market liberalization and deregulation, the elimination of protectionism, privatization of public services, and the promotion of competitiveness for export development. In the 1990s the strategy was strengthened by the country's involvement in Asia-Pacific Economic Cooperation (APEC), as well as by initiatives to boost innovation through promotion of collaboration between businesses and academia and strong public support for national centers of excellence. The past decade has seen a series of incentives (some preexisting) under the moniker "Backing Australia's Ability" designed to boost innovation in agroindustry, mining, biotechnology, and ICT. A new national strategy began being discussed in 2008 following the election of a Labor Party government. This new government launched two initiatives to address long-term challenges facing the country. The first was to arrange a summit between February and April 2008, the aim of which was to outline Australia's long-term development strategy. This initiative fostered a discussion of ideas about the direction of policies and the matters on which policy should focus up through 2020. The second initiative, under the assumption that innovation would be a keystone in spearheading growth, was creation of a working group charged with proposing the reform of the national innovation system. The group's proposal is contained in a document entitled "Powering Ideas: An Innovation Agenda for the 21st Century."

Czech Republic

Before 1989 the Czech Republic was part of the Soviet bloc and had a centrally planned economy. Independence resulted in a loss of traditional markets and suppliers, while economic stagnation and crisis combined with democracy, liberalization, and the introduction of market mechanisms. The country's association with the European Union (EU) in 1993, the deepening of market reforms, and an industrialization strategy based on FDI attraction resulted in an economic recovery. The country joined the European Union in 2004 after fulfilling certain economic goals in a series of three-year plans that provided a financial framework for achieving them. Between 1998 and the world economic crisis, the country's economic strategy gradually became more structural, with emphasis on selective FDI attraction through incentives, local business development, and the promotion of a knowledge-based economy. This approach was reinforced in 2006 with the adoption of an export-oriented strategy based on innovation and a focus on specific markets. Unstable political coalitions have often handicapped follow-through.

Finland

Following World War II, Finland's industrial development was partly determined by the rebuilding of the Soviet Union and the trade in primary mining and forestry products with countries of the Council for Mutual Economic Assistance (COMECON). Both factors, along with the high priority Finland gave to education, served to strengthen the engineering and metal industries as well as the mining and forestry clusters. Between the 1970s and the end of the 1980s, Finland's industrial strategy was geared toward export development. It protected local industry by restricting foreign investment, by granting subsidies, targeting government procurement, and carrying out frequent devaluations to boost exports. The macroeconomic disequilibria and unemployment in the early 1990s, resulting from the collapse of the Soviet Union, changed the country's long-term vision and strategy. Finland then embarked wholeheartedly on developing knowledge as an engine for structural change and economic growth. Industrial policy oriented toward innovation was reflected in public programs designed to integrate science and technology, further strengthen education, forge closer links between industry and academia to improve the commercialization of innovation, and to embed a national system of innovation itself (which is now considered one of the best in the world). Finland's current innovation strategy seeks to respond to what it perceives as the new challenges for growth and competitiveness. The aim is to diversify innovation activities beyond leading sectors and technologies as well as to redirect the strategy toward an innovation policy based more on demand—though without disregarding policy directed at supply. The approach seeks to establish a multifaceted and wide-ranging innovation policy with enhanced efforts to strengthen implementation.

Ireland

Over the past 25 years, Ireland has experienced radical changes to its strategy for growth and employment. The protectionist strategy that had been in force since the 1930s was frequently in crisis throughout the 1960s and 1970s. This problem, along with the opportunity to join the European Union, prompted the country to liberalize the economy and draw up plans for the use of various EU development funds. Then, the debt and unemployment crises of the mid-1980s gave way to social partnership agreements that shifted strategy toward structural change based on education and export diversification beyond agricultural products. The first strategic partnership program was centered on stabilizing the economy and introducing guidelines for structural change aimed at stronger growth along with social equality. Once the economy stabilized, the strategy became even more focused on education (including higher education) and on attracting foreign investment, especially from the United States, for export-led industrialization. To attract such investment, Ireland made the most of its EU membership; its English-speaking population; its educated workforce with relatively low wages; and incentives, including a relatively low corporate tax rate. At first, FDI was sought indiscriminately, although with time attraction programs targeted higher-technology sectors and those with greater value added. Export development therefore became specialized in a few sectors (pharmaceuticals, biotechnology, chemical products, and electronics) and in services, while local businesses were later supported by policies aimed at achieving links with international export chains.[34] The strategy at the turn of the century shifted to aggressive programs of incentives to stimulate science and technology in support of innovation; the integration of local business into the world economy; and the strengthening of production, commercialization, and innovation networks. The current strategy—which has had the extremely difficult task of sharing space with crisis management of the economy—aims to reorganize economic priorities in the next five years. The aggressive strategy, known as "Building Ireland's Smart economy," aims to build an intelligent, business-driven economy that creates high-quality jobs, ensures security of energy supplies, and provides first-class infrastructure, an area that lagged in the Irish economy when first priority was given to education.

Korea

The aftermath of war in Korea left the country devastated and dependent on economic aid from the United States to rebuild the nation. Five-year economic development plans began to be implemented in the 1960s. The first plans emphasized industrialization based on protecting local industry and restricting foreign direct investment, while promoting exports and developing the chaebols (industrial conglomerates) along with their trading companies. The model was a reflection of many of the strategies of postwar Japan. In the early 1980s external debt and inflationary pressure prompted the country to implement a five-year stabilization program based on gradual market liberalization. At the end of the 1980s, once chaebols were more economically independent and technological prowess was on the rise, the country began to focus on innovation, with a five-year plan that continued to liberalize markets and limit public support actions for the large firms. At the same time, the country joined the OECD and continued to open up the economy. The new millennium saw the beginning of competition with China and an appreciating exchange rate, which forced Korea to focus on developing an economy based on innovation, knowledge, and more internationalization. All of this was particularly relevant for SMEs, which had previously had been in the shadow of the chaebols. More recently, the strategy has included the negotiation of free-trade agreements (the first of which was signed with Chile).

Malaysia

In the middle of the 1900s, Malaysia was an agricultural economy that exported raw materials. There were four stages in its industrialization process. First, an import substitution strategy in place between 1957 (when the country gained independence) and 1970 resulted in an industry focused on producing low-technology, finished consumer goods. Special incentive regimes were set up for the indigenous Malay population to increase its relative position in this multiethnic economy. That was followed by an export industrialization strategy, characterized by the creation of duty free zones, strong incentives to attract multinationals, and the reduction of the economy's protectionist barriers. Between 1980 and 1985, the growth strategy took a new direction, with the reintroduction of an import substitution policy, especially focused on support of heavy industry. The fourth and final phase of industrialization promoted a renewed focus on export development based on another phase of liberalization with active participation in the Association of South-East Asian Nations (ASEAN) and free trade agreements. Industrial policy was guided by two plans. The first Industrial Master Plan, covering the period 1986–95, involved industrialization through investment attraction, privatization of public enterprises, lower trade tariffs, and proactive management of the exchange rate. Although this strategy achieved its objectives, it had structural weaknesses: labor-intensive production was losing competitiveness because of wage increases and inadequate production links and technology deployment. Since the mid-1990s, the second Industrial Master Plan has promoted the internationalization of services, ICT corridors, value added in certain manufacturing exports, and the development of a knowledge society.

New Zealand

The fall in the prices of raw materials during the crisis of 1930 encouraged New Zealand to implement an import substitution strategy that remained in place until the mid-1980s. As in Latin America, economic crisis, high inflation, and indebtedness prompted economic liberalization, openness, and generally speaking the policies associated with the Washington Consensus. New Zealand is also active in the APEC free trade initiative. Modest growth at the end of the 1990s, increasing concern about relatively low levels of productivity (below the OECD average), deterioration of the social situation, a widening current account deficit, and disequilibria pushed the country to seek a new, more strategic thrust that combined elements of the market with public sector interventions. This strategy aimed for innovation and structural change to promote productivity growth and sustainable and integrative export development. In 2002 the framework for "Growing an Innovative New Zealand" was established, but it ran into problems at the implementation stage because of a weak underlying public-private alliance. In 2005 the strategy was reconfigured as one of "Economic Trans-formation" and prevailed until 2008, when a more conservative govern-ment took office. It appears that the strategy has since been scrapped for a more traditional focus on macroeconomics and infrastructure.

Singapore

The country's separation from Malaysia in 1965, along with the announce-ment of the withdrawal of British forces in 1967, accelerated the search for an alternative development model that was not dependent on the small domestic market. The government therefore gathered together busi-ness and union representatives to work on new directions. The general ingredients of the resulting strategy, which has been in place ever since, was an open economy, stability in a multiethnic society, and a vigorous FDI-attraction policy drawing on comprehensive incentives, a population with English language skills and (initially) low salaries, a British-style legal system, and a strategic geographical position in Asia. In light of competition from countries with a lower-wage workforce, the government adjusted its strategy from one of indiscriminate FDI attraction toward activities with higher levels of value and knowledge. In the 1980s this focus gave rise to the development of electronics, information technology, and new service clusters, in which local businesses integrated with inter-national value chains or became suppliers to multinational corporations, or both. In the 1990s the country pushed forward with internationaliza-tion, including participation in ASEAN, APEC, and free trade agreements. At the same time, the strategic orientation has moved to higher educa-tion and innovation, especially in the areas of biotechnology, electronics, environmental industries, and global business promotion. Although this strategy persists in broad terms, the government has convened a Strategic Economic Committee comprising representatives of the public and private sectors to review the specific strategies for developing the various sectors on which national growth is based. The task is to review their potential, find new ways of attracting FDI, and secure new and creative responses to the 2008–09 crisis, especially its long-term impact on the world economy.

Spain

Between the end of the Second World War and the end of the 1970s, Spain was governed by an authoritarian centralist state with an inward-oriented and protectionist strategy. The advent of democracy brought about two economic changes that had a profound effect on the country's economic system. First, in 1986 Spain joined the European Union, which meant that the country had to adopt collective EU policies that resulted in mod-ernization of the economic rules, market liberalization and elimination of monopolies, privatization of public enterprises, and a reduced public-sector role in the economy. These reforms combined with a substantial rise in promotion instruments for the private sector and in financial resources allocated to that end. Second, Spain went from being a centralist country to a quasi-federal state where the Autonomous Communities have been legally awarded considerable power over economic promotion, FDI attraction, and SME support, including the integration of local businesses into the world economy. Over the past 20 years, the strategy has varied from an export-promotion focus to one of FDI attraction and international integration of local business, including reverse FDI. Following EU guidelines, the current strategy is focusing on innovation. However, fiscal retrenchment in the middle of a severe economic crisis raises challenges for implementation of that strategy.

Sweden

Between 1870 and 1970 Sweden was the second-fastest-growing country in the world, with a strong emphasis on educating its population. Growth subsequently came to a standstill for 30 years. During the first period of industrialization, growth was spearheaded by forestry (cellulose and paper) and mining. The country's strategy (which was protectionist at first) enabled the technological enhancement of production processes, while differentiating and adding value to its natural resources. Technology that was initially imported was then developed domestically, in a process that produced a much more diversified economic structure. This development was based on the export orientation of industry; the use of export income for technological development; industrial promotion resulting from government procurement; a constant effort to improve the education and health of the population; and a permanent drive to reduce costs through mechanization, process automation, and incremental innovation led by major Swedish transnational corporations competing in mainly mid-technology markets. In the mid-1970s the protectionist policy against foreign investment was toned down and the development of ICT and electronics began. In the 1990s strategy focused on joining the European Union and the knowledge society. An innovation strategy became the focus of the policy for structural change and productivity growth; the national innovation system was strengthened; and the development of the chemical, pharmaceutical, and biotechnology sectors was promoted. Start-ups have also been promoted more recently. To deal with the crisis and its long-term consequences, the Swedish organization responsible for innovation policy, VINNOVA, made a proposal to the government: the strategy was called Development and Innovation: A Strategic Proposal for Sustained Growth. This set of policies is meant to attenuate the crisis and also is geared to the long term. The policies center on the adaptation of Sweden's automotive industry, innovation in SMEs, mobilization of resources and actors to support innovation and competitiveness in the regions, and the further internationalization of economic growth and employment.

Annex Table 2A National Strategies: Selected Landmark Events

	First period	Second period	Third period	Fourth period
Australia	1920	1983	2000–	
	Import substitution.	Washington Consensus–type trade and political liberalization.	Push forward in the area of innovation and FDI attraction.	
Czech Republic	Up to 1989	1990	2005–	
	Centrally planned industrialization.	Introduction of market mechanisms. Washington Consensus orientation. Privatizations and emphasis on business development. FDI attraction. Institutional development and strengthening of competitiveness.	Incentives oriented toward high-technology goods and services. Boosting the development of microinstitutions. Promoting innovation, institutionalization, and collaboration between industry and the academic world. Formulating a strategy for innovation and export development. More selective attraction of FDI.	
Finland	1970	1993	2006–	2008
	Industrialization based on natural-resource-intensive sectors. Protectionism, government procurement, and subsidies for emerging industries. Continuing emphasis on education.	Joins the European Union. Liberalization of trade and external capital, together with increased attention to long-term microeconomic trends. Toward an innovation society. Strengthening and coordination of industry and the innovation system. R & D approach guided by the growth of industry.	Strengthening the capacity for renewal of the innovation system. Increasing the knowledge base. Improving the quality and goals of scientific and technological research. Increase the marketing of innovation.	Emphasize the role of users and market demand as equally important drivers of innovation, growth, and renewal, and as central elements of the innovation policy. Also pursue nonscientific and nontechnological innovations in services, business models, branding, and work-life innovations.

Ireland	1970	1986	1993	2006
	Change from import substitution and a protected economy to openness to foreign capital and trade related to EU entry in 1973.	Program for National Recovery adopted to promote social stability and cohesion. Industrial policy based on attracting export-oriented FDI.	Capacity building for improvements in competitiveness, focusing on sectors or market niches, SMEs with export capacity, and incentives for a more selective attraction of FDI, in addition to an aggressive education program and a state modernization plan	Entry to a knowledge-based society, emphasizing high value-added activities. Ambitious program of incentives for the development of innovation and the internationalization of local businesses, as well as strengthening networks for production, marketing, and innovation.
Korea, Rep.	1964	1970	1981	2001–
	Industrialization in low-technology goods with a focus on exports.	Industrialization based on dual-purpose military/heavy industry and increased export values. Emphasis on technology imports.	Stabilization, liberalization. Development of the electronic sector. Move from creative imitation phase to innovation.	Knowledge-based economic development. Industrial policy emphasizing innovation. Internationalization of small and medium firms.

(continued)

Annex Table 2A National Strategies: Selected Landmark Events *(continued)*

	First period	Second period	Third period	Fourth period
Malaysia	1960	1970	1980	1986
	Industrialization oriented toward import substitution.	New Economic Policy (1970–80). Industrial policy based on attracting export-oriented FDI, adding value to manufactured exports, and initiating development of technology corridors.	Reorientation of the industrialization process toward import substitution once more (heavy industry). Developing targeted protection policies, direct state participation in the production process and the development of complementary industries.	Export promotion based on trade liberalization, active participation in free trade agreements, and industrial development. 1986–96: export revival based on FDI attraction, lower tariffs, and managing the exchange rate to maintain competitiveness. 1996 onward: developing the knowledge-based economy, guided by a long-term vision based on the development of international services, ICT, value added in export manufactures, and technological innovation corridors.
New Zealand	1960	1984	2006	
	Industrialization oriented toward import substitution.	Washington Consensus–type trade and political liberalization.	A 10-year economic transformation agenda focusing on globally competitive firms, world-class infrastructure, stimulating innovation and productivity, environmental sustainability, and promotion of Auckland as a city able to compete on the world stage.	

	1965	1979	1990	2001–2005
Singapore	Industrialization through import substitution. Exports of light manufactures and FDI attraction.	Policy of orientation toward medium- and high-technology industry and services. Wage increases in labor-intensive sectors to provide incentives for the achievement of the above goal.	Internationalizing manufacturing aimed at neighboring countries, followed by expansion toward China, India, and the Middle East. Initiating the development of industrial and service clusters (including local businesses with state participation). Development of a platform of financial and business services.	Development of existing clusters, identification and development of new ones through investment attraction, strong support for innovative businesses, technological development in areas of existing capacity and in a selective number of new areas. Internationalization of SMEs. Creation of new geographical spaces for investment and exports.

	1950	1978	1990	2005
Spain	Inward-oriented and protectionist policies.	Trade liberalization, entry to the European Union and adhesion to its policies. Beginning of economic internationalization process. Strong infrastructure development, support for internationalization of small and medium firms. Decentralization of certain economic responsibilities to the Autonomous Communities. Attraction of FDI.	Promotion of Spanish FDI.	Strengthening of innovation.

(continued)

Annex Table 2A National Strategies: Selected Landmark Events *(continued)*

	First period	Second period	Third period	Fourth period
	1900	1930	1975	1990
Sweden	Export-oriented industrial development. Promotion of forestry and mining commodity exports.	Construction of the welfare state. Exports of processed raw materials. Endogenous technological development. Differentiation of export products. Trade liberalization, protection from foreign investment.	Industrial policy designed to support major corporations (including via state procurement). Development of ICT and services sectors. Reduction of protectionist policies against FDI. Promotion of exports from the electronics, machinery, engineering, services, and mining sectors.	Technological development and innovation. Strengthening of the national innovation system. Development of chemicals, pharmaceuticals, and biotechnology.

Source: Authors, based on official data.

Notes

1. There are many definitions of industrial policy (Chang 1994; Peres and Primi 2009). We think that basically IP involves the state, with a medium- to long-term perspective, strategically and proactively intervening in markets with a variety of instruments to promote or directly develop new industrial and techno- logical capacities of a higher order than those prevailing in an economy in order to accelerate economic transformation and growth beyond what static market forces might provide. A key feature of industrial policies is strategic selectivity, whether through focused, goal-oriented horizontal policies supporting several sectors or vertical policies focused on a specific sector. While IP's focus traditionally has been on industry, it should include services as well. Importantly, IP also can assist the "death" of sunset industries to free up resources for new activities with minimal damage to accumulated capabilities that still may have relevance for the perfor- mance of new activities in the economy.

2. Fajnzylber (1990) observes that obstacles to economic transformation can be particularly damaging in natural-resource-based economies.

3. As Rodrik (2008) notes, the new growth theory also recognizes the exis- tence of multiple market failures, as does the new trade theory. See also Lall (2000).

4. The Republic of Korea has used an extensive battery covering many of the instruments, which can be perused in Chang (1994, 115–16).

5. Adam Smith's *Wealth of Nations,* published in 1776, was in some ways countering ideas of state activism and mercantilism inspired by Louis XIV's famous finance minister, Jean-Batiste Colbert. Meanwhile, Alexander Hamilton in the United States and Friedrich List in Germany were famous 18th century antagonists of Smith's laissez faire theory of capitalism.

6. As pointed out by authors like Sabel (2009a). Even Michael Porter (2008), who formerly argued that only firms, not countries, have strategies, Porter (2007) now counsels that the United States needs a strategy if it is not to fall behind.

7. For an interpretation of how Latin America has viewed structuralism, see Di Filippo (2009).

8. Chang (2003) and others argue that successful countries become free trade proponents only after they reach the top, in effect attempting to eliminate for other more backward countries the "ladder" of industrial policy that they used to get ahead. But even after reaching a category of a liberal economy the remnants of industrial policy, albeit more subtle, are present. As the head of France's Strategic Investment Fund recently commented: "We consider it legitimate for the public authority to worry about the nature and evolution of the industrial fabric of our country.... The state has a right to have a vision" (Peggy Hollinger, "Dirigisme de rigueur," *Financial Times,* June 4, 2009, p. 7).

9. China's growth spurt started so late (1978), and China was so far behind the United States, that, despite rapid growth over the past 30 years, it did not qualify for the elite club in this World Bank database. However, China would now seem likely to pass the threshold based on independent estimates of purchasing power parity. See Martin Wolf, "In the Grip of a Great Convergence," *Financial Times,* January 5, 2011, p. 9.

10. An intellectual culture has its own language and norms, which inform, stimulate, and constrain the way one thinks about economic policy (Jung-en Woo 2007).

11. For example, some studies dismiss Korea's heavy industry development policy drive of the 1970s, even though, albeit with mistakes, it proved over time to be largely successful in supporting economic transformation and profitability. This critique arose because at the time the ambitious program distorted relative prices

and drew resources away from light industry, which (temporarily) reduced the net competitiveness of manufacturing and global efficiency (see Jong-ho 1990 and Kim 1990. From the different perspective of IP, the successful shifting of the economy from light to heavy industry represented the building of new capacities as well as a generation of public signals encouraging commitment to investment in new upgraded activities and learning. As Amsden (1989) famously observed, catch-up has often involved getting the prices "wrong" from the neoclassical perspective. Jong-ho and Kim also attribute the heavy industry drive to macroeconomic instability. However, others point out that temporary problems were not caused by IP as such, but rather by external shocks or excessively rapid capital account opening (Wade 2004).

12. One could look at this from an angle of "dynamic" efficiency, in which the gains from IP would outweigh, in discounted terms, the temporary consumption losses of IP policies (Harrison and Rodriguez-Clare 2009). However, while this perspective is conceptually neat, problems of precision confront measurement of the impact of IP, as noted earlier.

13. Frame (1958), p. 243.

14. For instance, the Asians have been enormously goal-oriented and strategic. As a contemporary illustration, the Chinese have a goal of making Shanghai an international fashion center by 2015; another goal is to raise the country's research and development expenditure to 2 percent of GDP by 2020 (Devlin 2008). Meanwhile, Singapore planned to raise its R&D expenditures from 2 percent to 3 percent of GDP by the end of 2010.

15. Moreover, in a new activity learning can be intense, allowing countries to move up the quality scale fairly quickly. In Korea, Hyundai Motors is a good example of learning. Behind a heavily protected domestic market, this industry within 30 years became a major player in the international auto industry.

16. Where dynamism lies in the world product space has been a point of debate. Most feel that it is in industrial manufacturing and certain knowledge-intensive services, but some argue that natural resources are equally attractive. For more discussion, see ECLAC (2008).

17. See Peres and Primi (2009). The breach emerges from questions about the real world relevance for public policy of the neoclassical paradigm's efficiency benchmark.

18. If the firm exports, the world market is big enough for more than one player. Moreover, new entrants can create intraindustry spillovers from which they themselves benefit. These spillovers are the outcome in some cases of export discovery analyzed in Sabel and others (forthcoming).

19. But as seen in the Asian crisis of 1997, and recent problems in Ireland and Spain, successful practitioners of IP can be periodically seduced into macroeconomic stances that are counterproductive to economic transformation.

20. Export development has several dimensions, which can be combined. It can include exporting greater quantities of products that already have a share of the world market, and doing so with increased productivity. Another dimension would be horizontal diversification based on existing comparative advantages, which are relatively easy to identify but for some reason are not fully exploited. It can also involve improvements in the quality of export products that are already exported to increase unit values in existing areas of production. Last, it can mean the creation of truly new comparative advantages.

21. In some countries, membership in the European Union (EU) coincided with a convergence process. In Finland, convergence was interrupted by the fall of the Soviet Union and picked up again after Finland made reforms in the mid-1990s, which also coincided with entry into the European Union. The convergence of Spain also coincided with its entry into the European Union. Sweden experienced a long process of losing its superior ground but began to regain its footing at around the same time as its entry into the European Union (1995), while the Czech

Republic showed signs of convergence as it prepared to join in 2004. Nonetheless, policies and strategies to exploit opportunities are important—countries such as Greece and Austria did not achieve convergence even with EU entry.

22. What is not conveyed in table 2.3 is that New Zealand and, especially, Australia have increased the productivity and added value to goods and services around their natural resources.

23. For a very clear and intelligent official statement on how Singapore uses industrial polices to overcome these obstacles and effectively "enable markets," see Menon (2010).

24. Singapore has "rebranded" its strategy on a number of occasions. See table 2.4 and Kumar and Siddique (2010).

25. Excluding Sweden, which industrialized in the 19th century and was already one of the richest countries in the world in 1970 (Andersson, 2010), in the postwar era almost all of these countries initiated liberalization with the international economy after periods of import substitution industrialization with domestically protected markets. In some cases, especially in Korea and Finland, that did not rely on FDI, this industrialization process was especially critical for building basic knowledge and technological capacities that contributed to their progressive march to the technological frontier.

26. This phenomenon is, of course, to be expected in smaller countries, but, interestingly, it has also occurred in medium-size and even large countries such as China. The role of export development as a growth factor comes as no surprise, since for decades the world has been witnessing a rapid globalization process in which foreign trade has generally been growing much faster than world GDP. This favorable development has given countries an opportunity to boost productivity and growth both directly and indirectly by moving into external markets. Amsden (2007) argues that in Asia the move from low- to medium- and high-tech exports depended on first "practicing" in protected home markets. However, Asian strategies pressured firms to initiate an export drive at early stages of the learning process.

27. Again, an intelligent reflection on this can be seen in Lee (2009). Ireland has undertaken a formal review of its strategy with reflections that aim to stabilize the economy, invest even more in R&D (with more incentives for local multinationals to do so), incorporate a new "green accord" around fossil fuels, and upgrade the country's infrastructure to world class (Government of Ireland 2008). The capacity of the govenrment to fully pursue this strategy clearly will be challenging because of the severe fiscal crisis the country has been facing since the 2008–09 recession.

28. Countries such as Ireland, Finland, and Korea have very actively tried to anticipate demands for skilled labor based on forward-looking development strategies. Expenditures on education, and priorities given different levels, are adjusted accordingly to prepare for a new phase of productive transformation.

29. Funding mechanisms vary considerably. In Ireland, for example, the allocation of resources is a "hard" budget commitment, while in Finland, the volume of resources allocated in the plan, like the plan itself, is only a guideline for the government, albeit a highly influential one.

30. The situation varies considerably among countries, especially in foreign direct investment; as mentioned already, a number of countries have had a history of restrictions in that area.

31. Taiwan, China, was also a latecomer in attracting FDI. China, meanwhile, has relied very much on FDI to gain a base for learning.

32. For insights on the early story of Singapore's FDI attraction, see Schien (1983).

33. This was a problem for the Czech Republic's successful FDI attraction program.

34. Compared with Singapore, Ireland was slow to recognize the need to combine FDI attraction policies with programs to integrate local businesses into the world economy (Ruane and Ugur 2006).

References

Adelman, Irma. 2000. "Fifty Years of Economic Development: What Have We Learned?" Paper presented at the World Bank ABC Conference, Washington, DC (June).

Agosin, Manuel. 2009. "Export Diversification and Growth in Emergent Economies." *CEPAL Review* 97 (LC/G.2400-P), Economic Commission for Latin America and the Caribbean, Santiago, Chile (April).

Amsden, Alice. 1989. *Asia's Next Giant*. Oxford, U.K.: Oxford University Press.

———. 2007. *Escape from Empire*. Cambridge, MA: MIT Press.

Andersson, Thomas. 2010. "Building Long Term Strategies and Public-Private Alliances for Export Development: The Swedish Case." Project Document 295. Economic Commission for Latin America and the Caribbean, International Trade and Integration Division, Santiago, Chile.

Bairoch, Paul. 1993. *Economics and World History*. New York: Harvester.

Bora, Bijit, Peter Lloyd, and Mari Pangestu. 2000. "Industrial Policy and the WTO." Policy Issues in International Trade and Commodities Study 6, United Nations Conference on Trade and Development, Geneva.

CAF (Corporación Andina de Fomento). 2006. *Camino a la transformación productiva en América Latina*, Economic and Development Report Series. Caracas: CAF.

Chang, Ha-Joon. 1994. *The Political Economy of Industrial Policy*, New York, St. Martin's Press.

———. 2003. "Kicking Away the Ladder: The 'Real' History of Free Trade." FPIF Special Report, Inter-Hemispheric Resource Center, Silver City, NM (December).

Cimoli, Mario, Giovanni Dosi, Richard Nelson, and Joseph Stiglitz. 2006. "Institutions and Policies Shaping Industrial Development: An Introductory Note." Working paper 2006/2, Laboratory of Economic Management, St. Anna School of Advanced Studies, Pisa.

de Oliveira Campos, Roberto. 1964. "Economic Development and Inflation with Special Reference to Latin America." In *Leading Issues in Economic Development*, ed. Gerald Meier. Oxford, U.K.: Oxford University Press.

Devlin, Robert. 2008. "China's Economic Rise." In *China's Expansion into the Western Hemisphere*, ed. Riordan Roett and Guadalupe Paz. Washington, DC: Brookings Institution.

Devlin, Robert, and Graciela Moguillansky. 2009. "Public-Private Alliances for Long- Term National Development Strategies." CEPAL Review 97 (LC/G.2400-P), Economic Commission for Latin America and the Caribbean (ECLAC), Santiago, Chile (April).

DiCaprio, Alisa, and Kevin Gallaher. 2006. "The WTO and the Shrinking of Development Space." *Journal of World Investment and Trade* 7.

Di Filippo, Armando. 2009. "Latin American Structuralism and Economic Theory." CEPAL Review 98 (LC/G.2404-P), Economic Commission for Latin America and the Caribbean, Santiago, Chile (August).

ECLAC (Economic Commision for Latin America and the Caribbean). 1990. *Transformación Productiva con Equidad, La Tarea Prioritaria del Desarrollo de América Latina y el Caribe en los Años Noventa*. S.90.II.G.6. Santiago, Chile.

———. 2008. *Structural Change and Productivity Growth Twenty Years Later*: *Old Problems, New Opportunities*. LC/G.2367 (SES.32/3). Santiago, Chile.

EPU (Economic Planning Unit). 2006. "Ninth Malaysia Plan, 2006–2010." http://www.epu.jpm.my/rm9/html/english.htm.

Evans, Peter. 1995. *Embedded Autonomy. States and Industrial Transformation*. Princeton, NJ: Princeton University Press.

Fajnzylber, Fernando. 1983. *La industrialización truncada de América Latina*. México, D.F.,: Nueva Imagen.

———. 1988. "International Competitiveness, Evolution and Lessons." CEPAL Review 36 (LC/G.1537-P), Economic Commission for Latin America and the Caribbean, Santiago, Chile (December).

———. 1990. *Industrialización en América Latina: de la "caja negra" al "casillero vacío*. Cuadernos de la CEPAL 60 (LC/G.1534/Rev.1), Economic Commission for Latin America and the Caribbean, Santiago, Chile.

Fernandez-Arias, Eduardo. 2010. "Industrial Policy in Latin America." In *The Age of Productivity: Transforming Economies from the Bottom Up*, ed. Carmen Pagés. Washington, DC: Inter-American Development Bank.

Frame, Donald. 1958. *The Complete Essays of Montaigne*. Stanford, CA: Stanford University Press.

Government of Australia. 2008. "Powering Ideas: An Innovation Agenda for the 21st Century." http://www.innovation.gov.au/innovationreview/Pages/home.asp.

Government of Finland. 2009. "Finland's National Innovation Strategy." http://www.tem.fi/index.phtml?l=en&s=2411.

Government of Ireland. 2008. "Building Ireland's Smart Economy: A Framework for Sustainable Renewal." http://www.taoiseach.gov.ie/BuildingIrelands-SmartEconomy_1_.pdf.

Government of the Czech Republic. 2004. "National Innovation Strategy of the Czech Republic." http://www.mpo.cz/zprava11688.html.

Harrison, Ann, and Andrés Rodriguez-Clare. 2009. "Trade, Foreign Investment and Industrial Policy." MPRA Paper 15561, University Library of Munich.

Hausmann, Ricardo, and Bailey Klinger. 2006. "Structural Transformation and Patterns of Comparative Advantage in the Product Space."Faculty Research Working Paper RWP06-041, John Kennedy School of Government, Harvard University, Cambridge, MA (September).

Hausmann, Ricardo, and Dani Rodrik. 2006. "Doomed to Choose: Industrial Policy as a Predicament," Kennedy School of Government, Harvard University, Cambridge, MA (September).

Hausmann, Ricardo, Dani Rodrik, and Charles Sabel. 2008. "Reconfiguring Industrial Policy: A Framework with an Application to South Africa." CID Working Paper 168, Center for International Development, Harvard University, Cambridge, MA (May).

Hee, Yol Yu. 2006. "Korea National Innovation System, Korea Institute of S&T Evaluation and Planning." http://www.scj.go.jp/ja/int/kaisai/jizoku2006/paper/pdf/41_hee-yol-yu.pdf.

Hughes, Alan. 2007. "Hunting the Elusive Snark of Innovation, Some Reflections on the UK Experience with Small Business Support Policy." *Proceedings of the Innovation Leadership Group Forum on Innovation and SMEs* (September).

Imbs, Jean, and Romain Wacziarg. 2003. "Stages of Diversification." *American Economic Review* 93, no. 1 (March).

Yoo, Jung-ho. 1990. "The Industrial Policy of the 1970s and the Evolution of the Manufacturing Sector." KDI Working Paper 9017. Korean Development Institute, Seoul.

Jung-En Woo, Meredith, ed. 1999. *The Developmental State*. Ithaca, NY: Cornell University Press.

———. 2007. "After the Miracle: Neoliberalism and Institutional Reform in East Asia." *In Neoliberalism and Institutional Reform in East Asia*, ed. Meredith Jung-En Woo., ed. New York: Palgrave.

Katz, Jorge, and Bernardo Kosacoff. 1998. "Arendizaje tecnológico, desarrollo institucional y la microeconomía de la sustitución de importaciones." *Desarrollo Económico* 37, no. 148 (January-March).

Kim, Ji Hong. 1990. "Korean Industrial Policy in the 1970s: The Heavy and Chemical Industry Drive." KDI Working Paper 9015. Korean Development Institute, Seoul.

Klinger, Bailey, and Daniel Lederman. 2006. "Diversification, Innovation and Imitation inside the Global Technological Frontier." Policy Research Working Paper 3872, World Bank, Washington, DC.

Kosacoff, Bernardo, and Adrián Ramos. 1999. "The Industrial Policy Debate." CEPAL Review 68 (LC/G.2039-P), Economic Commission for Latin America and the Caribbean, Santiago, Chile.

Krueger, Anne. 1990. "Government Failures in Development." Working Paper 3340, National Bureau of Economic Research, Cambridge, MA.

Kumar, Sree, and Sharon Siddique. 2010. "The Singapore Success Story: Public-Private Alliance for Investment Attraction, Innovation and Export Development." Serie Comercio International 99, Economic Commission for Latin America and the Caribbean, Santiago, Chile (March).

Lall, Sanjaya. 1993. "Policies for Building Technological Capabilities: Lessons from the Asian Experience." *Asian Development Review* 11, no. 2.

———. 1997. *Learning from the Asian Tigers: Studies in Technology and Industrial Policy*. London: MacMillan.

———. 2000. "Selective Industrial and Trade Policies in Developing Countries: Theoretical and Empirical Issues." Working Paper 48, Queen Elizabeth House, University of Oxford, Oxford, U.K. (August).

Lee, Hsien Loong. 2003. "Remaking the Singapore Economy." Speech at the annual dinner of the Economics Society of Singapore (April).

———. 2009. "Transcript of Prime Minister Lee Hsien Loong's Speech in Parliament." Singapore (May 27).

Lin, Justin Yifu, and Célestin Monga. 2010. "Growth Identification and Facilitation: The Role of the State in the Dynamics of Structural Change." Policy Working Paper 5313, World Bank, Washington, DC (May).

McClelland, Peter. 1975. *Causal Explanation and Model Building in History, Economics and the New Economic History*. Ithaca, NY: Cornell University Press.

Menon, Ravi. 2010. "Markets and Government: Striking a Balance in Singapore." Opening address of the Permanent Secretary of the Ministry of Trade and Industry at the Singapore Economic Policy Forum, October 22.

Ministry of Economic Development 2002. "Growing an Innovative New Zealand." www.gif.med.govt.nz.

Nambiar, Shankaran. 2007. "Public-Private Partnerships for Innovation and Export Development: The Malaysian Model." Paper presented at the seminar "Public-Private Partnerships for Innovation and Export Development," held by the Economic Commission for Latin America and the Caribbean and the Iberoamerican Secretariat, Seville, September 13–14.

National Research Foundation website. http://www.nrf.gov.sg/nrf/strategic. aspx?id=134.

National Research Foundation, Singapore. No date. "The National R&D Agenda." http://www.nrf.gov.sg/nrf/aboutus.aspx?id=92.

Nelson, Richard R. 1987. *Understanding Technical Change as an Evolutionary Process*. Amsterdam: North Holland.

Newfarmer, Richard, William Shaw, and Peter Walkerhorst. 2009. "Breaking into New Markets: Overview." *Breaking into New Markets*, ed. R. Newfarmer, W. Shaw, and P. Walkenhorst. Washington, DC: World Bank.

Noland, Marcus, and Howard Pack. 2002. "Industrial Policies and Growth: Lessons from International Experience." Working Paper 169, Central Bank of Chile, Santiago.

Pack, Howard, and Kamal Saggi. 2006. "Is There a Case for Industrial Policy? A Critical Survey." *World Bank Research Observer* 21, no. 2.

Peres, Wilson, and Annalisa Primi. 2009. "Theory and Practice of Industrial Policy: Evidence from the Latin American Experience." Productive Development Series 187 (LC/L.3013-P), Economic Commission for Latin America and the Caribbean, Santiago, Chile (February).

Pérez, Carlota. 1992. "Cambio técnico, reestructuración competitiva y reforma institucional en los países en desarrollo." *El trimestre económico* 59, no. 1 (January-March).

———. 2001. "Technical Change and Opportunities for Development as a Moving Target." CEPAL Review 75 (LC/G.2150-P/E), Economic Commission for Latin America and the Caribbean, Santiago, Chile (December).

Porter, Michael. 2007. "La ventaja comparativa de las naciones." *Harvard Business Review* (November).

———. 2008. "Why America Needs an Economic Strategy." *Business Week* (October 30).

Reinert, Erik. 2004. "How Rich Nations Got Rich." Working Paper 2004/01, Center for Development and the Environment, University of Oslo.

———. 2009. "Emulation vs. Comparative Advantage: Competing and Complementary Principles in the History of Economic Policy." *The Political Economy of Capabilities Accumulation: The Past and Future of Policies for Industrial Development*, ed. M. Cimoli, G. Dosi, and J. Stiglitz. Oxford, U.K.: Oxford University Press.

Rodrik, Dani. 2004. "Industrial Policy for the Twenty-First Century." Kennedy School of Government, Harvard University, Cambridge, MA (September).

———. 2008. "Normalizing Industrial Policy." Working Paper 3, Growth and Development Commission, World Bank, Washington, DC.

Ruane, Francis, and Ali Ugur. 2006. "Export Platform FDI and Dualistic Development." *Transnational Corporations* 15, no 1 (April).

Sabel, Charles. 2009a. "Changing Relations among Firms, and How Governments Can Learn to Support the Development They Make Possible." Paper presented at the seminar on policies and instruments to promote development of private sector during the world recession, Inter-American Development Bank, September 18.

———. 2009b. "What Industrial Policy Is Becoming: Taiwan, Ireland and Finland as Guides to the Future of Industrial Policy." Columbia Law School. http://idb-docs.iadb.org/wsdocs/getDocument.aspx?DOCNUM=1843147.2009a.

Sabel, Charles, and others. Forthcoming. *Self-Discovery as a Coordination Problem: Lessons from a Study of New Exports in Latin America*. Washington, DC: Inter-American Development Bank.

Sarel, Michael. 1996. "Growth in East Asia." International Monetary Fund, Washington, DC.

Schein, Edgar. 1983. *Strategic Pragmatism*. Cambridge, MA: MIT Press.

Todesca, Jorge A., Horacio Larghi, and Pablo Besmedrisnik. 2006. "Instituciones públicas de apoyo a la competitividad: un análisis de casos." Working Paper 114 (LC/BUE/L.210), Economic Commission for Latin America and the Caribbean, Buenos Aires.

Ul Haque, Irfan. 2007. "Rethinking Industrial Policy." Discussion Paper 183, United Nations Trade and Development Conference, Geneva.

Wade, Robert. 1986. "The Organization and Effects of the Development State in East Asia." Paper presented to the conference "Development Strategies in Latin America and East Asia: a Cross-Regional Comparison," Institute of the Americas, La Jolla, CA.

———. 1990. *Governing the Market. Economic Theory and the Role of Government in East Asian Industrialization*. Princeton, NJ: Princeton University Press.

———. 2004. *Governing the Market. Economic Theory and the Role of Government in East Asian Industrialization*, 2nd ed. Princeton, NJ: Princeton University Press.

Weiss, John. 2005. "Expert Growth and Industrial Policy: Lessons from the East Asia Miracle Experience." Paper presented at second annual meeting of economy and trade of Latin American and the Caribbean and Pacific ASEAN (LAEBA), Buenos Aires.

3

The Second Principle:
Create Public-Private Alliances for
Effective Development Strategies
and Industrial Policies

Development strategies based on a neostructuralist approach arise, in the first instance, from a systematic examination and assessment of key opportunities for market positioning and upgrading over the longer term. Obstacles that must be reduced or removed should be identified and appropriate priorities and sequences established to ensure that the country can access those opportunities. Obviously, the chosen objectives must be based on real capacities of the economy, either already existing or capable of being developed, as well as on the short-, medium- and long-term trends detected in the external environment.[1]

Meanwhile, specific public policies and programs designed to help overcome identified primary constraints must be aligned with the political and institutional realities of the country concerned, the specific capacity of the agents in the public and private sectors, and the types of incentives that will best motivate the private sector to make decisions conducive to achieving the strategic goals. Last, to effectively combine market signals with government incentives, the strategy's goals and programs at the macroeconomic and horizontal levels must be aligned with goals and programs relating to specific activities or sectors (figure 3.1).

How can this task be undertaken? In the early postwar era, even in many capitalist industrial countries, the state often had a commanding view of the market because the public sector owned or controlled a core of major enterprises. In many countries this ownership facilitated state-led planning—often indicative in nature rather than prescriptive (Shonfield 1965). Today, in contrast, the means of production in most developing

Figure 3.1 Alignment of Strategic Policies and Programs

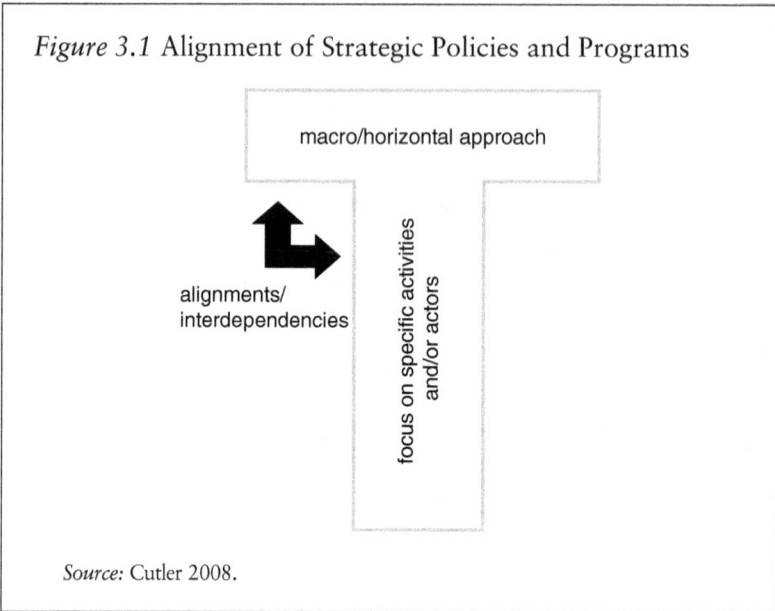

macro/horizontal approach

alignments/
interdependencies

focus on specific activities
and/or actors

Source: Cutler 2008.

countries are basically in private sector hands. Consequently, it is the private firm, not the government, that has the contextual market information that, however incomplete, can serve to identify opportunities and obstacles (including those related to public policy) to economic transformation. Firms can be shortsighted, however, when it comes to making decisions and undertaking measures that might yield markedly upgraded performance. This shortsightedness is caused by inertia, or "status quo bias," arising from uncertainty (Culpepper 2001), which can be aggravated by so-called market failures—problems assessing first-mover advantages and the appropriation of the benefits of innovation and technical developments, optimum coordination of investments, and the like, all of which take on special importance in a fast-changing globalized world.

Although governments have their own shortcomings, and are not very good at assessing the contextual information of markets that house the private sector, they have advantages in observing and assessing aggregate outcomes (Culpepper 2001). Moreover, a government's political leadership can stimulate proactive and forward-looking strategic thinking about the country's position in the international hierarchy of production and export. Governments also can help coordinate collective actions in pursuit of national or sectoral objectives and motivate investment and risk taking. Thus, when private and public sectors work together, they can enhance their separate potential for supporting mechanisms and programs that can identify and overcome primary constraints on economic growth and transformation, including government failures.[2] In short, in an effective enabling environment, group thinking can be smarter than isolated individual approaches.

The neostructuralist approach adds some important requirements, however, to public-private collaboration. First and foremost, public-private alliances can be an effective tool of development strategies only if the state collaborates closely with the private sector but retains its autonomy to protect the public's welfare. Only by retaining what Evans (1995), a pioneer in modern industrial policy, calls "embedded autonomy" can the state be a proactive partner of the private sector and at the same time avoid "capture" by special interests. The second point is that both elements of the equation—embedded autonomy and a successful public-private alliance for economic development—depend on an effective institutional design for a "social process" of public-private collaboration (Muñoz 2000). This institutional design must help the parties overcome their respective barriers of asymmetric information so that socially beneficial opportunities, primary constraints, and effective promotional support, including distribution of functional rents, can be identified without the state being captured. In this sense, getting "right" the institutional setting and social process of public-private collaboration is central to modern industrial policy because it raises the likelihood that smart public interest–oriented strategies will emerge.

Given the mistrust between public and private sectors that often exists in developing countries, constructing these alliances is not necessarily easy.[3] Strong and effectively focused political leadership, aimed at building a consensual national vision, coupled with the formation of a technically credible public bureaucracy armed with the finance and modern tools of industrial policy, are essential ingredients in bringing the parties together in a partnership.

In many cases, alliances may incorporate other social groups.[4] For example, depending on the area of interest, noncommercial agents, such as academics (including researchers), trade unions, or nongovernmental organizations (NGOs), may hold some of the information required for diagnostics and intelligent strategies. Moreover, building consensus, or at least a public understanding that generates sufficient public acceptance of policy, is necessary to ensure that strategies and their financing have the necessary political support to survive and coherently evolve over the longer term.[5]

In sum, an alliance can be seen as a "bridging tool" that can bond different intersectoral interests into a common vision for collective action that mobilizes a country's fullest capacity for the cause of economic transformation. The neoliberal school is skeptical about collective action because of fear that instincts for private gain will dominate and ultimately lead only to "cheap talk" (Ross Schneider 2009) or in the worst case "spell disaster for collective benefits" (Sandler 1992, 193). In this view individuals cannot be socially embedded in the alliance in a way that is beneficial to the functioning of a group objective (Storper 2005). There is certainly evidence that group structures can turn socially perverse. However real these risks, bad outcomes can be reasonably checked by institutional design and modalities, coupled with politically dedicated leadership. And as we show, there are countries that do this reasonably well.

The Scope of Public-Private Alliances

The scope of public-private alliances is set out schematically in figure 3.2. The dynamic for involving an alliance in building a strategy is shown on the left. As displayed in the figure, the construction of an alliance, the role it will play in formulating and implementing strategies, and the institutional setting clearly depend on the political, historical, and cultural context of the country.[6] In certain political settings, a mature and effective alliance can lead to a veritable public consensus. In other cases, the nature of the political context may lead to a mature alliance that is best described as an expression of public understanding, or passive acceptance, of the strategy. But, in one way or the other, it is the consensus or understanding, and the different ranges and nuances involved, that condition the formulation and implementation of a strategy as well as its sustainability as a tool for economic transformation.

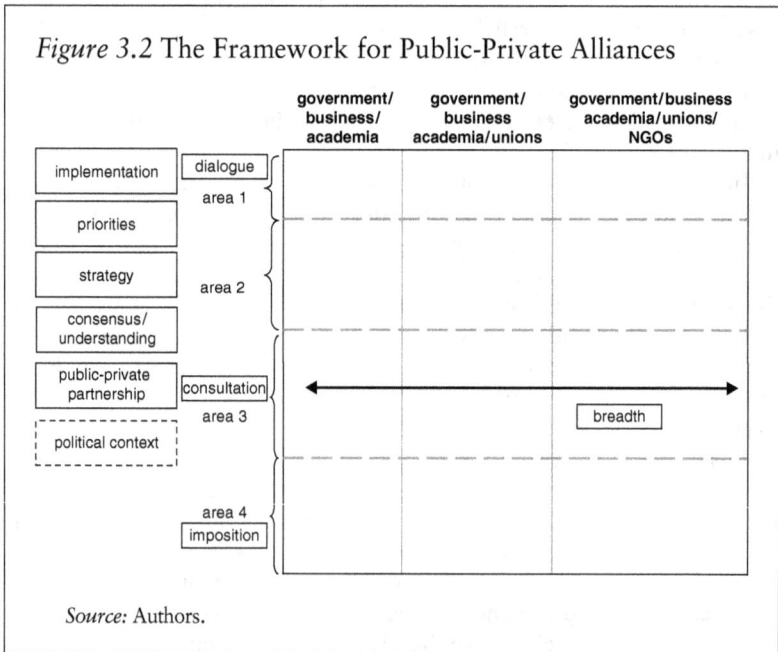

Figure 3.2 The Framework for Public-Private Alliances

Source: Authors.

In achieving consensus and understanding, the interaction between the parties of an alliance may vary both in the form of the discourse and in its scope. The left (vertical) axis of figure 3.2 shows that the discourse between government and private-sector stakeholders may range, along a nondiscrete scale, from a true dialogue, to a consultation of the private sector by the government, to a situation where the government imposes its strategy without any great attempt at dialogue or public consultation but in a way that commands public-private collaboration underpinned by a system of rewards and punishment.

The extent of social participation in the alliance may also vary. The horizontal axis of figure 3.2 shows that the spectrum may range from a trilateral relationship between the government, business, and academia to a very broad partnership including practically all the main social groups.

Finally, a third dimension, not reflected in figure 3.2, must also be taken into account: the general operational structure. In this case three stylized variants may be identified: first, an alliance that operates through formal and permanent structures; second, an alliance that operates with formal structures that emerge on an ad hoc basis; and third, an alliance that functions as an informal network or through tacit agreements. In practice, the three structures coexist in any public-private alliance, although one or more (that is, a hybrid) structure is likely to dominate.

Alliances in the 10 Success Cases

Annex table 3A.1 sums up the nature of alliances for formulating national development strategies in our extraregional success cases by highlighting for each country the predominant structures of the partnership, its main stakeholders, and the principal means of engagement. Annex table 3A.2 does the same at the level of national strategy implementation but through the prism of our four strategic orientations for strengthening integration with the world economy and export development.

Figure 3.3 illustrates the nature of national alliances for the studied countries using the information in annex table 3A.1 and the potential areas of interaction indicated in figure 3.2. In Finland and Ireland, the alliances are characterized by their formal structuring, breadth, and depth, with extensive coverage in the public sector hierarchy of strategy formulation and implementation. While governments always make the policy decisions in any alliance, these two alliances are a real force, having resulted in something that is tantamount to a social dialogue and agreements on strategies that transcend political cycles.[7] Therefore, these countries may be placed in area 1 of figure 3.3, with Ireland having the broader alliance of the two countries.

Figure 3.3 Public-Private Alliances: The Playing Field

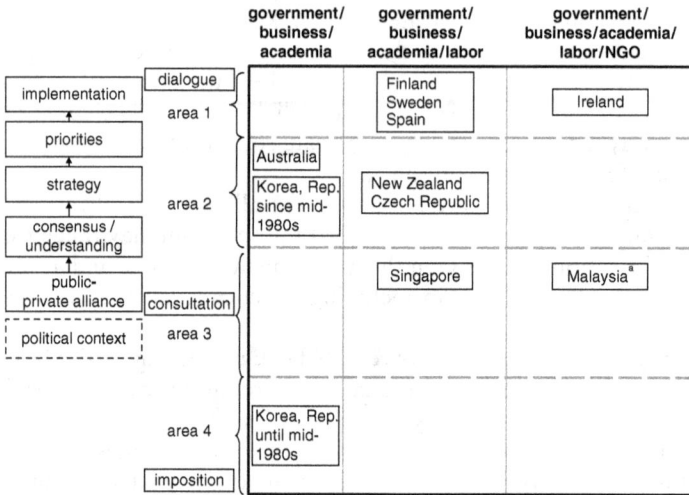

		government/ business/ academia	government/ business/ academia/labor	government/ business/academia/ labor/NGO
implementation	dialogue / area 1		Finland Sweden Spain	Ireland
priorities				
strategy	area 2	Australia / Korea, Rep. since mid-1980s	New Zealand Czech Republic	
consensus / understanding				
public-private alliance	consultation		Singapore	Malaysia[a]
political context	area 3			
	area 4	Korea, Rep. until mid-1980s		
	imposition			

Source: Authors.

a. Malaysia also incorporates representatives of political parties but excludes union representation.

Singapore also has a relatively broad, well-structured alliance, and Malaysia's is even broader, including representatives of nongovernmental organizations (NGOs) and political parties but excluding unions.[8] In both cases, the government consults extensively with its alliance partners rather than engaging in dialogue as such; the government then comes to a decision and announces its strategy without pretensions of a consensus. The result is a public understanding of what the government's strategy is. Both countries are thus positioned in area 3 of figure 3.3.

The depth of the alliance in these four countries is important for the degree of interaction with the government bureaucracy (especially in Ireland and Singapore), contributing to the flow of information, coordination of processes, and the building of consensus or understanding. Figure 3.4 illustrates the institutional framework established in Singapore, where the interaction with the private sector is very comprehensive, with representatives of firms participating on boards of directors, including the Economic Development Board (EDB), which traditionally has been the "brain" behind the country's development strategies.[9] Multinational companies with operations in the country (and foreign academics in the case of the Agency for Science, Technology and Research, or A*STAR) are represented, reflecting their importance in the country's productive apparatus

Figure 3.4 Singapore: Board Members of the Agencies That Support the Global Integration Strategy

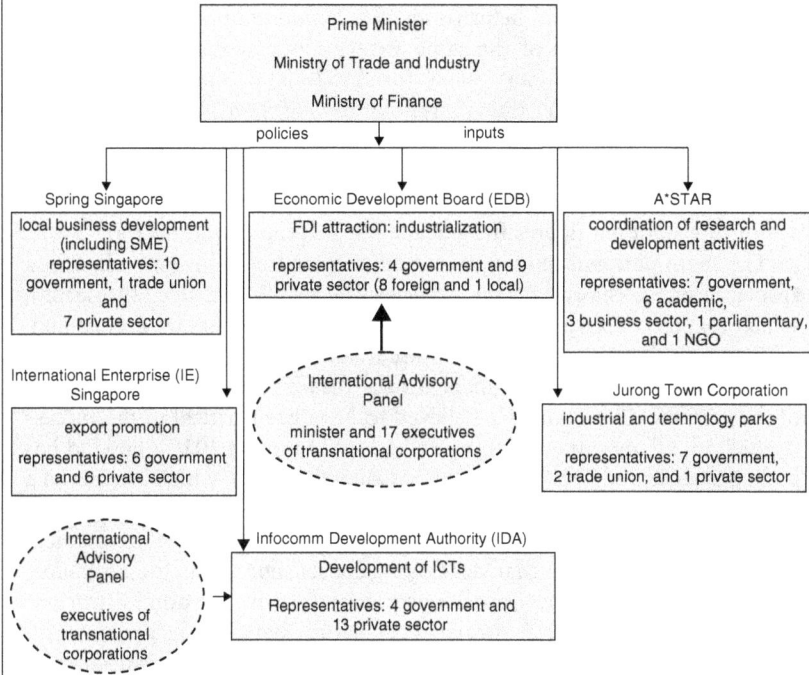

Source: Authors, based on official data.

Note: SMEs = small and medium enterprises; ICTs = information and communications technologies.

but also showing that the government attaches a high priority to gathering international intelligence from these firms relevant for its strategy. The profile for Ireland is similar with the exception that the boards of directors in Singapore only comment and make periodic appraisals of policies and programs, whereas in Ireland, directors also have operational responsibilities.

Singapore (and to a lesser degree Ireland and Malaysia) has another strategically valuable modality to strengthen its international public-private alliance—international advisory panels for Singapore's EDB and its Infocomm Development Authority (see figure 3.4). Each year the EDB organizes a meeting at which private discussions are held between high government officials and chief executive officers of major multinational companies on subjects such as globalization trends, developments in the

Southeast Asia region, and technological and commercial issues. At the end of the meeting a press report is issued. This event, which also includes social events, not only provides a venue for exchanging information relevant to national strategies but also creates a network of contacts in the international market and helps to identify concrete opportunities for the country.[10] An example of the same strategy, but at the academic level, is the international advisory panel for A*STAR, a high-level executing body that operates under the umbrella of the National Research Foundation, the agency that leads the country's innovation strategy; the panel includes Nobel Prize winners.[11] In 2005 Malaysia formed a similar international council to advise on its latest national plan; the council includes senior international figures from academia and the private sector.

The main national public-private alliance of Ireland is embodied in a special council, chaired by the office of the prime minister (Taoiseach), which regularly convenes representatives of the major social groups and, with technical support, engages in discussions to reach consensus on recommendations to the government for the future socioeconomic direction of the country. This council is believed to have been critical to the success of the Irish alliance and economic model (O'Donovan 2010). Finland has had its Science and Technology Policy Council (STPC), which has served a similar purpose. These forums are discussed in more detail later.

Australia and New Zealand are intermediate cases within the classification of figure 3.3. Rather than developing consensus as such, these alliances are related to the political coalitions constructed by the administrations in power. The alliance in Australia exists mainly between the government, business, and academia. New Zealand had an alliance with businesses and academia up to 1999, when a new government headed by the Labor Party included and gave more attention to the labor sector. The conservative government elected in 2009 may have different ideas about the nature of the alliance. In any event, predominant structures and participation in the alliances of these two countries are fluid and unstable, reflecting in part a certain aversion to corporatism, albeit for different reasons.

In Australia, until 2009, the governments in power assumed a neoliberal economic policy stance. In New Zealand the Clark government that came to power in 1999 following a long period of relatively neoliberal economic policies found it difficult to firmly establish a consensus with the business sector and the political opposition around a new structuralist approach partly inspired by Ireland. It even encountered skepticism in pockets of the government bureaucracy (Haworth 2008). This case illustrates the obstacles to change that stem from "path dependency" as well as the point made earlier that forming an alliance between a government and the private business sector is not necessarily an easy task. In any event, this inability to establish full legitimacy for a new approach caused the government to move slowly in fits and starts. Although two strategic and complementary medium- and long-term initiatives were launched to promote economic transformation,[12] the government ultimately failed in its effort to install an Irish-style model of alliances and consensus in support of a strategy for economic transformation. In effect, the hybrid structure of the New Zealand alliance did not have either the stability or the coherence to generate lasting agreements at the national level conducive to the implementation of a well-structured strategy relatively insulated from electoral cycles.

In both countries, a more structured and deeper alliance does exist in certain specific areas and is especially striking in the fields of innovation in natural resources exploitation and in marketing, where the corporate sector and academic representatives assume operational responsibilities on the boards of specialized public executing agencies. Nevertheless, the vagaries of their national alliances place Australia and New Zealand in the intermediate area (area 2) of figure 3.3.

Spain, for its part, has been able to build consensus on its national strategy during the process of democratization and integration into the European Union with forums, committees, working groups, and so forth. While that consensus was valid at least up to the crisis of 2008–09, the predominant modality for interaction of the alliance at the level of the central government and its specialized agencies is an informal one that functions principally with trade unions and business associations, some of which originate in, and are partly funded by, the public sector (Bonet 2010).[13] Spain is probably located in area 1 of figure 3.3. In Sweden, where a high level of consensus is traditional, the alliance between government and business has been so informal/tacit that it is not easy to describe.[14]

Before the 1990s the Republic of Korea would have been located at the extreme bottom left of figure 3.3 (area 4), because strategy formulation and implementation were almost exclusively the domain of the government and its technocrats. Before democratization in Korea, the national plan guided the activities of the major conglomerates (*chaebols*), involving strong public-private collaboration sustained with a range of unilaterally applied incentives and penalties.[15] Now a sophisticated economy, Korea has dispensed with national plans, and the chaebols have a large degree of business independence. While today's democratic framework includes growing government recognition of the value of the public-private alliances for supporting strategies, the country is still in a transition in this regard. It is now located in the intermediate area, as is the Czech Republic. This country has fairly well-structured formal forums, with broad participation and active interaction between the public and private sectors, both for setting and for implementing national strategies. However, their political relevance and importance in decision making have been strongly influenced by the ideology of the different government coalitions that have assumed power since the introduction of democratic rule.[16]

To conclude, the most complete and functional alliances for supporting the formulation of medium- and long-term strategies with sufficient public consensus or understanding to avoid pendulum swings are found in Finland, Ireland (at least until the recent crisis), Malaysia, Singapore, Spain (also until the recent crisis), and Sweden. The alliances in Australia, New Zealand, and the Czech Republic are less solid or effective. Korea is still in transition from a bureaucratic development model to a more open social model based on modern industrial policies.

Consensus Building

Intelligent medium- and long-term strategies based on a high degree of consensus between the public and the private sectors can give better results for a number of reasons. Consensus facilitates consistency in the strategy between electoral cycles because the process that builds and maintains a consensus achieves a "buy-in" of stakeholders (especially elites) (Campos and Root 1996) and serves as an implicit public evaluation of the effectiveness of such strategies and associated public policies. Even more important, processes geared to building consensus can mobilize and incorporate the country's best information, perspectives, and skills, as well as engender credibility for the strategy through agreement on financing of its priorities.

Unfortunately, building consensus takes time and is no easy task. It is a process rather than an event. The nature of the process depends on many factors, such as cultural dispositions, political institutions, the configuration and power of the different social groups, leadership and political vision, and the sense of urgency.[17] Nevertheless, appropriately structured and governed institutional frameworks for alliances can, over time, help to build consensus.

As mentioned, there are no formulas for the structure and functioning of alliances; they are by their nature idiosyncratic, based on the particular conditions of each country. But theory and experience suggest some basic considerations about governance that can contribute to the effective operation of an alliance. Successful alliances at the national level that deliberate and make recommendations to government about the direction of national strategies are likely to:[18]

- Ensure representation of the civil stakeholders with the market-based and scientific or technical information necessary to build a strategy and of those with political power to legitimize resource allocation. It is advisable that civil appointments be of a very high level sufficient to garner the respect of the communities they are meant to represent. To avoid degrading the authority of the civil membership, the appointments should be for a set period, and substitute representatives should not be allowed.

- Include government representation at the highest level to signal to civil participants that the alliance can seriously address their and the nation's issues. But governments also should take care to include the ministries and agencies that lead or coordinate the formulation and implementation of strategies (Herzberg and Wright 2005). The government, as a member of the alliance, moreover must continually demonstrate its political leadership, its commitment to the process, and its respect for the alliance's recommendations for strategies underpinning public policy; only in that way will the alliance attract and maintain top civil participation.
- Minimize politicization of the deliberations. Alliances thus should probably not include representatives from political parties, which can observe and discuss recommendations from their seat in the legislative branch. It is difficult for politicians to take off their party "T-shirt," even in private deliberations.
- Ensure that the alliance membership, while representative, is not overly large in number to facilitate interpersonal trust and manageable dialogue (Ross Schneider 2009).
- Make mandates clear, concrete, and realistic given the stage of maturity of the alliance and the state of the economy. Indeed, realistic and manageable mandates over the term of the alliance facilitate "successes" that can give the alliance creditability. Initially, mandates might focus on what Herzberg and Wright (2005, 22) term "low-hanging fruit." At the launch, then, the alliance may want to limit mandates to information exchange, coupled with very specific problem solving and recommendations at a lower level of aggregation, and then progressively aim at consensus building on big issues and directions (Ross Schneider 2009).
- Establish a funded, quasi-independent secretariat to support deliberations. It should not just be administrative in nature, but rather have a high-level, objective, respected technical capacity to encourage fact-based discussion and problem solving.[19]
- Set deliberations at regular intervals—every month, every other month, or every quarter—so that discussions maintain their relevance and a commitment to the process is demonstrable to the alliance participants and the public (Ross Schneider 2009).
- Keep deliberations confidential to encourage frankness and an environment where compromise is possible. Public reports can be periodically released concerning fulfillment of the alliance's mandates.
- Insulate civil membership from political retribution.
- Set clear and transparent criteria and procedures for appointment to the alliance forum.
- Institutionalize explicit rules of conduct for members of the alliance to guard against conflicts of interest and rent seeking. Capture is

also minimized if the alliance has adequate transversal social representation while avoiding a dysfunctional size.

- Ensure that the alliance body, or a sister institution, has a capacity to
  monitor the degree to which policy makers adopt its recommendations.
- Use independent mechanisms to periodically evaluate consensus
  positions in the alliance to avoid the risk of "locked-in" strategic
  vision that may be losing relevance.

Ireland's experience in this regard is quite interesting. Once one of the
poorest countries in Europe, Ireland, starting in the late 1980s, managed
to build a consensus for its development and integration into the global
economy that led to one of the greatest economic transformations in the
postwar period. Even in its current severe economic crisis, it still maintains an above-average European income. Annex tables 3A.1 and 3A.2
show that the alliance's institutional framework covers many dimensions
of the formulation and implementation of medium- and long-term strategies. One entity in particular, the National Economic and Social Council
(NESC), throughout its decades of work, evolved from a publicly sponsored "talk shop," which allowed representatives of the various social
groups to exchange ideas, into a forum that facilitated the generation of
consensus on the future course of the economy. In the next section, we
examine the council in more detail. We also comment on the governance
of other alliances.

Alliances in Practice

In this section we sketch out the governance of the alliances in three of our
success cases and then look at a fourth, the Irish alliance, which is one of
the most mature and sophisticated.[20]

A Snapshot of the Nature of Three Alliances

Finland.   Finland's development strategy has been led by the country's
Science and Technology Policy Council, founded in 1987. It is chaired by
the prime minister and has seven additional ministers. Two industry representatives and one labor representative, of the highest level, participate
in a personal capacity. Another seven members are from the academic and
science community. Members serve for a four-year term, and nongovernmental members receive a small honorarium. The council meets four times
a year and is supported by two subcommittees (science and education),
which work on specific topics, as well as a secretariat with four employees
linked to the Ministry of Education. Every three years the council publishes a consensus-based report analyzing the opportunities and challenges
the economy is facing in a globalized economy and concluding with an

outline of a recommended path for the national economy. The council also recommended amounts of resources to allocate to the strategic areas set out in the report. Ministries and executing agencies in charge of specific areas addressed in the council's outline and then prepare a series of one-year operational plans, which are executed and monitored under the umbrella of the STPC's strategic guidelines.

The council was renamed the Research and Innovation Council in January 2009, reflecting some changes in its operation. As its name suggests, the body is now more intensively focused on the issue of innovation, a key dimension of Finland's most recent development strategies. Membership remains at 18, but the number of experts in innovation policy is higher, and fewer nominations are socially based. Meanwhile, the two subcommittees were replaced by a science and education subcommittee and a technology and innovation subcommittee.

New Zealand.   In 2008 New Zealand's Growth and Innovation Advisory Board had 20 members from civil society, including 14 high-level business representatives, 5 technical or academic members, and 1 labor union representative. The members are nominated by ministers and discussed and endorsed at the cabinet level; they are paid a modest honorarium for each day's work and their expenses are paid. One of the business representatives is designated as chair and leads the interaction with the prime minister and other ministers. A board term is up to three years; the board meets about six times a year. The Ministry of Economic Development provides administrative secretariat functions.

The growth and innovation board is expected to carry out constructive debate, arrive at consensus recommendations, and give policy advice to the prime minister and relevant ministers. When consensus cannot be reached, the board's recommendations can reflect the different perspectives of members, or the topic can be assigned to a "work stream" to further develop perspectives.

The board was set up by the Clark government to create a social buy-in to its emerging neostructuralist initiative for economic transformation. Its mandate covers broad issues on the overall direction of the economy, specific issues, and the promotion of consensus on what needs to be done to stimulate growth and innovation. However, the board is not expected to focus on detailed policy advice, implementation, or monitoring issues. The board's authority and interaction with government is less structured than the Finland's council is, and it is less bound by consensus building. Hence, its influence on policy seems to ebb and flow according to the domestic political dynamics of the government (Haworth 2008).

The Czech Republic.   The Council of Economic and Social Agreement (RHSD) was established in 1990 to parallel the democratic transition. It is made up of eight members of government, seven trade union representatives, and seven business sector representatives. This plenary group is supported by an executive body in charge of following up on the work of the plenary and by a number of expert working groups.

The mandate of the RHSD is the widest of the three alliances discussed here; it is what Ross Schneider (2009) calls an open-ended forum of discussion. This format is not necessarily a powerful tool for guiding development strategies as such, but it can and has served as a mechanism to bring together for social dialogue major groups with little contact during the previous Communist regime.

In January 2009 the National Economic Council was formed. It is an apolitical, 10-member expert body, made up largely of economists, chaired by the prime minister. It initially made recommendations on ways to manage the impact of the world recession and financial crisis and was also charged with recommending measures to accelerate growth and development. The council's procedures were a work in progress at the time of writing.

A Closer Look at the Achievements and Limitations of the Irish Alliance

Ireland's National Economic and Social Council dates to the early 1960s and started as an exercise in bringing together representatives of employer associations, trade unions, farmers' organizations, and senior public officials to discuss the country's economic and social development.[21] More recently NGOs joined the group. In the 1970s and 1980s the NESC served as a peaceful, closed-door "talk shop" for discussion and information exchange. After a crisis involving severe macroeconomic imbalance, recession, and substantial unemployment in the second half of the 1980s, the NESC evolved into a genuine forum for common understanding and social agreements on an economic policy aimed at high and sustained growth with social cohesion.

Duties and Structure of the Alliance.   The NESC analyzes medium- and long-term strategic socioeconomic issues and reports its findings to the prime minister along with recommendations on the future course of national plans, policies, and programs. The council is chaired by the secretary-general of the Department of the Prime Minister, and the public representatives are the secretaries-general of certain plan-relevant government departments (ministries) plus five representatives from the business sector; five from the trade unions; five from farmers' organizations, five from NGOs, and five independent representatives (normally technical experts or academics). The government selects members from nominations made by the respective social groups. The five independent participants are appointed directly by the government, and their policy orientation may have some affinity with that of the government. All the members act in a personal capacity; their term of service is three years. Nongovernment members receive reimbursement for their travel expenses where relevant.

The NESC receives technical and administrative support from a semi-autonomous secretariat of nine persons, most of whom are technical experts, all with master's degrees or doctorates. The current director is an economist held in high esteem in Ireland and recognized as politically impartial. The officials are contracted through competitive examinations and granted contracts as temporary employees of the state. The NESC budget for 2007 was 1.1 million euros.

The council typically meets once a month for a half or full-day session, and its decisions are made by consensus. Nongovernment members must recuse themselves when subjects present a potential conflict of interest. Risks of capture are also lowered by the transversal nature of membership. In any event, the NESC triennial report is the strategic input for negotiation of the National Social Agreement between the government, business, and trade unions, and it has served as a highly influential guide for the government in the formulation of the National Plan.[22]

The effectiveness of the NESC was politically consolidated in 1986, when it successfully laid the foundations for the negotiation between the government and various social actors that led to a three-year agreement on wages, taxes, and social spending within the framework of a program of growth, employment, and fiscal balance. Once the country's macroeconomic imbalance had been overcome, subsequent reports focused on other strategic issues, including competitiveness policies, supply-side policies, industrial and service policies, and the knowledge economy, all explicitly underpinned by a concern for social cohesion.

As the NESC agenda evolved, the government in 1993 created another forum for the partnership, the National Economic and Social Forum (NESF), which was responsible for long-term issues particularly related to employment and social cohesion (for further information on NESF and other specialized social dialogue forums in Ireland, see Doyle 2005). With the incorporation of NGOs into the partnership, a clearer division of labor was established between the two entities, giving the NESC exclusive responsibility for the national strategic vision and NESF the responsibility for monitoring implementation policies.

The two forums are coordinated by the National Economic and Social Development Office. With time more forums have been created for the alliance. The National Competitiveness Council (NCC) emerged in 1997, headed by the prime minister and heavily weighted with business representation. The National Center for Partnership and Performance (NCPP) was created in 2006 to promote a discussion between business and unions on labor relations.

A Method of Discourse for Consensus Building.   The NESC over time developed a methodology of discourse to facilitate consensus building. Rather than entering into discussions on current issues, the council makes recommendations based on broad principles relating to Ireland's medium- and long-term socioeconomic policies and programs. The aim is to agree on an analytical framework that will facilitate adoption of a social agreement, orientations for a national strategy, and the introduction of supporting government programs under the National Plan. The alliance expressed in the NESC has two dimensions: consultation and covenants between partners who share a functional interdependence; and a sense of solidarity, social cohesion, and participation. The alliance incorporates both these dimensions because depending exclusively on the first would give too much importance to the relative power of the partners, while depending only on the second could be an overly simplistic vision of inclusion, reducing the process to a consultation in which the interested parties merely express their points of view and needs.

There is, however, an important third dimension: negotiation. Building consensus implies that the partners must come to the table willing to set aside the goal of maximizing their individual interests and instead be part of a process of deliberation that has the potential to formulate and reformulate agreement on problems and solutions; the expected result approximates the creation of a public good. Thus, the process of developing partnerships depends on the capacity to promote an understanding and to approach deliberations with a view to jointly solving a problem and producing a consensus.

Indeed, the key to the NESC process may be the method of deliberation. First, problem solving is assumed to be the central mandate of participants. Second, the mechanism for deliberation is geared to solving one or more problems through a dialogue supported by inputs from impartial experts and working groups that help to create a common definition of problems. The particularity of this approach is that partners do not argue over a definitive point of view. Rather, faced with empirical evidence presented by an impartial technical secretariat and the mandate to solve a problem, a sort of joint decision may emerge among the partners. Participants are bound, given the facts laid out by the secretariat, to explain and give justifications to their partners in the alliance, their affiliates, and the general public and to take responsibility for their proposals. Thus, understanding and consensus are not a prerequisite for the alliance but rather the result of a problem-solving process that fosters it. Another important element in consensus building is social cohesion, which is a constant objective throughout the deliberations on the management and content of future strategies.

The experience of the NESC demonstrates that pragmatic deliberations geared toward the solution of a specific problem can produce consensus even in the presence of underlying conflicts of interest and absent an initial understanding. Another key aspect is that consensus achieved through the NESC is always provisional. In other words, consensus allows interlocutors to proceed with a recommendation for pragmatic action, while reserving the right to review goals, ways and means, and the analysis itself. Deliberations are private, the process is supported by the prime minister, and different participants are involved in the deliberations depending on the agenda—all of which facilitate consensus. Another advantage is that the approach is forward looking, rather than retrospective or focused on the present; as a result, government representatives tend to be less defensive.[23]

It must be recalled that the positive results of NESC and its methodology are the outcome of a long process based on "trial and error," stemming from the public sector's decision decades ago to provide the interested social groups with a neutral, high-level forum with quality technical support for discussing, in private and under the aegis of the prime minister, views on the direction of the country's development. Because this institutional process aiming at national consensus had been in place for many years, the alliance was able to jell into a true forum of national consensus to deal with the severe economic crisis that struck at the end of the 1980s.

A Fall from Grace.   The onset of the big economic crisis of 2008–09, with roots in a latent macroeconomic disequilibrium, witnessed the collapse of the Irish public-private alliance, expressed in the inability to renew the social pact on wages. A major factor was the reluctance of labor unions—especially in the public sector—to sacrifice wages for fiscal balance after a large public bailout of the banking system. The NESC and its secretariat have been working on bridging the differences.

The effectiveness of the NESC appears to have weakened during the course of the past decade, in part because of a progressive "balkanization" of the Irish alliance. With the creation of the National Competitiveness Council, business, aiming to achieve a degree of exclusive dialogue with the prime minister, began to give its primary attention to this forum rather than the NESC. Meanwhile, after the creation of the National Center for Partnership and Performance, the dialogue between business and labor migrated to this forum from the NESC. As a consequence the discourse in the NESC was dominated by labor unions and NGOs, which progressively distanced themselves from issues of industrial policy (which were taken up more intensively in the NCC) and labor relations (dominated by the NCPP) in favor or social policies (O'Donnell 2009). At the same time a type of rivalry developed between the technical secretariat of the NESC and Forfás (the technical secretariat to the NCC) over promoting a national strategic vision of development. Finally, the coordinating role of the National Economic and Social Development Office was quite ineffective.

With the balkanization of the alliance, public sector unions gained more space to promote their agenda, often in conflict with the recommendations for reform of the NESC secretariat, which was directed to focus almost exclusively on social issues. Meanwhile, the representatives in the different forums of the alliance began to be captured by the macroeconomic bubble that was developing in the real estate and construction markets in the 2000s: the boom provided a short-term win-win environment through employment, acquisition of first and second residences, profits, fiscal income, and public support for the government. Indeed, the internal dynamics of NESC in the described balkanized setting was not conducive to sounding alarm bells about the direction of the economy or deflating the bubble and even more aggressively adjust policies to counteract eroding international competitiveness.[24]

Perhaps the lesson here is that a national alliance forum like the NESC needs to incorporate suballiances for those players that have strong bilateral agendas to discuss, such as business and labor or business and the government. These more intimate forums, however, perhaps should take place in special "rooms" under the single roof of the national forum, in this case the NESC. This arrangement would allow the subdialogues to filter up to the NESC plenary, permitting more coordination, counterpoints, and cross-checks among the partners, and perhaps even the sounding of an alarm bell. Nevertheless, under any circumstances there is always the risk that a consensus vision will become "locked in," to the detriment of flexibility and adjustment of strategies to changing realities. It seems in this case that, although the NESC fostered a useful national consensus for the great economic expansion of the 1990s, that consensus did not evolve sufficiently fast enough to account for the emerging dangers of the real estate bubble and eroding competitiveness that developed during the next decade. The excessive compartmentalization of the alliance may have contributed to this short-sightedness.[25]

Finally, another weakness may have been that the NESC operated with an excessively national view of the economy. As the productive transformation and complexity of the economy progressed over the years, it probably would have been wise to link the national forum's deliberations more closely to regional and more decentralized perspectives.

Annex Table 3A.1 The Nature of Public-Private Alliances in National Strategy Formulation, 10 Success Cases

Country	Type of alliance	Participants	Means of engagement
Australia	Formal ad hoc	Government-business-academia-trade unions (pre-1996) Government-business-academia (1996–2008)	Ad hoc convening of summits, committees, and councils.
Czech Republic	Hybrid (formal structured; formal ad hoc)	Government-business-academia-trade unions	Council for Economic and Social Agreement, as well as forums and formal consultation meetings. In 2008 a National Economic Council was formed to advise the prime minister.
Finland	Formal structured	Government-business-academia-trade unions	Participation in the Science and Technology Policy Council (STPC).[a] The STPC was reformed in January 2009 to become the Research and Innovation Council.
Ireland	Formal structured	Government-business-farmers-academia-trade unions-nongovernmental organizations (NGOs)	Permanent forums at a national level, such as the National Economic and Social Council, the National Competitiveness Council, and the National Expert Group on Future Skills Needs. In addition, the National Plan is discussed at length with other representatives of society.
Korea, Rep. (post-1990)	Hybrid (formal ad hoc; informal/tacit)	Government-business-academia	Ad hoc committees of experts to fulfill specific tasks, public forums, and informal communication, especially between the government and the *chaebols*.
Malaysia	Hybrid (formal structured; formal ad hoc; informal/tacit)	Government-business-academia-NGOs-political parties	The National Economic Consultative Council, which gives views and provides inputs to the government's Economic Planning Unit for the preparation of the National Plan. In preparation for the Industrial Master Plans, a high-level steering committee was set up for the business sector to coordinate working groups. Other views are also received through forums, meetings, and informal communications.

(continued)

Annex Table 3A.1 The Nature of Public-Private Alliances in National Strategy Formulation, 10 Success Cases *(continued)*

Country	Type of alliance	Participants	Means of engagement
New Zealand	Hybrid (formal structured; formal ad hoc; informal/tacit)	Government-business-academia (pre-1999) Government-business-academia-trade unions (post-1999)	Formal mechanisms, such as the Growth and Innovation Advisory Board; ad hoc arrangements (meetings, working groups, and consultancies), and informal communications.
Singapore	Formal structured	Government-business-academia-trade unions	The private sector participates in the boards of three important bodies responsible for strategy development: the Economic Development Board; the National Science Foundation; and the Research, Innovation and Enterprise Council[a].
Spain	Informal/tacit	Government-business-academia-trade unions	Mainly informal/tacit through communication with trade unions and business associations, some with joint financing by the government. In the 1980s, in preparation for entry into the European Union, extensive formal consultation arrangements helped to build consensus on the strategy for internationalization, which exists to this day.
Sweden	Informal/tacit	Government-business-labor-academia	The government has had a tight informal/tacit relationship with large Swedish transnational corporations and academia and until relatively recently a formal link with the trade unions (in the context of wages). Academic advice strongly influences policy.

Source: Authors, based on official data.
a. Renamed the National Research and Innovation Council in 2009.

Annex Table 3A.2 Nature of Public-Private Alliances for Strategy Implementation, 10 Success Cases

Country	Type of partnership	Participants	Means of engagement
Australia	Hybrid (formal structured; informal/tacit)	Business sector and academia	The private sector participates very actively with operational responsibilities on the boards of public agencies supporting R&D/innovation. Informal contacts are predominant in other areas.
Czech Republic	Formal structured	Business sector, academia; some monitoring committees include trade unions and NGOs	Participation on the board of directors of Czech Invest (only in an advisory capacity) and on program monitoring committees.
Finland	Formal structured	Business sector, academia, and trade unions	Participation on boards of executing agencies with operational responsibilities
Ireland	Formal structured	Business sector and academia	Participation on boards of executing agencies with operational responsibilities, including Forfás (the "brain" of the public sector in the area of strategies for international integration).
Korea, Rep.	Informal/tacit	Business sector and academia	Informal/tacit
Malaysia	Hybrid (formal structured; informal/tacit)	Business sector and academia	Participation on boards of executing agencies, with advisory responsibilities plus informal communication.
New Zealand	Formal structured	Business sector; in some cases, trade unions	Participation on boards of executing agencies with operational responsibilities

(continued)

Annex Table 3A.2 Nature of Public-Private Alliances for Strategy Implementation, 10 Success Cases (*continued*)

Country	Type of partnership	Participants	Means of engagement
Singapore	Formal structured	Business sector and academia	Participation on boards of executing agencies (in an advisory capacity only) and on councils.
Spain	Hybrid (formal structured; informal/tacit)	Business sector, unions, and academia	Formal in the area of export promotion through recent participation on the board of directors of ICEX; informal channels with business and trade unions including in the area of innovation.
Sweden	Informal/tacit	Business sector and academia	Informal/tacit.

Source: Authors, based on official data.

Notes

1. As Cutler (2008) observes, the development of an effective vision of the future requires an assessment, among other things, of long-term trends. Nonetheless, to truly determine the underlying long-term trend, past trends must be borne in mind; it would be unusual for future changes to be unaffected by former trends.

2. The primary constraints on sustained growth may be concentrated in the macro-, meso-, or microeconomic spheres. Hausmann, Rodrik, and Velasco (2005) have come up with some ideas for diagnosing the subject systematically and setting priorities.

3. Thanks to Manuel Agosin for reminding us of this potential obstacle in Latin America.

4. As pointed out by Prats i Català (2005), the weakest stakeholders may require technical support in order to become effective actors in a dialogue.

5. A strategy that does not have some degree of public acceptance, or understanding, runs a risk of popular political resistance to the allocation of scarce resources for its implementation. Some areas of a strategy—for example, public spending in support of research and development and innovation—may not be readily understood and accepted politically by the public, in comparison with other more easily grasped expenditures such as poverty reduction programs. Thus, an explicitly constructed public understanding, or consensus, might be a necessary condition to legitimize a strategy in the public's mind.

6. According to a joint study by the World Bank, the Economic Commission for Latin America and the Caribbean (ECLAC), and the International Institute for Democracy and Electoral Assistance (IDEA) (2005, 3), "The process of building a national vision does not have a unique format but must be adapted to the country situation and the particularities of the participating stakeholders."

7. However, in the middle of the Irish crisis of 2008–09 employers and unions were unable, for the first time in many years, to reach a wage agreement.

8. It should be noted that trade unions in Singapore have links with the government.

9. Schein (1996) extensively examines the EDB and its role in the development of the country. More recently innovation agencies have taken the lead role.

10. General managers of multinational companies may also be attracted to the meeting by the opportunity to learn about topics of interest for doing business in East Asia.

11. The private representatives serving on the board of directors of the National Research Foundation and the Research, Innovation and Enterprise Council are exclusively Singapore nationals.

12. Office of the Prime Minister (2002); Ministry of Economic Development, New Zealand (2005).

13. In some of the autonomous communities, such as Andalusia, the alliance is formal, structured, and essentially tripartite.

14. Sweden's alliance may be in part a democratic version of the big firms–government alliance that prevailed for many decades in Korea.

15. Campos and Root (1996) give a good description of how such a collaboration can work.

16. The European Union has had a positive influence on the alliances by insisting on a broad social dialogue about the use its cooperation funds.

17. One fairly common factor in the selected countries is that the consensus (or understanding) has often emerged during a crisis that has served, together with other factors, as a catalyst for constructing a common vision.

18. As mentioned, alliances also can function at the level of sectors and specific activities. The main difference in this case vis-à-vis the national forums is that the

group will be more homogeneous. Homogeneous membership facilitates consensus (Ross Schneider 2009).

19. For an analysis of the dynamics of various evidence-based, consensus-building strategies, see Caillaud and Tirole (2007).

20. Herzberg and Wright (2005) examine public-private competitiveness alliances in a wide range of countries in a study that is also instructive on governance issues.

21. This section relies in part on a background paper by O'Donovan (2010).

22. As noted, other dimensions of the Irish alliance penetrate the agencies that are responsible for providing inputs and executing the National Plan. These agencies are overseen by ministries represented in the NESC.

23. The deliberations on the national recovery strategy for 1986, when stabilizing the economy was a matter of urgency, illustrate the NESC methodology. At the monthly meetings of the council, in-depth analyses of the issues involved were carried out under the guidance of the council chairman and on the basis of studies prepared by the secretariat. To arrive at a common understanding, the focus of the discussion was shifted from the annual fiscal deficit to the debt-to-GDP ratio. This focus facilitated a more constructive exchange of opinions than focusing exclusively on socially controversial issues of tax increases or expenditure reductions. First, it was observed that, despite cuts in public spending, the fiscal situation was continuing to deteriorate and the record-high world interest rates then prevailing were giving rise to a heavy debt-servicing burden. The multiyear debt buildup was therefore a more important issue than the deficit in any given year. Second, it was noted that the Irish crisis went beyond fiscal deterioration and stemmed in part from the sluggish rate of growth in the economy. Furthermore, based on this understanding, the members realized that the poor performance resulted not just from the macroeconomic problem but also from the agriculturally based style of development in the country. In addition to formulating macroeconomic recommendations, the council also emphasized the challenges of structural change and productivity growth: the need to develop comparative advantages beyond that of agriculture. To promote policies in this area, the group also analyzed the primary constraints on growth and recommended industrial policies for overcoming them. With the restoration of macroeconomic equilibrium, this last dimension of the NESC approach gained an even higher profile in subsequent reports.

24. As mentioned in chapter 2, industrial policies had been addressing competitiveness issues, principally through large investments in R&D and by focusing on attraction of hi-tech FDI.

25. Another factor may have been the euro, which could have provided a false sense of security in bond markets.

References

Bonet, Antonio. 2010. "Alianzas publico-privado. Fomento de la exportación en PYMES: el caso de España." Serie Comercio Internacional 95, Economic Commission for Latin America and the Caribbean, International Trade and Integration Division, Santiago, Chile (March).

Caillaud, Bernard, and Jean Tirole. 2007. "Consensus Building: How to Persuade a Group." *American Economic Review* 92, no. 4 (September).

Campos, José Edgardo, and Hilton Root. 1996. *The Key to the Asian Miracle.* Washington, DC: Brookings Institution.

Culpepper, Pepper. 2001. "Employers, Public Policy, and the Politics of Decentralized Cooperation in Germany and France." *Varieties of Capitalism*, ed. Peter Hall and David Soskice. Oxford, U.K.: Oxford University Press.

Cutler, Terry. 2008. "Public and Private Sector Alliances for Innovation and Export Development: The Australian Experience." Economic Commission for Latin America and the Caribbean, International Trade and Integration Division, Santiago, Chile.

Doyle, Mary. 2005. "Irlanda." In *National Visions Matter: Lessons of Success.* Washington, DC: World Bank.

Evans, Peter. 1995. *Embedded Autonomy. States and Industrial Transformation.* Princeton, NJ: Princeton University Press.

Hausmann, Ricardo, Dani Rodrik, and Andrés Velasco. 2005. "Growth Diagnostics." In *The Washington Consensus Reconsidered*, ed. J. Stiglitz and N. Serra. New York: Oxford University Press.

Haworth, Nigel. 2008. "Breaking with the Past: Growth and Innovation in a Post-Market Fundamentalist Economy." Economic Commission for Latin America and the Caribbean (ECLAC), International Trade and Integration Division, Santiago, Chile.

Herzberg, Benjamin, and Andrew Wright. 2005. "Competitiveness Partnerships." Working Paper 3683, World Bank, Washington, DC.

Ministry of Economic Development, New Zealand. 2005. "Economic Transformation." Auckland.

Muñoz, Oscar. 2000. *El Estado y el sector privado*, Latin American Social Science Faculty (FLACSO). Santiago. Chile.

O'Donnell, Rory. 2009. "Ireland's Public-Private Alliance—from Success to Crisis—Again." Economic Commission for Latin America and the Caribbean, International Trade and Integration Division, Santiago, Chile.

O'Donovan, David. 2010. "Private-Public Partnerships for Innovation and Export Development: The Irish Model of Development." Serie Comercio International 96, Economic Commission for Latin America and the Caribbean, International Trade and Integration Division, Santiago, Chile (April).

Office of the Prime Minister. 2002. "Growing an Innovative New Zealand." http://www.executive.govt.nz/minister/clark/innovate/innovative.pdf.

Prats i Català, Joan. 2005. "Las bases de un consenso político nacional de largo plazo." In *National Visions Matter: Lessons of Success*. Washington, DC: World Bank.

Sandler, Todd. 1992. *Collective Action.* Ann Arbor, MI: University of Michigan Press.

Schein, Edgar. 1996. *Strategic Pragmatism: The Culture of Singapore's Economic Development Board.* Cambridge, MA: MIT Press.

Ross Schneider, Ben. 2009. "Business-Government Interaction in Policy Councils in Latin America: Cheap Talk, Expensive Exchanges, or Collaborative Learning?" Department of Political Science, Massachusetts Institute of Technology, Cambridge, MA (March).

Shonfield, Andrew. 1965. *Modern Capitalism.* Oxford, U.K.: Oxford University Press.

Storper, Michael. 2005. "Society, Community and Economic Development." In *Reimagining Growth*, ed. S. de Paula and G. Dymski. London: Zed Books.

World Bank, ECLAC (Economic Commission for Latin America and the Caribbean), and IDEA (International Institute for Democracy and Electoral Assistance). 2005. *National Visions Matter: Lessons of Success.* Washington, DC: World Bank.

4

Operational Principles for Supporting Public Sector Leadership

So far we have reviewed two key dimensions of the most successful of our country cases: development of a medium- to long-term national strategy for structural transformation and establishment of public-private alliances. In the next two chapters, we focus on the remaining necessary dimension for success—public sector implementation.

Figure 4.1 shows that strategic public policies should be aligned with programs and incentives that support them. Moreover, both the strategy and the supporting programs and incentives should emerge from a public-private alliance that takes into account opportunities and constraints in the context of the current capacities of the public and private sectors in their respective institutional settings as well as those that might be realistically realized in a relevant planning horizon for the future. The decisive factor for success or failure, however, is public sector implementation of the package. In other words, as in sports, good strategies are winning strategies only if they are well executed.

In other words, smart strategies are important, but effective implementation will determine actual outcomes at all levels. Moreover, while successful outcomes are important in themselves, they also are important for the coherence and sustainability of the alliance: without effective implementation and successful outcomes, the public sector will lose legitimacy as a partner of the private sector. Hence, this chapter and the next present operational principles geared toward the implementation issue.

Figure 4.1 The Importance of "How" in Public Policies and Programs

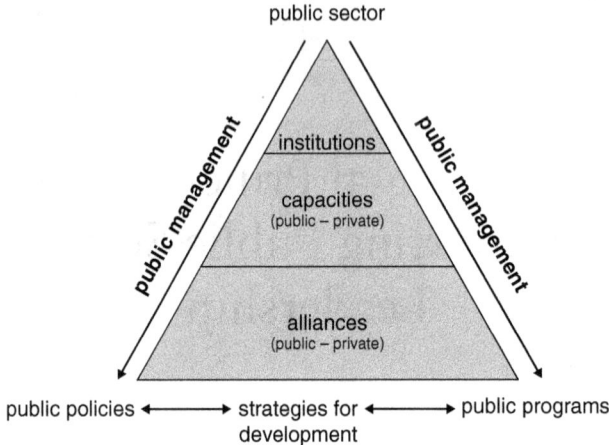

Source: Authors.

The Third Principle: Give the Baton to the "Real" Sector Ministries

The technical leadership for a strategy of economic transformation should be in the hands of the ministries and their executing agencies charged with fundamental oversight of industrial activity, services, and innovation. Although the finance ministry is an extremely important authority in a country, with primary responsibility for maintaining macroeconomic balance, administering tax policies, coordinating and controlling spending, and maintaining the solvency of financial services, it is not the most appropriate entity for assuming this leadership role.[1] Aside from the issue of competency in strategic issues of economic transformation, personnel in the ministry of finance may not have the "cultural" disposition for selective interventions that industrial policy often demands. In Latin America today ministries of finance tend to dominate policy making much too much at the expense of leadership in the ministries responsible for real sector activities.[2]

The strategies of our successful extraregional countries with relatively well-defined goals for structural transformation have been led by one or two ministries responsible for the "real" sectors of the economy. As shown in table 4.1, in six of our success cases, the entities generally responsible for implementing the strategy are the powerful ministries of industry and trade, education, and science and technology (when

Table 4.1 Government Entities Responsible for Implementing the Strategy of Structural Change and Productivity Growth

Country	Design and implementation agencies
Czech Republic	1. Ministry of Industry and Trade 2. National Council on Research and Development
Finland	1. Science and Technology Policy Council of Finland[a] 2. Ministry of Trade and Industry[b]
Ireland	1. Department of Enterprise, Trade, and Employment 2. Forfás
Korea, Rep. (to 1993)	Economic Planning Board
Korea, Rep. (after 1993)	1. National Science and Technology Council 2. Ministry of Science and Technology (MOST)
Malaysia	1. Ministry of International Trade and Industry 2. Ministry of Science, Technology, and Innovation 3. Economic Planning Unit
Singapore	1. Economic Development Board 2. Research, Innovation and Enterprise Council 3. National Research Foundation

Source: Authors, based on official data.
a. In January 2009 this body became the National Research and Innovation Council.
b. Starting in January 2008 this ministry's mandate was transferred to a new Ministry of Employment and the Economy.

innovation is the very top priority), or a special executing agency or entity appointed for this purpose.

The power of these entities depends on several factors: first, as the previous chapter emphasized, the strategy must be built on the broadest possible consensus (or public understanding), especially regarding the key vehicles for the country's development (such as integration into the world economy, export development, and innovation).

Second, ideally, an institution with recognized and respected authority should be available to manage the development and implementation of the strategy. This authority can be aided if the ministry, or one of its executing agencies, has the technical capacity to serve as the public sector's respected "brain" for strategic thinking and implementation.[3] One good example is the Department of Enterprise, Trade and Employment (DETE) in Ireland, whose agency Forfás is a sort of strategic "think tank" with analysis that is highly influential in orienting Ireland's precise insertion into the world economy. The Economic Development Board played this role in Singapore for many decades (before the National Research Foundation took on the task), as has the Science and Technology Policy Council in Finland and the Ministry of International Trade and Industry in Malaysia.

Third, the highest political level of government must support the priority strategic initiatives headed up by ministries or government agencies. This strong political signal can ensure the necessary budget allocations and can help to focus the actions of specialized agencies on strategic priorities.

These three elements are seen in a number of our success cases:

Czech Republic. The National Research and Development Council is made up of 14 prestigious members of the scientific community nominated for a four-year term by the prime minister.[4] The council is highly influential in the formulation of the research, development, and innovation strategies that have been a new priority thrust of Czech development policy; to reflect that priority, the prime minister has chaired the council since 2007. The country also has had a very effective and influential agency called Czech Invest, which was responsible for two crucial and successful aspects of recent strategy: attraction of foreign direct investment (FDI) and development of local business. In 2007 a political disagreement within the parent ministry (Industry and Trade) precipitated an internal crisis in Czech Invest. Some commentators have remarked that Czech Invest could have avoided such problems if it had had a more direct link with the prime minister (Benáček 2010).

Finland. Innovation is the country's national strategy. As discussed in more detail in chapter 3, the entity that developed the guidelines for strategy and proposed the allocation of resources was the Science and Technology Policy Council of Finland (now the Research and Innovation Council), chaired by the prime minister.

Ireland. In Ireland, research and development and innovation are now lead areas of the national strategy. The Inter-Departmental Subcommittee on Science, Technology and Innovation receives reports from the Advisory Council for Science, Technology and Innovation (ACSTI), which is composed of nationally renowned technical experts and academics. Along with contributions from the chief scientific adviser to the Irish government, the subcommittee formulates strategy and defines relevant programs. The prime minister participates in the subcommittee, which falls under the Department of Enterprise, Trade and Employment. DETE in turn is in charge of a constellation of agencies—Enterprise Ireland, Industrial Development Agency–Ireland (IDA), and Science Foundation Ireland—that manage a large proportion of the total public sector budget for research and for support of export-oriented innovation. DETE also oversees Forfás, which produces studies for the Inter-Departmental Subcommittee on Science, Technology and Innovation and ACSTI, while also providing major technical contributions for the formulation of national strategy. All of these activities contribute to DETE's leadership in the cabinet.

Republic of Korea.   The country's strategy is geared toward innovation, now including small and medium enterprises (SMEs). In 1999 the National Science and Technology Council was created with maximum power to define strategies and programs and to allocate resources. The council is composed of representatives of several ministries plus nine representatives from the scientific community and is chaired by the country's president. In 2004 the position of minister for science and technology was elevated to deputy prime minister. The ministry is responsible for planning and coordinating all science and technology programs. Last, some of the most prestigious public research centers working in strategically defined areas are sponsored by the prime minister.

Malaysia.   In its recent national plans, development of information and communications technology (ICT) has been the country's top strategic area. The Implementation Council, chaired by the prime minister, has been the most senior governmental decision-making body in the field. The initiative focuses on the development of a multimedia corridor managed by an agency of the Ministry of Science, Technology, and Innovation. The prime minister also appoints the members of a high-level International Council of Experts that advises on sectoral strategy. Meanwhile, the Economic Planning Unit is a technical body responsible for formulating the national plan in consultation with ministries. The power and legitimacy of this body is strengthened by its location in the Office of the Prime Minister.

Singapore.   The focus of the country's national strategy has shifted toward a new priority: knowledge creation and innovation, under the leadership of the Research, Innovation and Enterprise Council, chaired by the prime minister, and a subordinate agency, the National Research Foundation, whose director is also the deputy prime minister. The foundation has replaced the Agency for Science, Technology and Research as the country's strategic "brain" for innovation policy; that agency had more resources but less political power. The foundation was allocated $5 billion of the $13.5 billion budget for public sector research and development in the period 2006–10.

Another factor that determines the power of entities implementing such strategies is the appointment of politically or technically renowned directors. Such appointments have been the practice in, among others, Singapore (both for the Economic Development Board and A*STAR), Malaysia (the Ministry of Trade and Industry), and the Czech Republic (in Czech Invest up to 2007). Of course, the determining factor in the power of the strategy-implementing authority is whether financial and capable human resources are allocated in accordance with the relevant mandates.

Last, the formal presence of the highest political authority in and around a ministry or agency charged with a priority initiative does not guarantee it leverage; the political authority must exercise real political leadership on behalf of the initiative. Moreover, putting a highly respected person at the helm of the initiative is no guarantee that the power of the public agency implementing the strategy will be sustained in the medium or long term. Such longevity, where relevant for a country's development, requires that the priority and culture of leadership become institutionally rooted and publicly respected. In other words, initiatives and bodies that rely exclusively on the political power of an individual public figure can easily lose their legitimacy and momentum, even if they are successful, when the strong personality departs. This phenomenon appears to explain the crisis that occurred at Czech Invest when its head was dismissed and at Vision 2020 in Malaysia with the departure of Prime Minister Mahathir Mohamad. A subnational lesson along these lines involving a major hydrocarbon innovation strategy in the Province of Alberta, Canada, can be found in annex 4A.

The Fourth Principle: Promote Medium- and Long-Term Policy Strategic Thinking

Government bureaucracies, as participants in an alliance, need to promote a long-run perspective; in principle this responsibility is part of their comparative advantage in a public-private alliance. Politicians tend to focus on the next election cycle. Business can be either myopic and attracted to the siren call of market bubbles and fashions, or victims of status quo inertia. But a government bureaucracy also can get caught up excessively in day-to-day management and undermine its comparative advantage. So while government has a role in helping a country be forward looking, it needs institutional structures and processes to exploit its advantage.

Boyle, O'Donnell, and O'Riordan (2002) point to some steps bureaucracies can take:

- Structure spaces and time for longer-term policy thinking in government. Special units embedded in ministries or agencies dedicated to a long-term perspective create such space. We showed earlier that some success cases have special agencies or government-sponsored research centers that do this type of strategic thinking. However, these technical agencies must have additional space and time to interface with ministers and politicians on long-term issues.
- Launch initiatives within government and in academia that set an agenda for research on longer-term themes that are crosscutting and strategic in nature.
- Train a supply of technicians with the skills and capacities in associated methodologies and practices to think about the future as well as support networks of long-term thinkers.

Foresight exercises—systematic analyses of possible future scenarios—support formulation of strategies and orient activities and thus have proved to be a helpful tool in promoting long-term perspectives. These exercises are used not so much for projecting an increasingly uncertain future but rather for socializing information to create networks of stakeholders and expert analysts who contribute to the search for inputs to strategy definition and policy making. In effect, foresight exercises provide a structured platform for a broad public-private discussion of the future that can involve a large number of social actors. The process tries to detect weaknesses, opportunities, and challenges, while also building a common understanding of the most important determining factors. These systematic efforts attempt to "light up" potential paths for progress in various areas such as developing new markets, or protecting existing ones, and defining priorities for science, technology, innovation, the development of labor supply and skills required by the market, demographics, and the environment, all with the same aim of improving the standard of living of the population.

Although foresight analysis organizes a society-based reflection on the future direction of the economy, in areas such as technological development, changes happen so quickly that policy cannot be a "slave" of any particular exercise. Not only do foresight studies have to be carried out with some frequency, but authorities must also be alert and adaptable between exercises. In addition, information and analysis contained in foresight studies carried out in more developed countries can be helpful inputs too.

The most systematic application of forward-looking analysis at the country level was undertaken during the 1990s in nations such as Austria, France, Germany, Japan, the Republic of Korea, Sweden, and the United Kingdom. Today almost all members of the European Union have engaged in such work, while the Asia-Pacific Economic Cooperation forum has promoted the practice in Asian countries.

In most of our success cases, foresight analysis is being implemented in an increasingly systematic and formal way by stable, dedicated agencies that maintain a constant dialogue with the authorities on defining strategies and policies to face the future. As part of this process, governments have applied foresight analysis to many areas in various ways. Some countries use the methodology through agencies working in specific areas, such as technological foresight studies. As Finland's experience illustrates, foresight analysis is also a way to create public consensus around possible scenarios and to prioritize strategies in various parts of the economy; the practice subsequently spread to other aspects of economic strategy.

The Finnish Example

Foresight analysis was first used by the Finnish Funding Agency for Technology and Innovation (TEKES) in the 1990s to formulate its technological strategy and guide the technology programs for which it is responsible. In 2001 the Ministry of Trade and Industry (later folded into the Ministry of Employment and the Economy) began to use foresight analysis more broadly, coordinating a project to analyze future scenarios and visions for innovation policy, track the development of various processes, and develop new focuses for long-term analysis. In the process, several networks of experts and ministers were established, along with an administrative committee with representatives from the Ministry of Trade and Industry, TEKES, and the Technical Research Center of Finland.

In 2005 TEKES and the Academy of Finland launched a joint foresight project called Finnsight 2015. The aim was to identify future competencies in the fields of science and technology, society, business, and industry, and then to prioritize them. The project helped to identify the country's centers of excellence in science, technology, and innovation, in keeping with the government's decision to develop a public research system, mainly to advance export development and social well-being. The project also strengthened relations between TEKES and the Academy of Finland and created a climate of multidisciplinary discussion. The foresight analysis was carried out by panels of leading industry experts and researchers with multidisciplinary knowledge and experience working in different networks. Discussions were constructive, and each panel produced its own report, all of which were summarized in the publication *Finnsight 2015*.

In 2006 TEKES launched the Signals 2006 foresight project, which was focused on discovering new opportunities and challenges involving industry and society. The project partners included, among others, the Ministry of Industry and Trade, the export credit agency Finnvera, the Finnish Innovation Fund, the Academy of Finland, and the Technical Research Center of Finland. For the government, such an exercise facilitated decision-making processes in a constantly changing environment. The project also helped TEKES to define its strategy for technological programs. The process involved recruiting 7,000 people, with the collaboration of foreign parties, to develop qualitative long-term scenarios through networking, workshops, Delphi surveys, and virtual platforms to carry out benchmarking of the country's innovation environment.[5]

Foresight Analysis in Other Success Cases

Others of our success cases have centers of foresight studies, but these centers have only an informal relationship with government bodies. Such is the case in Sweden, where high-level foresight agencies (such as the Institute for Futures Studies, Royal Swedish Academy of Sciences, Swedish National Board for Industrial and Technical Development, Swedish Foundation for Strategic Research, and the Swedish Industry Association) act independently in choosing their agenda, experts, working methods, funding, and in drawing conclusions from their analyses (Paillard 2005;

Lübeck 2001). These bodies expect the government to take their analyses into account, however, and indeed that is the case. These exercises have become an important tool for the Swedish government because they contribute to public debate and alert the population to future challenges, serve as a means of consultation on social reform, and help to define strategic priorities (especially in the realm of science and technology).

Other countries in our group have made efforts at foresight studies, with some creating government agencies for that purpose. However, these initiatives seem not to have had much impact owing to the dominance of a culture of short-term thinking in government decision making. For example, in Australia the first foresight analysis agency, the Australian Commission for the Future, was created in 1985, but its significance and budget decreased as the years passed. Then in the 1990s, the Australian Science, Technology, and Engineering Council, which had been set up in 1979 to advise the government on science and technology policy, began trying to prepare for the future by applying long-term foresight analysis. Its proposals, however, did not have much impact. Other public agencies in Australia also carry out foresight analysis, but they too have had little nationwide impact (James 2001; Conway and Stewart 2004).

Despite this poor track record the new Labor government in 2008 initiated the "Australian Summit 2020." This project was an attempt to ingrain a culture of long-term thinking into society. The exercise involved a great number of actors across all of civil society who were asked to think about and analyze the challenges of the decades ahead. The discussion was far-reaching in the sense that hundreds of proposals in different thematic areas were debated and evaluated. It remains to be seen whether, in the euphoria of China's current high demand for Australian commodities, this ad hoc exercise has any effect in promoting long-term strategic thinking and policy.

The Fifth Principle: Each Priority Area or Activity in a Strategy Should Have at Least One Dedicated Implementing Agency

In applying this principle, it is important to strike a balance between dispersion of specialization and the demands of coordination. As table 4.2 shows, some of our most successful extraregional cases have a range of main agencies working in the four strategic orientations of international integration and export development. The institutional structure of these agencies is dynamic and functional, that is, it is adapted to the evolution and priority content of the strategies in question. For example, in Ireland one large institution (the Industrial Development Agency) originally covered all four strategic areas. However, economic progress and an increasing focus on structurally specific strategies resulted in a "rebranding," with the development agency spinning off more specialized agencies. The

Table 4.2 Main Agencies Implementing Programs and Policies for Integration with the World Economy

Country	Attraction of FDI	Internationalization of SMEs	Export promotion	Innovation
Australia	AUSTRADE (part of the Department for Foreign Affairs and Trade)	Various	AUSTRADE	Various
Czech Republic	Czech Invest	Czech Invest	CZECH TRADE	Various
Finland	Invest in Finland	n.a.	Ministry of Foreign Affairs, FINPRO	Academy of Finland, TEKES
Ireland	Industrial Development Agency	Enterprise Ireland (EI)		Science Foundation Ireland
Korea, Rep.	Korea Trade-Investment Promotion Agency (KOTRA)	Various	KOTRA	Various
Malaysia	Malaysian Industrial Development Authority (MIDA)	Various	Malaysia External Trade Development Corporation (MATRADE)	Various
New Zealand	NZ Trade and Enterprise (through Invest New Zealand)	NZ Trade and Enterprise		Various

Spain	Autonomous communities	Central export promotion agency (ICEX) and autonomous communities	ICEX and autonomous communities	Center for the Development of Industrial Technology and autonomous communities
Singapore	Economic Development Board	Spring Singapore	International Enterprise Singapore	A*STAR, Economic Development Board
Sweden	Invest in Sweden Agency	National Board for Industrial and Technical Development	Swedish Trade Council	Swedish Research Council, Swedish Governmental Agency for Innovation Systems

Source: Authors, based on official information.
Note: One common characteristic in export promotion not included in the table is that other export insurance and credit agencies often exist.
n.a. = Not applicable.

same story is seen in Singapore where the Economic Development Board divested functions to new specialized agencies as the economy's structure and objectives became more sophisticated. This structure displayed a kind of Tinbergen's Rule, with each main function covered by a clearly identified responsible agency.[6]

Some countries such as Australia, Korea, Malaysia, New Zealand, and Spain have a diverse array of institutions that may indicate degrees of specialization that complicate effective coordination. For its part, the Czech Republic's Czech Invest—a very successful multipurpose agency—may have reached a stage where rebranding should be considered.

The Sixth Principle: The More Structured and Specific a Strategy, the Greater the Need for Coordination among Ministries and Agencies and the More Likely Cabinet-Level Coordination Will Not Be Enough

Coordination is a central element of effective execution but a difficult objective for government to achieve. The successful extraregional countries with relatively structured strategies have used a multiple of coordinating mechanisms. As figure 4.2 shows, the greater the complexity and selectivity of policies and programs in a development strategy, the greater the demands for integrated management by ministries and executing agencies.

A clear mandate and hierarchy of functions for each agency is obviously fundamental. Giving institutions their own clear mandate limits the risks of duplication of efforts and tensions over the territorial distribution

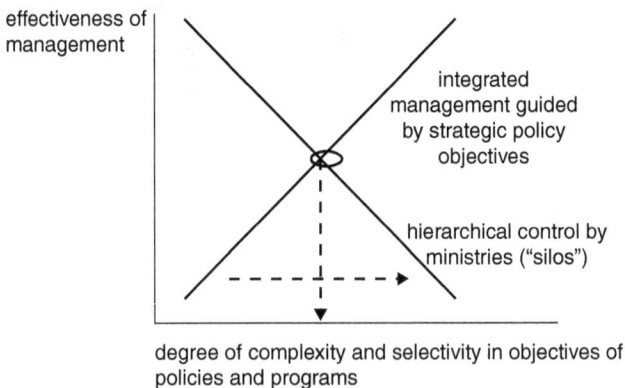

Figure 4.2 Coordination for Effective Public Management

effectiveness of management

integrated management guided by strategic policy objectives

hierarchical control by ministries ("silos")

degree of complexity and selectivity in objectives of policies and programs

Source: Marshall 2009.

of tasks. In any event, collaboration and coordination are always required. For instance, the Industrial Development Agency of Ireland must coordinate its FDI attraction programs with Enterprise Ireland because the strategy also calls for the development agency to promote links with local suppliers. Ireland has multilayered mechanisms for facilitating coordination. The role of coordinating the country's three agencies described in table 4.2 is assigned to Forfás, which along with these agencies all come under the Department of Enterprise, Trade and Employment. The authority of Forfás as a coordinating mechanism is strengthened by its renown as a strategic think tank for integration with the world economy and its influence over budget allocations to the executing agencies.

Moreover, although the representation on the boards of directors of executing agencies and committees in the export development constellation include various public sector entities (as well as private sector representatives), coordination is facilitated by the presence of extensive cross-representation by Forfás or its parent department (figure 4.3).

Figure 4.3 Ireland: Cross Representation on the Boards of Agencies and on Councils Implementing the Export Development Strategy

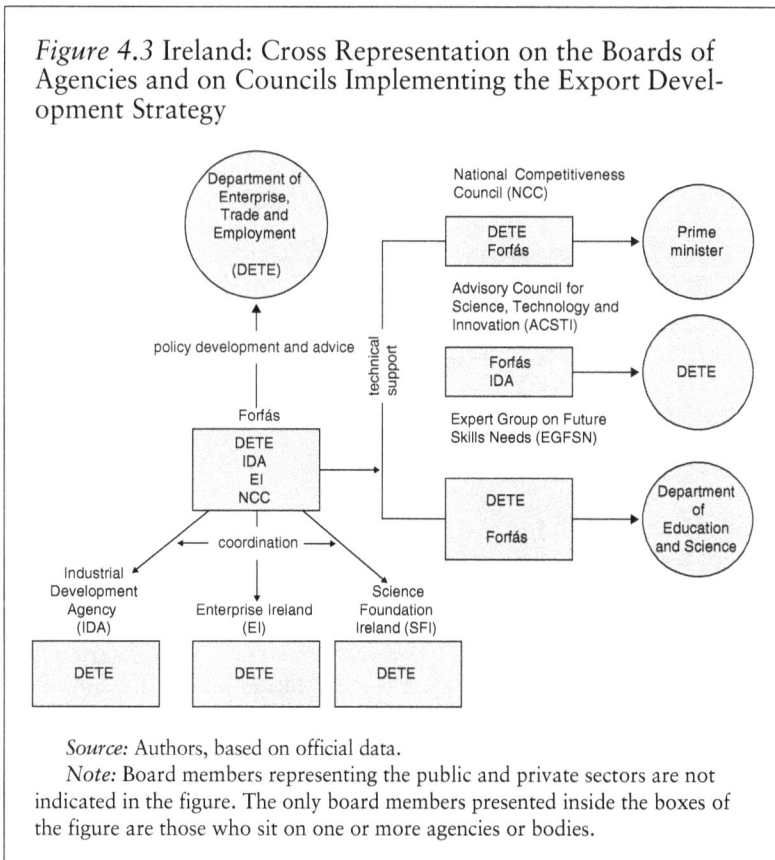

Source: Authors, based on official data.

Note: Board members representing the public and private sectors are not indicated in the figure. The only board members presented inside the boxes of the figure are those who sit on one or more agencies or bodies.

Figure 4.4 Singapore: Coordination of Innovation Institutions

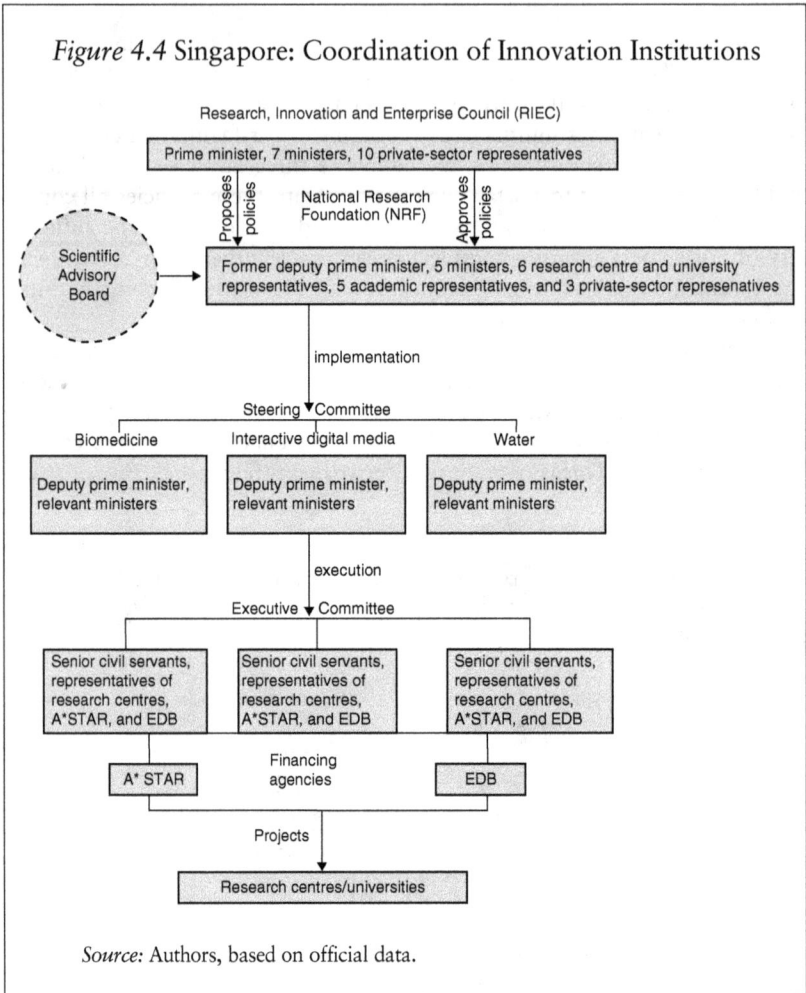

Research, Innovation and Enterprise Council (RIEC)

Prime minister, 7 ministers, 10 private-sector representatives

Proposes policies

National Research Foundation (NRF)

Approves policies

Scientific Advisory Board

Former deputy prime minister, 5 ministers, 6 research centre and university representatives, 5 academic representatives, and 3 private-sector represenatives

implementation

Steering Committee

Biomedicine | Interactive digital media | Water

Deputy prime minister, relevant ministers

Deputy prime minister, relevant ministers

Deputy prime minister, relevant ministers

execution

Executive Committee

Senior civil servants, representatives of research centres, A*STAR, and EDB

Senior civil servants, representatives of research centres, A*STAR, and EDB

Senior civil servants, representatives of research centres, A*STAR, and EDB

A* STAR | Financing agencies | EDB

Projects

Research centres/universities

Source: Authors, based on official data.

In addition, the formal assessment of the performance of agency officials makes reference to internal coordination and external coordination with other agencies. Finally, the buildings of Ireland's export development agencies are in the same complex, thereby facilitating informal day-to-day communication.

In Singapore there is some cross-representation on boards, but much of the coordination takes place through structured committees and informal networks within a stable cadre of professional civil servants who have worked together for a long time in the various agencies and bodies. Figure 4.4 illustrates the formal network of coordination among committees and agencies (as well as their members) responsible for promoting research and development (R&D) and innovation. There is a noticeable "cascading" specialization of responsibilities the nearer a decision gets to the final disbursement of resources to beneficiaries.

As mentioned, Finland's national economic development strategy is concentrated on innovation. Coordination is facilitated by the strategy's relatively singular focus and clear mandates as part of a simple division of labor between the Finnish Funding Agency for Technology and Innovation (which drives applied research) and the Academy of Finland (which promotes basic research). Furthermore, each agency submits an annual plan (with periodic monitoring of results) to its parent ministry that, when approved, forms a signed agreement for the execution of the actions recommended in the three-year guidelines prepared by the public-private alliance's Science and Technology Policy Council (see chapter 3). Figure 4.5 summarizes this coordination in Finland.

In Malaysia the agencies are conventionally coordinated by the relevant ministries and through regular interministerial meetings involving the prime minister as ultimate arbitrator. In addition to the Small and Medium Industries Development Corporation, at least 12 ministries and 38 agencies are charged with implementing strategic lines of action related to SMEs. Each agency has explicit objectives identified in the national strategy. This in itself is a coordination mechanism. However, the National SME Development Council, a dedicated interministerial committee, was set up to improve coordination.

The Czech Republic has an implementation and coordination system for the achievement of strategic objectives assigned to a ministry or agencies

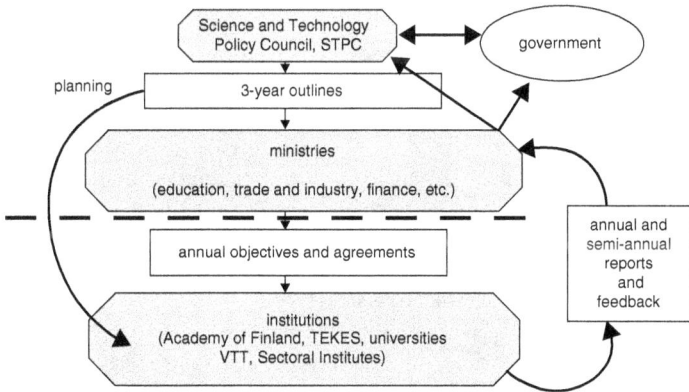

Figure 4.5 Finland: Planning and Coordination among Agencies

Source: Andersson 2010.

within a ministry. Unstable government coalitions in the age of democracy have created a continuous risk of fragmentation of tasks. In the first half of 2006 the Czech Council on Trade and Investment was established within the Ministry of Industry and Trade to coordinate government agencies and ministries working in these areas and monitor the 2006–10 export development strategy.[7] The council became operable in 2008. A discussion on the need to centralize the entities executing the country's innovation plan, rather than relying on 22 ministerial channels, suggests that coordination in this area has been quite inadequate.[8]

Since Korea abandoned national planning in the 1990s, each ministry devises its own plan. Initiatives to create new coordination mechanisms within a very complex, proactive state apparatus and sophisticated economy have not always been successful. Organization in support of R&D and innovation is especially fragmented, which in turn has resulted in a duplication of efforts and bureaucratic tensions.

Korea's experience also demonstrates the importance for effective coordination of hierarchical positioning in the government bureaucracy. The National Science and Technology Council had a mandate to coordinate innovation planning and implementation among relevant ministries and agencies. Until 2004, however, it shared hierarchy with the Ministry of Planning and the National Assembly, which diluted the council's authority and the effectiveness of the principle mechanism of coordination. Only after a reform that gave the council a preeminent place in the bureaucratic hierarchy did it gain the needed leverage for achieving unchallenged responsibility for coordination (figure 4.6).

New Zealand implements its strategy through a small number of agencies with responsibility for a wide range of policies and programs. This structure suggests that the economic transformation strategy of the Labor government was somewhat path dependent on the relatively entrenched liberal horizontal approach of the past, which made it difficult to implement a more focused, structurally oriented strategy. Agency coordination is traditionally carried out through a lead ministry. The economic transformation strategy was formulated by the Ministry of Economic Development, which used interministerial committees as part of the official framework intended to promote an integrated government. As in Ireland and Singapore, some specialized executing bodies have cross-representation on boards of directors.

Australia, Spain, and Sweden have faced serious coordination challenges. In Spain implementation responsibilities are relatively easy to assign and coordinate, thanks to a strategic approach to export development that, until recently, was fairly horizontal. Serious shortcomings have, however, arisen in coordination between the central government and the 17 autonomous communities, which have a high degree of independence as far as strategies and implementation are concerned (see Annex 4B for the case of Andalusia). In effect Spain has 18 strategies counting the central government! In an effort to improve coordination, ICEX (the

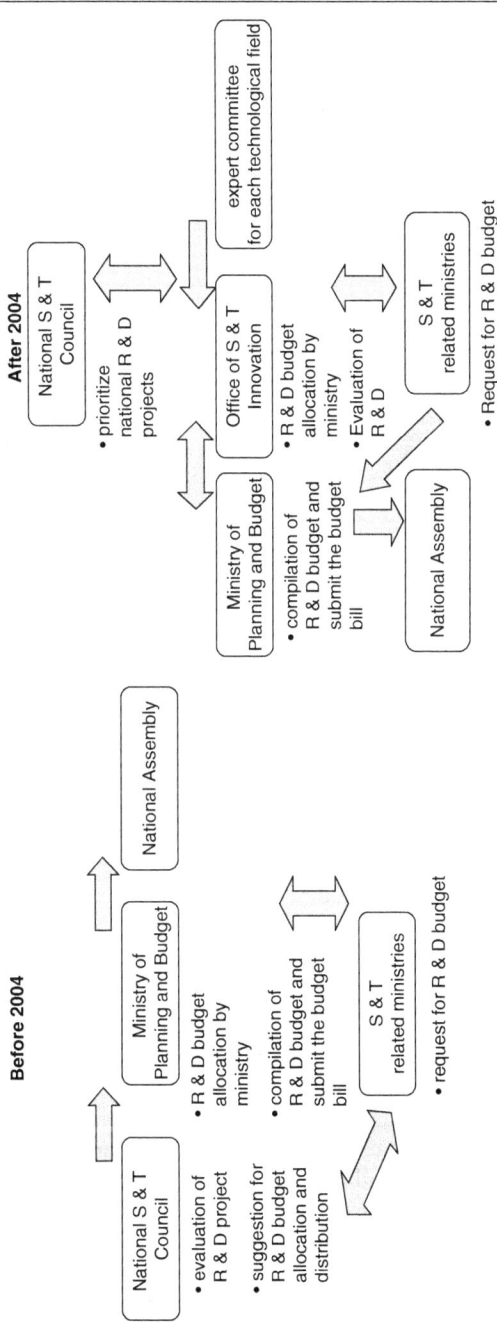

Figure 4.6 Reform of Korea's National System of Innovation

Before 2004

National S & T Council
- evaluation of R & D project
- suggestion for R & D budget allocation and distribution

Ministry of Planning and Budget
- R & D budget allocation by ministry
- compilation of R & D budget and submit the budget bill

National Assembly

S & T related ministries
- request for R & D budget

After 2004

National S & T Council
- prioritize national R & D projects

expert committee for each technological field

Office of S & T Innovation
- R & D budget allocation by ministry
- Evaluation of R & D

Ministry of Planning and Budget
- compilation of R & D budget and submit the budget bill

National Assembly

S & T related ministries
- Request for R & D budget

Source: Hong 2010.

Figure 4.7 Administrative Structure of the Main Innovation Programs and Agencies in Australia

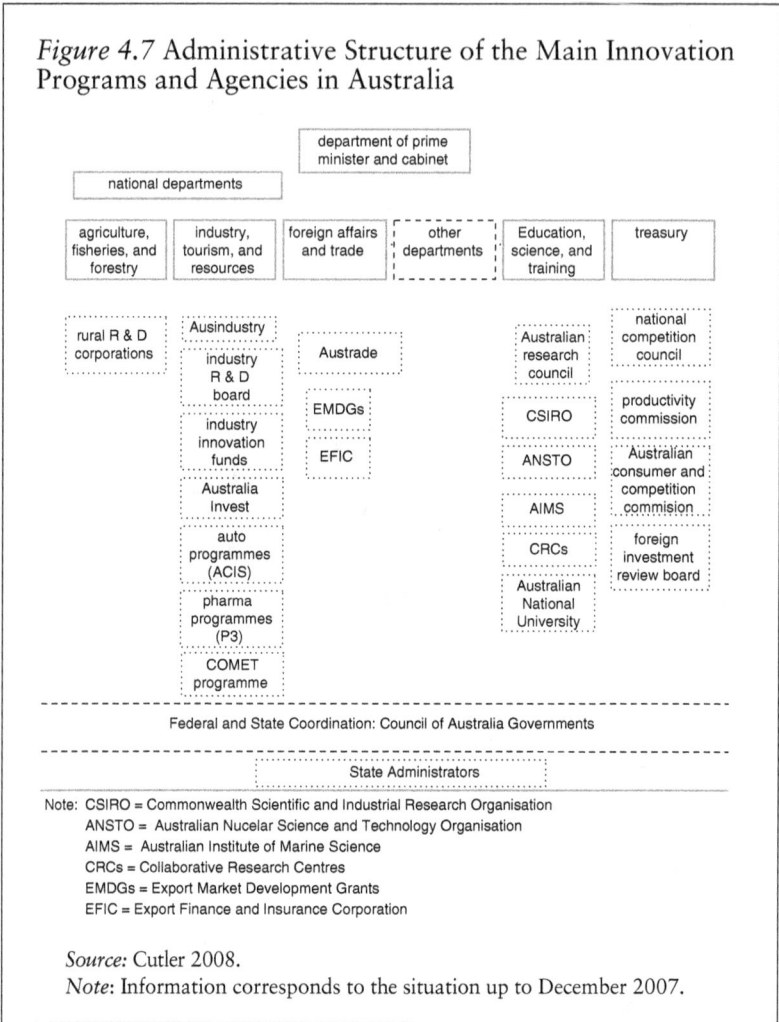

Note: CSIRO = Commonwealth Scientific and Industrial Research Organisation
ANSTO = Australian Nucelar Science and Technology Organisation
AIMS = Australian Institute of Marine Science
CRCs = Collaborative Research Centres
EMDGs = Export Market Development Grants
EFIC = Export Finance and Insurance Corporation

Source: Cutler 2008.
Note: Information corresponds to the situation up to December 2007.

central government export promotion agency) has attempted to join the boards of sister agencies in the communities.

Although Australia has a relatively liberal horizontal development strategy, it is much more structured in the support of innovation, an area that covers multiple sectors and activities. Implementation has therefore been fairly spread out among specialized agencies and ministries. This structure could be interpreted as leaning toward a system of "open innovation" (a broad network of informal relations between agents contributing to innovation), but it also creates a huge demand for effective coordination mechanisms. Ministries and specialized agencies have traditionally operated without much interaction, thereby creating a series of isolated "silos" that hampers the development of integrated management (figure 4.7).[9] Second, like Spain and its relations with the autonomous communities in the country, Australia faces the challenge of aligning federal programs with state programs, a task that is further complicated by the size of the country.[10]

The Seventh Principle: For Medium- and Long-Term Strategies to Be Effective, Public Sector Personnel Must Be Highly Professional, Career Oriented, and Nonpoliticized

A technically competent, motivated, and honest public workforce in which career advancements are based on merit is essential for successful strategies underpinned by industrial policies. Strong, competent public bureaucracies are an important element in "state capacity" and have been cited as a key ingredient in the success of catch-up countries (Evans 1995).

As mentioned in chapter 3, capable public-private alliances that give birth to effective strategies need the "embedded autonomy" of the state. A necessary, but not sufficient condition for this is the availability of a highly professional public bureaucracy motivated by national development objectives. A professional and capable bureaucracy, moreover, will be a credible partner of the private sector, allowing effective interaction on the basis of trust. A professional bureaucracy also can serve as an institutional "memory" over political cycles, instilling consistency in development strategies over time. And effective implementation of strategies, especially where Sabel's (2009) "open industrial policy" is relevant, demands delegation of authority that only a capable professional civil service can undertake successfully.

The central role of a strong, technically competent public bureaucracy has been a key characteristic of the Asian countries that have succeeded in catch-up (Evans 1995; Wade 2004; Jung-En Woo 1999; Karagiannis and Madjd-Sadjadi 2007; Chang 1994; World Bank 1997).

In East Asia recruitment is typically competitive and based on merit. The aim is to recruit the "best and brightest" either from local elite universities or among nationals studying abroad in top schools. Bringing in and retaining the best and brightest generates prestige for civil service, which in turn facilitates on-going recruitment of top talent. Once in the civil service system, recruits are put on a career path and given training. Promotions are based on merit, which encourages continuity, deepening of learning experiences, coordination, teamwork, and an esprit de corps. The civil service is technically driven and largely insulated from politicization. In some cases salaries are competitive with the private sector, while in others national prestige, job experience, and security are sufficient for recruitment and retention. Interestingly, in some East Asian countries, technicians outside the economics profession dominated the most influential policy-making groups during the period of intensive industrial policy and catch-up (Wade 2004; Chang 1994).[11]

Salaries and incentives in our success cases are varied. In most countries public sector salaries are below those for equivalent work in the private sector. The exceptions are Ireland and Singapore; both countries have had a conscious policy to make public salaries equivalent to those in the private sector in order to recruit and retain a quality public workforce[12] Singapore is especially committed to parity (Schein 1996). As a Singaporean minister commented in 2007 about public sector salaries: "We do not aim to lead private sector salaries, but we must keep pace. If we are not responsive, we will lose our ability to recruit and keep able people. This will do great harm to Singapore as we should have lost one key advantage over other countries—a clean, competent and effective civil service."[13] Singapore also has an innovative merit pay system based on the country's annual economic performance.

Singapore's public sector human resource management encourages a corporate culture in its specialized agencies. The aim is to motivate not only individuals but also to facilitate the teamwork and delegation that is so vital for a system that implements strategic activities through a network of agencies. Two strains run through this efficient civil service. One is the British tradition of "clean civil service," or honesty (Schein 1996). The other, inspired by the French system of the Grands Corps de l'Etat (Kumar and Siddique 2010), is an elite body of about 250 public servants that serve as upper management in the public bureaucracy.[14] Future senior managers for this elite corps are recruited from the country's best students and receive special dedicated academic and business training at home and abroad throughout their careers, so that they are able to technically lead the public bureaucracy in the development and implementation of strategies. The elite corps also facilitates consensus and informal coordination.

In Spain, pay in specialized agencies tends to be lower than pay in the private sector but somewhat better than that in central government. Korea and Malaysia have depended more on a sense of national pride and the prestige of public service to recruit and motivate top professionals. Salaries in the civil services of Australia, Finland, and New Zealand also do not match their counterparts in the private sector.

Two organizational models prevail in our success cases. In the first model, the central government directly controls specialized agencies. This system is in place in the Czech Republic, Finland, Korea, and Sweden. In the second model, agencies are semiautonomous, with legally delegated mandates, and operate at arm's length from the executive (often as a statutory body). This structure is used in countries with a commonwealth tradition (Australia, Ireland, Malaysia, New Zealand, and Singapore) and also in certain areas of the Spanish central government.

In the first model, historical convention has given rise to agencies that are protected from political cycles (and have some autonomy in certain operational aspects), as in Finland. Czech Invest (responsible for FDI attraction and SME development strategies) enjoyed almost 15 years of relative autonomy based on the professional excellence of its executive directors and professional team; however, it was unable to establish a sufficiently firm tradition within the public administration and public awareness. Czech Invest underwent a bureaucratic and political crisis in 2007 and lost its autonomy.

In the second model, functions are delegated more explicitly and agencies are better protected from political cycles. This system also has the advantage of raising the specialized professional profile of the agency, by giving it more flexibility than central government offices have in professional recruitment, salaries, procedures, and the promotion of cooperation.

Such semiautonomy encourages delegation and may also make the agency more accountable for the results of its programs. Autonomy remains relative because the government is represented on the board of directors and usually appoints the directors, stipulates periods of rotation, and allocates funding. Agencies are also subject to public auditing procedures.

Annex 4A Alberta Oil Sands Technology and Research Authority: Leading Innovation to Exploit the Oil Sands in Alberta, Canada

The Province of Alberta, Canada, is home to one of the world's largest petroleum reserves.[15] Trapped in sticky layers of sediment known as oil sands, the petroleum is difficult to extract. Of the total reserves, 80 percent has to be drilled in situ, which requires a high level of technological development.

In 1984 the premier of the province made a key contribution to developing this resource when he created the Alberta Oil Sands Technology and Research Authority (AOSTRA), designed to promote the costly technological development needed to extract the oil in situ and ensure benefits for the local population. AOSTRA was run by an independent board; at least one of the board members was a political representative, while the remaining members (including the chair and vice-chair) were private sector technical experts recruited through competitive processes. Within this set-up, the political representative provided an essential strategic link between the objectives of AOSTRA and the world of politics. Similarly decisive for the future of the organization was the election of a highly experienced and respected engineer from the region's private oil sector to serve as chair of the board of directors, a full-time job.

The provincial premier mobilized Can$235 million to cofinance the initiative (around half of the funding requirements) and to attract research projects with industry partners. He also introduced one the most striking characteristics of the new organization: the rights on the new technologies developed remained the property of the provincial government. The involved private sector enterprises had the right to use the inventions in their place of operation but were barred from commercializing them. Any company that did not collaborate would have to buy the technology at a price reflecting its development costs. Information on new inventions would be kept by the government for 35 years. In the early stages of AOSTRA, this was the main bone of contention between the provincial government and the industry. Although only one company initially signed on to the requirement that the new technology would be owned by the provincial government, the rest of the industry eventually followed suit.

AOSTRA spent its first two years consulting with industry and academia. It then devised a five-year work program, which consisted of collaborating with industry to field-test the most advanced technologies developed by the private sector at that time. Devising the Underground Testing Facility and developing and commercializing the petroleum extraction system known as Steam Assisted Gravity Drainage was costly and discouraging. At the same time, international oil prices collapsed in 1982 and the private sector pulled out. The provincial government maintained its long-term vision of innovation and the sector's potential profitability and decided to continue to implement the testing facility alone. The facility opened in 1987, and in 1993 AOSTRA announced that it was about to overcome the obstacles to commercializing the extraction system. Furthermore, over 100 patents or invention requests and reports had been produced in support of commercial licences.

The AOSTRA vision, however, began to fade in the second half of the 1980s. Peter Lougheed, the premier who had been the main promoter of the initiative, left office. Clem Bowman, the respected chairman of the board, also departed after 10 years. These departures coincided with economic problems at the national level. In this context, AOSTRA lost its political and financial independence in 1994 when its functions were subsumed under a new division affiliated with the Ministry of Energy.

Several lessons can be gleaned from this experience:

- Political leadership is crucial.
- Ambitious initiatives, especially in the sphere of technology, need long-term vision to be brought to fruition.
- When technological development costs are high and the results uncertain, funding must be long term and independent of electoral cycles.
- Implementing agencies should be semiautonomous with mainly technical staff and subject to the proper checks and balances.

- An alliance between academia and science and industry is vital.
- The long-term vision should be created by building consensus and institutional agreements that transcend political cycles and a "big person."

Annex 4B The Autonomous Community of Andalusia: Another Subnational Case

In 2003 the Autonomous Community of Andalusia launched a development strategy known as the Second Modernization of Andalusia.[16] Export promotion, FDI attraction, industrialization of SMEs, and innovation were the central hubs of this strategy. The resulting programs and policies were implemented by two agencies: the Trade Promotion Agency of Andalusia (Extenda), which focuses on traditional export promotion activities, and the Innovation and Development Agency of Andalusia (IDEA), which deals with the other areas of export development.

The relationship between the public sector (agency executives) and the private sector (business, trade associations, and chambers of commerce) has been a smooth and easy one, irrespective of the political party in office, with no serious differences of opinion between the public and private sectors. There is an unwritten understanding about their roles and how to interrelate, with the public sector systematically consulting the main private organizations on issues of internationalization policy and, albeit to a lesser degree, on support for SMEs and innovation. The execution of promotion policies is decidedly sectoral. Private associations and organizations play a very active role in the design and execution of policies and plans. There are also frequent meetings (especially informal ones) between the sectors.

In time this relationship has become increasingly formal. One example is the admission of business organization representatives into the export promotion institutions of the Autonomous Community.

The capital of Extenda is 88 percent owned by the government of Andalusia, with the remainder owned by 12 of the region's 14 chambers of commerce. The government has limited involvement in the day-to-day running of Extenda. Its strategic positioning and the design of instruments and programs are defined by the 12-member management board, 10 of whom represent various public administration bodies. These include ICEX, the central government export promotion agency (a formal policy-coordination link is being forged between ICEX and Extenda). The two remaining members of the management board are elected by the chambers of commerce of Andalusia.

The government has guaranteed increasing levels of minimum budgetary income over time, enabling Extenda to plan for the medium and long term. Extenda has also relief on instruments that have had low budgetary requirements but maximum visibility in addressing businesses needs: information, training, advice, promotion, and support abroad. Extenda often carries out surveys and studies on the value of its business services, and the results point to a very high level of satisfaction with the services offered. In contrast to ICEX, the Extenda promotion programs have been part of the agency's multiyear strategic plans since 1998. Strategic plans are produced by an external consultancy firm with the input of Extenda and then reviewed and presented to the managing board for discussion and approval. In terms of subnational public-private alliances, IDEA has an advisory board made up of representatives of the community's socioeconomic agents. Meanwhile the agency's strategic support is subject to consultations under the community's Social Cohesion Accords.

The autonomous communities, Andalusia in particular, are assuming growing responsibilities in developing their business networks and boosting cooperation between government and the private sector. The fact that regional administrations are closer to local companies means they find it easier than the central government to understand business needs and thus have a key role to play in innovation and research and development. However, autonomous administrations have problems similar to those of the central government, such as slow and bureaucratic management and limited coordination with other bodies in the central government and within the region. In Andalusia, the regional government's autonomy and room for maneuver in the design and implementation of innovation and SME support policies have been influenced by European Union practices in this area.

To a certain extent, the Autonomous Community of Andalusia could be said to have a higher level of institutional development for industrial policy than the central government, because the former has a medium-term strategy based on a guiding, formally structured public-private alliance, thereby driving the institutional reform needed to strengthen program and policy coordination, all with a view to achieving more integral growth for the region.

Notes

1. In Ireland the Ministry of Finance coordinates other ministries and leads the public consultation on the strategy.

2. This dominance probably stems from the period when finance ministries took over the leadership of the economies during and after the debt crisis and were usually the "port of entry" for the Washington Consensus.

3. A lack of a strategic "brain" in Spain was perhaps the reason that the country was slow to realize the effects of competition from low-wage eastern European countries when EU expansion occurred and also slow to realize the need to boost its meager expenditure on R&D and innovation.

4. They receive a part-time civil servant salary.

5. Elija (2003); Pulkkinen (2000); TEKES and the Academy of Finland (2006a, 2006b).

6. Under Tinbergen's Rule, each objective requires its own instrument. Ireland combines export development with the business development of SMEs in one agency, because multinationals do not need export support. Singapore keeps the two areas of responsibility separate.

7. The council consists of 9 government and 10 corporate representatives.

8. Nonetheless, the programming requirements for the use of EU funding is a positive factor in the coordination of strategies relating to export development.

9. Silos also hamper processes that could lead the development of effective national strategies. According to Cutler (2008), the new Australian Labor government announced its intention to strengthen coordination mechanisms within the federal system and between that system and individual states. It is not clear that much has been accomplished as yet.

10. One way of mitigating the problem of geographical dispersion would be for agencies to use regional offices more intensively. The gap between the federal government and individual states could be narrowed through cross-representation on agency boards of directors.

11. Economists in Japan, Korea, and Taiwan, China, especially foreign-trained ones, tended to be skeptical of industrial policy.

12. During Ireland's recent crisis, civil servants were forced to take a significant pay cut.

13. Zakin Hussain, "Ministerial Civil Service Salaries Expected to Go Up," *Straits Times*, March 3, 2007 (http://www.straitstimes.com/).

14. France's Grands Corps de l'Etat has led postwar industrial policy and has been a constant influential strategic force in business and government even in an era of reforms and liberalization (Loriaux 1999 and 2007).

15. Based on information in Hester and Lawrence (2010).

16. Drawn from Bonet (2010).

References

Andersson, Thomas. 2010. "Building Long-Term Strategies and Public-Private Alliances for Export Development: The Swedish Case." Project Document 295, Economic Commission for Latin America and the Caribbean, International Trade and Integration Division, Santiago, Chile (July).

Benáček, Vladimír. 2010. "Is the Czech Economy a Success Story? The Case of Czech Invest: The Strategic Promotion Agency in Czech Industrial Restructuring." Serie Comercio Internacional 101, Economic Commission for Latin America and the Caribbean, International Trade and Integration Division, Santiago, Chile (March).

Bonet, Antonio. 2010. "Alianzas publico-privado. Fomento de la exportación e innovación en pymes: el caso de España." Serie Comercio Internacional 95, Economic Commission for Latin America and the Caribbean, International Trade and Integration Division, Santiago, Chile (March).

Boyle, Richard, Orla O'Donnell, and Joanna O'Riordan. 2002. "Promoting Longer-term Policy Thinking." CPMP Discussion Paper 22, Institute of Public Adminstration, Dublin.

Chang, Ha-Joon. 1994. *The Political Economy of Industrial Policy*. New York: St. Martin's Press.

Conway, Maree, and Chris Stewart. 2005. "Creating and Sustaining Foresight in Australia: A Review of Government Foresight." Monograph Series 2004–8, Australian Foresight Institute, Swinburne University of Technology, Melbourne.

Cutler, Terry. 2008. "Public and Private Sector Alliances for Innovation and Export Development: The Australian Experience." Economic Commission for Latin America and the Caribbean, International Trade and Integration Division, Santiago, Chile.

Elija, Ahola. 2003. "Technology Foresight within the Finnish Innovation System." TEKES, Helsinki (February).

Evans, Peter. 1995. *Embedded Autonomy. States and Industrial Transformation.* Princeton, NJ: Princeton University Press.

Hester, Annette, and Leah Lawrence. 2010. "A Sub-National Public Private Strategic Alliance for Innovation and Export Development. The Case of the Canadian Province of Alberta's Oil Sands." Project Document 292, Economic Commission for Latin America and the Caribbean, International Trade and Integration Division, Santiago, Chile (March).

Hong, Yoo Soo. 2010. "Public and Private Sector Alliances for Export Development: The Korean Case." Serie Comercio Internacional 102, Economic Commission for Latin America and the Caribbean, International Trade and Integration Division, Santiago Chile (August).

James, Matthew. 2001. "Australia 2020: Foresight for Our Future." Research Paper 18, Department of the Parliamentary Library, Canberra (February).

Jung-En Woo, Meredith, ed. 1999. *The Developmental State.* Ithaca, NY: Cornell University Press.

Karagiannis, Nikolaos, and Zagros Madjd-Sadjadi. 2007. *Modern State Intervention in an Era of Globalization.* Cheltenham, U.K.: Edward Elgar.

Kumar, Sree, and Sharon Siddique 2010. "The Singapore Success Story: Public-Private Alliance for Investment Attraction, Innovation and Export Development" Serie Comercio Internacional 99, Economic Commission for Latin America and the Caribbean, International Trade and Integration Division, Santiago, Chile (March).

Loriaux, Michael. 1999. "The French Development State as Myth and Moral Ambition." *The Developmental State.* Meredith Jung: En Woo, ed. Ithaca: Cornell University Press.

———. 2007. "Development as a Political Culture and Liberalization in France." *Neoliberalism and Institutional Reform in East Asia.*, ed. Meredith Jung-En Woo. New York: Palgrave.

Lübeck, Lennart. 2001. "The Swedish Technology Foresight Project." United Nations Industrial Development Organization, Geneva.

Marshall, Jorge. 2009. "La Reforma del Estado: Vision y Proceso." Programa Expansiva, Instituto de Políticas Públicas, Santiago, Chile.

Paillard, Sandrine. 2005. "Futures Studies and Public Decision in Sweden." Project Aleph, Paris (November).

Pulkkinen, Raimo. 2000. "Finnish Manufacturing Foresight Exercises." Finnish Funding Agency for Technology and Innovation, Helsinki.

Sabel, Charles. 2009. "What Industrial Policy Is Becoming: Taiwan, Ireland and Finland as Guides to the Future of Industrial Policy." Columbia Law School. http://idbdocs.iadb.org/wsdocs/getDocument.aspx?DOCNUM=1843147.

Schein, Edgar. 1996. Strategic Pragmatism: *The Culture of Singapore's Economic Development Board.* Cambridge, MA: MIT Press.

TEKES (Finnish Funding Agency for Technology and Innovation) and the Academy of Finland. 2006a. "Finnsight 2015: The Outlook for Science, Technology and Society." Helsinki (September).

———. 2006b. "Signals 2006." http://www.tekes.fi/eng/innovation/foresight.htm.

Wade, Robert. 2004. *Governing the Market: Economic Theory and the Role of Government in East Asian Industrialization.* Princeton, NJ: Princeton University Press.

World Bank. 1997. *World Development Report, 1997: The State in a Changing World.* Washington, DC: Oxford University Press.

5

Principles for Managing Programs and Incentives

We examined in the previous chapter the issue of effective public sector organization for leadership in the formulation and implementation of strategies. In this chapter we draw insights and operational principles from our success cases on management of programs and incentives in support of the strategy.

The Eighth Principle: The Effective Application of Incentives Must Be Assessed Not only by How They Are Individually Managed But also by How They Are Coordinated for a Systemic Effect

To promote economic links with the world economy, public agencies support enterprises. Countries place more or less emphasis on the four areas of export development discussed in chapter 2 depending on their specific national strategies. This emphasis is conveyed through functional programs—the different types of technical assistance and support offered, including financing instruments, the most common being loans, grants, and tax incentives (table 5.1).

The strategic area of attracting foreign investment generally consists in establishing contractual arrangements under which governments offer tax breaks for given periods, supply public financing for infrastructure and training or education for needed local labor supply, and provide other incentives that can support the company's activity. For its part, the company undertakes to set up operations in the country, or to make significant reinvestments, and to comply with certain goals (for example, job creation). Under other programs, the foreign firms are encouraged to support the development of local input supply industries and to locate part of

Table 5.1 Typology of Programs and Instruments in Areas of Strategic Orientation

Policies	Programs	Incentives
International integration of local business	Training programs	Subsidies for participation in specific training programs
	Improvement of operation, management, training, quality, and adoption of new standards	Subsidies for consultancy, technical assistance, training, preparation of business plans, quality enhancement
	Support for new projects	Subsidies and competitive funding
	Programs to develop collaborative innovation	Subsidies for integration in networks and collaborative research
		Availability of consultants; R&D alert campaigns and technology transfer services
	Machinery and equipment	Tax discounts, exemptions, preferential rates, rebates on machinery and equipment
	Entrepreneurship	Subsidies, soft loans, venture capital
Export promotion	Assistance in gaining a foothold in external markets	Credit to generate export supply Organization of country brand initiatives and fairs
		Financing export loans and risk insurance for trade operations
		Competitive funding up to a percentage of the investment in promotion abroad

		Market alerts and research offices
		Overseas promotion offices
FDI attraction and reinvestment		Public financing
	For infrastructure (transport, industrial parks, buildings, technology corridors, technological cities) and training of labor and professionals for the industry in question.	
	Machinery and equipment	Tax incentives and import tariff rebates
	Encouragement for R&D activities	Tax incentives plus special competitive subsidized funding
	Other support services	Creation of a "one-stop shop" with representatives from different ministries and agencies to deal with problems concerning programs, public regulations, and postinvestment services
Innovation	Technical assistance	Technical assistance to companies through training in management and strategy design for innovation
		Availability of "pay-as-you-use" laboratory installations

(continued)

Table 5.1 Typology of Programs and Instruments in Areas of Strategic Orientation *(continued)*

Policies	Programs	Incentives
Innovation	Promotion of innovation in key sectors	Collaborative research funds for clusters or consortia
		Collaborative funding for links between companies and universities, research institutes, and centers of excellence
		Tax exemptions or tax credits
		Subsidies for conferences and workshops and for major researchers
	Attracting talent	Programs for recruiting high-level researchers from abroad or collaborating with them
	Scholarships	Various scholarship funds for education of locals
	Marketing of knowledge	Training in intellectual property
		Seed or venture capital
		Investor contact networks
		Training in corporate management for innovation

Source: Authors.

their research and development (R&D) activities in the country. As noted in chapter 2, countries where FDI attraction was a key component of their national export development strategy—the Czech Republic, Ireland, Malaysia, and Singapore—typically started out with incentives supporting general objectives such as employment. These countries first established themselves as attractive FDI hosts and then targeted their FDI incentives on achieving more specific objectives.

Local firms are supported to make them internationally competitive. The focus is often on small and medium enterprise (SMEs). Much attention is given to capacity building in areas such as management, scaling up production, upgrading product lines, R&D, and innovation. All 10 success cases actively promote "start-ups."

Export promotion strategies are designed to assist firms in gaining a foothold in external markets. The types of services offered are fairly common in all countries and any differences between one service and another lie more in their effective implementation than in the nature of the programs themselves. In most cases, some degree of subsidy is granted in ways that do not infringe on the rules of the World Trade Organization (WTO).

As for innovation, programs seek to promote the development of new products and services as well as new processes in industries or clusters defined by the strategy. Incentives for technical assistance in managing innovation are also offered, as is assistance in commercializing the results of innovation. Indeed, this last aspect is receiving increasing attention, especially through the creation of formal and informal networks of researchers and businesses. Besides educational initiatives, the priority instruments in this area are grants and tax credits. Whether direct subsidies are a more suitable instrument for innovation than tax credits has become a matter for discussion (see annex 5A). Singapore and, to a lesser extent, Ireland have active and generous programs for recruiting internationally renowned foreign researchers to work with their local counterparts (a kind of "twinning") to boost national capacities.

Figure 5.1 illustrates how the instruments and programs for integrating SMEs into the world economy should tie in with each other in the four areas of strategic orientation for export development. The application of a particular incentive may fail if it is not combined with other elements necessary for the success of the whole. For example, subsidies for consultancy and business management training in SMEs could be indispensable to the success of the special loans for international expansion granted by the export promotion agency. The programs of the agency in charge of internationalization of SMEs, which promotes links with transnational firms or with international value chains, must work together with incentives awarded to attract foreign investment that has the potential to stimulate demand for local suppliers and services.

Figure 5.1 Functional Links between Support Programs: The Example of SMEs

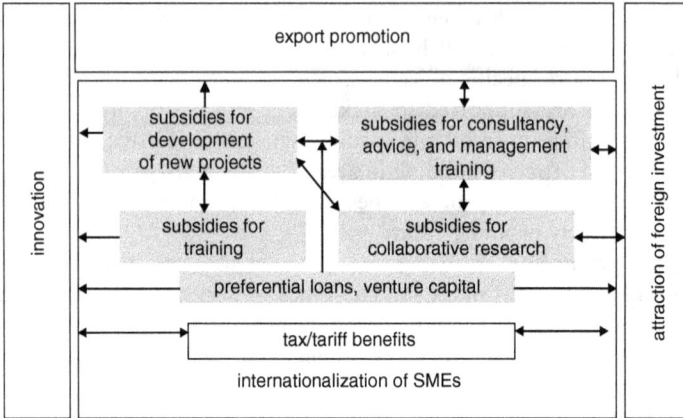

Source: Authors.

The implementation of Malaysia's strategy is a good example of this need for tie-in. One of the objectives of the Third Industrial Master Plan was to achieve stronger links between SMEs and the production chains headed by transnational corporations. The Small and Medium Industries Development Corporation (SMIDEC) is responsible for developing programs to achieve these objectives (SMIDEC 2006). The agency set up four programs to assist businesses in areas they need to improve, such as skills upgrading and industry networking, if they are to become exporters or suppliers for transnationals. In the sphere of innovation, the Strategic Business Intelligence Center, an agency in the Ministry of Science, Technology and Education, supports local industry through multidisciplinary technological programs (SIRIM 2005). Its R&D programs are geared toward new technologies and seek to bring companies to the technological frontier, transforming them into global players. The programs provide services mainly for SMEs, including strategic planning, business intelligence, technological development, and quality. This set of actions complements those developed by SMIDEC to provide SMEs with comprehensive assistance for integrating into the world economy. And, as mentioned in chapter 4, Malaysia also has a special interministerial committee to oversee the integration of programs for SMEs.

The innovation chain in Australia, shown in figure 5.2, is another way of illustrating the need for integrated coverage and coordination of incentives using as an example the chain of innovation in Australia.

Figure 5.2 Interventions in Support of Innovation: The Case of Australia

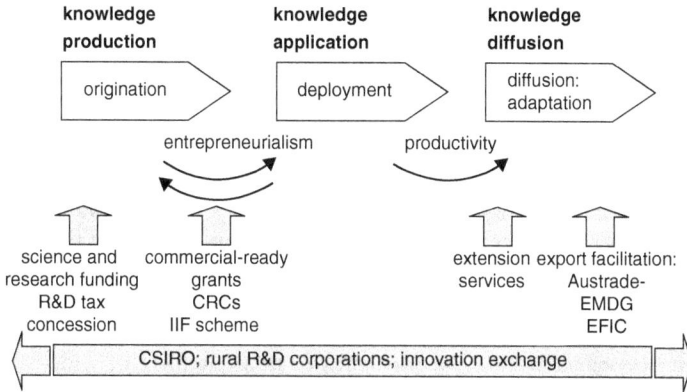

Source: Cutler 2008.
Note: The Commonwealth Scientific and Industrial Research Organisation (CSIRO), rural R&D corporations (RRDCs), and collaborative research centers (CRCs) support innovation. Austrade, the Agency for Export Market Development Grants (EMDC), and the Export Finance and Insurance Corporation (EFIC) support respectively the promotion of exports, loans, and export insurance.

The figure reinforces the idea that the case of innovation support must take into account interconnections between chains of key activities aimed at a central commercial objective, bearing in mind the primary constraints faced, on the one hand, and avoiding gaps in the coverage of support by agencies and programs, on the other. For instance, awarding tax breaks for R&D makes no sense if there is an unrelieved constraint on commercializing the results. Likewise, the return on the subsidy will underperform if there are impediments to the diffusion of the new knowledge or to identifying export opportunities.

Last, countries may implement programs and policies and grant incentives across the board or selectively. Some policies and programs are applied on a general basis and any company may opt for them; these include tax rebates for attracting FDI (when the investment is ruled eligible), subsidies for investment in integrating SMEs into the world economy, and tax credits for R&D. Other policies and programs are geared to clusters, selected sectors, or specific activities and investments, using a battery of instruments, such as targeted FDI attraction, sectoral investment funds, or innovation funding in activities considered key for the country's export future. The East Asian success cases have had the most selective strategies, but Ireland and the Czech Republic also became increasingly selective as their objectives for upgrading became more focused.

The Ninth Principle: The Effectiveness of Programs and Instruments Is Intimately Linked to the Way in Which the Process Is Managed

Figure 5.3 illustrates the relationship between the type of policy and the nature of private participation in the context of a public-private alliance. The left axis represents policy orientation. On one extreme of the left axis is the generic or horizontal policy (with its across-the-board incentives). In these types of policies, the private sector does not participate actively in the life cycle of the program because the program does not precisely identify beneficiaries. Interaction tends to take the form of wide-ranging consultations in the program design phase and a selective interaction during the operational phase.

At the other extreme is a selective policy, geared to developing a new sector(s) or specific activity(ies). In such cases, the nature of the public-private interaction is more active and collaborative in nature, including coinvestment (when the subsidies, credits, venture capital, or even the fiscal incentive granted are just a percentage of the cost) and specific performance agreements by the parties. This more intimate arrangement

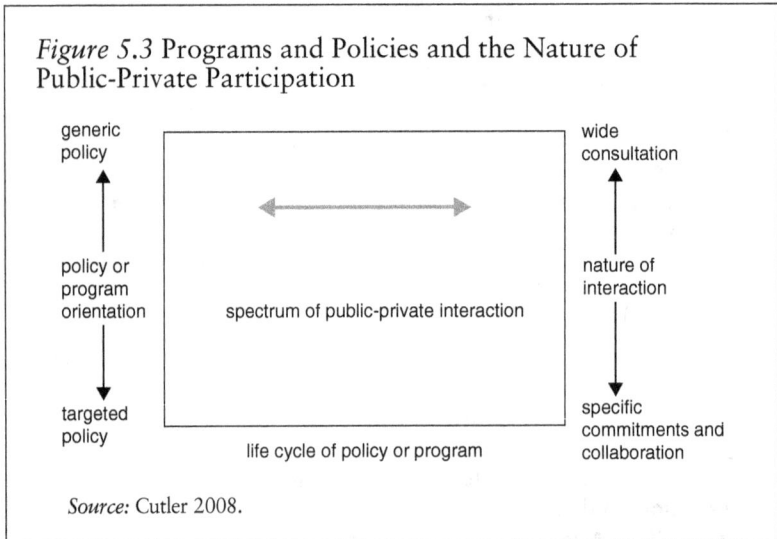

Figure 5.3 Programs and Policies and the Nature of Public-Private Participation

Source: Cutler 2008.

arises because the parties are targeted beneficiaries and hence there is greater specific interest in design and outcomes. Formal links are thus established between the private sector and the public agencies and their programs throughout the life cycle of the activity. The Rural Research and Development Corporations (RRDCs) in Australia are a good example of this collaboration—they are funded through joint investment by the government and the private sector, which contributes through a collective tax, and the sectors are represented on the board of directors of the RRDCs. Singapore also has special funding for specific technical support of SMEs financed by a collective tax on these firms.

Coinvestment and risk sharing may boost the efficiency of programs. Cofinancing tends to work best when the projects it supports are relatively close to market activities. Such is the case for the just mentioned RRDCs, the Collaborative Research Centers (CRCs) in Australia, and the technological programs for product and process innovation development in Finland and Sweden. In these cases, the investment funds contributed by the state complement the resources contributed by firms and industries for the purposes of a possible commercial application. Basic R&D, which tends to be a more strictly scientific activity, is further removed from profitable market activity and hence is generally supported by the state in the form of grants, competitive or otherwise.

Some of the other insights drawn from our success cases should be borne in mind:

Incentive programs are more likely to succeed if they correspond to industries or activities where the private sector already has some demonstrated interest and capacity in coordination (even if only incipient). This is an important consideration when transitioning into the world of industrial policy where legitimacy may depend on early demonstration of successes.

The availability of sufficient financing for the effective implementation of programs and policies is a critical issue. In many of our success cases, the government arranged funds, or agreements with financing covering several years, for new priority initiatives, which by their nature have a medium- to long-term gestation period. These arrangements help to increase the credibility of the initiative and to reduce uncertainty for the private sector. Support of innovation is characteristically an uncertain long-term endeavor. Science Foundation Ireland, Sitra in Finland, the National Research Foundation in Singapore (and the aforementioned subnational case of AOSTRA in Alberta, Canada) have credibly signaled a commitment to research and innovation through the availability of multiyear financing. Another point related to the funding issue is that financing should not be spread thinly across many programs; in the face of limited resources it may be better to prioritize and ensure that a critical mass of resources are available where they most count. Underfunding an initiative erodes the credibility and effectiveness of a program and industrial policy more generally.

A proactive attitude on the part of executing agencies is important. The most effective executing agencies are not "passive windows" waiting to be approached by users. In many of our countries the agencies actively seek to identify clients with potential and provide them with information and technical assistance for their business plans and investment. For example, one of the missions of Enterprise Ireland is to proactively search out businesses with potential and offer to conduct a rigorous analysis of the company with an eye to developing a business plan that encourages start-ups, upgrading of the existing firm's output or activities, increased productivity, and innovation and R&D. Assistance also helps companies to identify government support programs that may be relevant to them. Enterprise Ireland has proactively built its client base to more then 3,500 firms (Sinnamon 2009). Moreover, the agency's services are often subsidized or free.

Encourage accountability in awarding incentives to transnational corporations. In the Czech Republic, Ireland, and Malaysia, formal agreements are concluded to establish explicit conditions and commitments undertaken by the company and the promotion agency. The agreement establishes the terms under which the subsidies, tax incentives, or support investments are granted and specifies the obligations of the corporation in areas such as investment and job creation. These are long-term agreements (for example, in Ireland, they are for 10 years). In most cases (except Malaysia), the agreement includes a clause that provides for partial refund of the incentives should the investor fail to fully comply.[1] In Ireland, the incentive programs are divided into various stages, so that fulfilment of the targets can be monitored as a precondition for the next disbursement. The same holds true for incentives granted to SMEs to work with newly hosted FDI to develop local supply chains, a process that makes the country a more attractive host for the foreign firm.

In Ireland, a cost-benefit model is used to select and determine the exact incentives to be awarded to a transnational company. The calculation is made over a seven-year period and all public expenditure on FDI attraction is taken into account, including the cost of standardized tax exemptions and administration, plus an estimate of the benefit in terms of increased economic activity resulting from FDI. The benefits are discounted by 50 percent to take into account the possibility that the investment might have occurred in any event. Recently, special weighting has been applied to FDI in high-technology enterprises.

Meanwhile, in the year 2000, the Czech Republic established Investment Act 72/2000, which did away with the discretionary power in this area by spelling out the types of benefits available for FDI (and local investment). This act has served as the blueprint for awarding incentives, except in the case of two large-scale projects. The act had the disadvantage of limiting negotiation space for the attraction of FDI, but it did enhance transparency and reduce transaction costs (Benác̆ek, 2010). And of course when the potential investment was attractive enough, as in two large-scale automobile manufacturing projects, discretionary policy worked on the margins of the act. Meanwhile, Malaysia, a country recognized for the effectiveness of its FDI-attraction program, has a relatively high degree of discretionary power in offering incentives and limited transparency.

It is normal for support programs that entail a certain level of risk to sometimes fail. Indeed, in some areas a high success rate may be the sign of a bad program. This is especially the case in the area of innovation. In Finland, where public programs are particularly well managed, roughly one-fifth of supported innovation projects in 2002 failed outright or gave less than satisfactory results. It took some time for the Finnish innovation agencies to convince the Ministry of Finance that failure is inherent in programs encouraging learning and experimentation (Kotilainen 2008).

Too much red tape in a program can deter a company from participating. A balance must be found between rigorous administrative procedures, on the one hand, and promptly responding to a company's application and disbursement of funds, on the other. Time can be of the essence for a successful investment; moreover, too much red tape will debase the value of the incentive vis-à-vis the opportunity that the incentive is designed to support.

The countries that use strong incentives as part of their structurally oriented strategies consider them not so much as subsidies but rather as an investment in the country's growth, which will bring in returns for the treasury. This point is illustrated in figure 5.4 for the case of Finland, where subsidies for enterprise performance have been calculated to have generated a positive return to the fiscal accounts. Naturally, the returns depend on sound program design and management.

In program conceptualization and design, an explicit "checklist" of points to be covered may be useful in raising the likelihood of success and reducing risks by anticipating needs such as avoidance of excessive bureaucratic noise, identifying and terminating "losers," and ameliorating problems of potential capture and strategic behavior of beneficiaries, among other things. Box 5.1 illustrates a checklist.

Figure 5.4 The Cycle of Return on Incentives in Finland

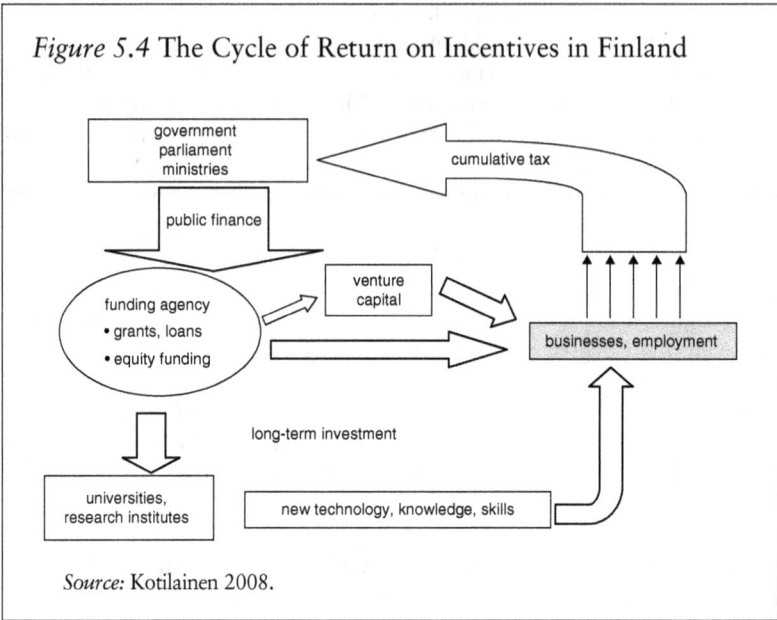

Source: Kotilainen 2008.

Box 5.1 Example of a Checklist for Program Conceptualization and Design

Clarity on the nature of the problem to be addressed

Have the objectives been clearly and unambiguously defined, with a view to overcoming any specific constraints?

Additionality

Is it clear that the program will encourage the desired behavior and be well received by the designated users, and does the scale of the financing match the expected actions and results?

Competition

Does access to the program need to be competitive? The answer to this question depends on a capacity to define objectives in terms of social benefits, the ability to assess the merits of alternative proposals, estimate administrative costs, and manage users' potential strategic behavior to obtain preferential treatment.

Consistency

What are the possible interactions with other programs, and how does the program fit into the overall set of support activities for the identified objective?

Duration

How long will the program need to continue to achieve the objective and produce sustainable results? Is there a natural cycle for the development of the objective, or should the program be introduced in segments? Is there a plan for ending the program?

Risk calculation

Is it clear what the risk of program failure is in relation to the potential benefits? If both the risk and the benefits are considered to be high, it may be better to begin with an experimental program and, if it proves satisfactory, expand the program to its full scale on a pilot basis before launching it as an official initiative.

Risk management

Have those involved remained alert to possible conflicts with the objectives of other programs, both within and outside the set of programs for the export activity being supported? Given the danger of capture by lobby groups, is there an exit plan for shutting down the program according to success or failure vis-à-vis the objective. One mechanism that can be considered for that purpose is a specific program duration (a sunset clause) that automatically triggers an assessment of whether it should be continued or not. Possible abuse of the program on the part of users must be anticipated by doing studies of the real behavior of agents in the market concerned.

Administration

Does the design of the administrative framework match the complexity of the program and its risks, so as to avoid excessive bureaucratic interference that would discourage its potential users? Examples of interference would include unnecessarily slow processing of requests and disbursement of funds. Insofar as accounts or reports are required from those who benefit from the program, efforts should be made to apply procedures that are familiar to, and not excessively burdensome for, those in the industry.

Source: Drawn from Cutler (2008).

The Tenth Principle: The Effectiveness of Strategies Is Dependent on an Objective Assessment of Implementation and Their Impact on the Objectives Set Out

In that regard, the former prime minister of Singapore, Lee Kuan Yew, has commented on that country's attitude about design of public support programs: "Does it work? Let's try it and if it does work, fine, let's continue it. If it doesn't work, toss it out, try another one."[2]

This may be a good pragmatic philosophy for a proactive and solvent government with medium- and long-term ambitions and strategies for structural change. Nonetheless, to be effective, governments must have the capacity to evaluate the impact of their support programs.

Many of our successful countries have a structured system for assessing and monitoring strategies from the programmatic viewpoint of the outputs of ministries and agencies. Ireland, for example, has a committee that monitors implementation of the national development plan. The committee itself meets every six months. In addition, each government department is required to prepare its own three-year strategy for implementing the national plan, as well as a yearly output plan with quantifiable performance indicators. In Finland, as mentioned, yearly operational plans are prepared and monitored by executing agencies.

However, outputs are not necessarily synonymous with impact and the attainment of the objective. Few countries systematically conduct impact assessments. Indeed, most governments have only recently begun to pay special attention to the systematic assessment of the impacts of strategies, projects, and programs.[3] Rigorous assessment based on an appropriate methodology and empirical evidence is quite difficult. Consequently, only a few of the challenges can be outlined here.

As Alan Hughes (2007) observes, it is vital to know what would have happened if public support had not been granted to an activity. One possible methodology for program assessment is to create control groups, comparing the performance of firms having similar characteristics with that of firms that benefited from the incentive. There is a problem, however: the firms that take advantage of programs may be the most astute, and without the incentives they would have done well anyway. To overcome this potential bias, the firms that enter the program can be modeled using an econometric exercise with a counterfactual. An alternative is to use a subjective counterfactual, where participating firms are asked what would have happened if they had not made use of the program. The advantage of this approach is that participating firms have the greatest amount of information about themselves. A strategy suggested by Hughes (2007) to overcome the methodological pros and cons is to combine methodologies. For example, in the case of an innovation program for SMEs in the

United Kingdom, a combination of paired control groups was used, with a selection model, along with a subjective counterfactual and case studies (a "mixed method").

Cutler (2008) points to three additional challenges. First, in addition to stating goals in a quantifiable way that can be evaluated,[4] a quantity of information and data must be collected on the firm's performance before and after the support program. To that end, the program must—without discouraging participation—require firms to provide a minimum of relevant data on performance when they enter the program and during a monitoring process, which also has to be organized. Second, some programs have quite long-term impacts, such as the field of innovation; as a result, the monitoring and data collection system may have to function for as long as 10 or 20 years. Third, better understanding is needed of the complex transmission mechanisms between an activity and its impact on aspects such as productivity, enterprise growth, and trade. Other considerations that can be added to those noted by Hughes and Cutler are the importance of using independent assessments, the need to strike a balance between the quality and benefits of an evaluation methodology, and the cost in financial terms as well as the time spent by officials.

Two countries with a culture of systematic and relatively rigorous evaluation of impacts, particularly in the difficult area of innovation, are Finland and Australia. Finland has been cited by the Organisation for Economic Co-operation and Development for the particular attention it pays to evaluations. For example, its ministries organize (generally independent) expert groups, which may include non-Finnish nationals, to evaluate the programs of certain sectors or clusters. The Academy of Finland evaluates both research programs and individual projects, but it now places more emphasis on the former. Programs are evaluated taking into account the initial conditions and goals and the level of financing, with an analysis of scientific results, impacts, and the efficiency of program administration. Another aspect that is monitored is the implementation of recommendations arising out of the evaluation. The academy's sister agency, the Finnish Funding Agency for Technology and Innovation (TEKES), uses goal-led indicators. There are also evaluations of the support bodies themselves. Program evaluations have been used as inputs for the analyses conducted by the former Science and Technology Policy Council (STPC) for the three-year strategic national guidelines. Annex 5.2 summarizes the evaluation of an R&D and innovation program in the field of electronics and telecommunications.

Another country active in evaluation, this time in the area of enterprise and export promotion, is New Zealand, which conducts both internal and external evaluations. For example, the various programs of New Zealand Trade and Enterprise are evaluated externally every three to five years; the agency also has its own assessment unit. The methodology used is a mixed method; for example, the evaluation of one program involved a review of documents and files; interviews with users and officials; and three surveys, two administered to user groups and one to a group of non-users. The respondents totaled 3,000.

In Ireland, incentive programs are justified to the public using cost-benefit analysis ("value for money"). However, the ex post assessment of program impacts does not yet appear to be particularly systematic. When requested by its ministry, Ireland's national economic development authority, Forfás, which is the coordinating agency for supporting integration with the world economy and export development, can evaluate a program three to five years after its inception. In its analyses, it uses a mixed method combining independent external consultancies with beneficiary interviews. The other selected countries also conduct, on a relatively ad hoc basis, evaluations with varying levels of rigor.

The Eleventh Principle: Structured Public-Private Alliances Representing a Diversity of Interests, with Well-established Rules, Transparency, and Evaluation, and Supported by a Professional Public Bureaucracy, Can Minimize the Risk of Private Sector Capture of the Government

It has been argued that medium- and long-term strategies *cum* industrial strategies can be more effective when developed in the context of an alliance between the public and private sectors. It is, however, essential that the government's collaboration with the private sector represent a public good. Special interest capture of the government is always a serious risk of industrial policy (but also of most any public policy) and the utmost attention, particularly to the design of modalities, is required to guard against the problem.

Constructing formal frameworks for primary interaction between the public and private sectors in the development of strategies and programs is one safeguard against private sector capture. An alliance dominated by informal channels of communication, without parallel control mechanisms, can easily lead to capture of the government by lobby groups. In addition, representation in the formally structured alliance by valid stakeholders with different roles in the economy can contribute to self-regulation. This diversity is harder to achieve the more narrow the scope of an alliance's policy purview.

Promoting public transparency is another way to prevent capture, but there are practical limitations. For example, publishing the cost of an agreed incentive to attract an FDI project can be effective, but it would not be advisable to reveal in real time the precise content of a negotiation on the subject, or to reveal it ex post, if there will subsequently be a need to negotiate with other businesses. The publication of precise information on, for example, the contributions to the investment project by the foreign company and the government may also encounter practical constraints associated with proprietary information not traditionally considered to be in the public domain. A failure to respect confidentiality in related areas could discourage other firms. This is why TEKES, the Finnish agency for business innovation, often performs its own in-house evaluations. In addition, to make public a very positive impact assessment on a horizontal subsidy program to which access is generally available might not be appropriate if it resulted in demand exceeding the available resources, leading to rationing.[5] The advisable degree of transparency in decisions by high-level committees depends on incentives and the institutional framework (Levy 2007). Nonetheless, despite exceptional reservations that may arise depending on the circumstances, transparency is usually a very important tool for avoiding the capture of government by special interests.

Clearly setting out the objectives of an incentive program, together with appropriate ex post evaluation based on evidence, can minimize the capture of a government by industry. This procedure guards against the continuation of programs that favor companies but that are not yielding satisfactory results. As mentioned, the presence of a sunset clause in the incentive program can avoid such problems

A highly professional and reasonably well-paid public bureaucracy, coupled with explicit rules of conduct for public servants and participants in the public-private alliance are also important to avoid a conflict of interest. Auditing of programs should be standard.

Notwithstanding the gradual emergence of serious weaknesses in the governance of the national alliance led by the National Economic and Social Council, addressed in chapter 3, some of the procedures at the level of executing agencies are illustrative of certain measures that can be adopted to ward off potential risk of capture. The private partners (with operational responsibilities) sitting on the board of directors of the executing agencies that manage the incentives for private businesses are appointed in an individual capacity by a government minister. They must be highly respected as experts in their fields and not act as representatives of their companies or associations. Appointments rotate over time. The private directors, like all the government officials, sign a code of conduct and the members submit annual declarations of their financial and commercial interests.[6] The private directors receive no documents and take part in no discussions that are directly linked to their own commercial or financial interests. The cost of fees, travel expenses, and per diem payments for the directors appear in the budget published by the agency.[7] As would normally be expected, auditing is carried out. The decisions of the board are almost always reached by consensus. Each year, the minister responsible for the agency is required to confirm that all procedures have taken place correctly. Public agencies in Ireland exhibit a high degree of transparency, while employees are channeled through a professional civil service that is reasonably well paid and subject to codes of conduct.

Although its system is less transparent, Singapore discourages capture by offering good wage levels for a professionally oriented civil service, a strong culture of accountability for decision making among public officials, and the existence of an independent anticorruption agency with extensive powers.

Annex 5A Efficiency of Tax Credits for Research and Development

Tax credits (or concessions) for R&D have been successfully used in countries such as Canada, the United Kingdom, and the United States, but they have not had the same success in less advanced countries. Studies have been carried out to compare the efficiency of tax credits in less advanced countries with that of direct subsidies in specific programs designed to boost corporate supply and demand for R&D (Maloney and Perry 2005).

Tax credits are said to be more useful than direct subsidies in avoiding conduct that might lead to government failures in the selection of projects. However, direct subsidies might be an advantage in some countries where relatively scarce resources make it necessary to prioritize certain activities or sectors. It is also argued, however, that tax credits occasionally support investments in R&D that would have been made in any event. Although direct subsidies theoretically support marginal projects that might not have been undertaken in their absence, the difficulty of identifying those types of marginal projects may in practice make this particular distinction about the advantages of direct subsidies less relevant. From another angle, tax credits do not take account of the difference between the social rate of return and the private rate of return, which may not be the same in all projects. So here subsidies might be advantageous because theoretically they could be granted only for projects with a high social rate of return, although in practice identifying such projects also can be difficult. Subsidies do have a clear advantage for sectors and activities that show promise but that have yet to generate profits, such as start-ups or some SME sectors or clusters.

Perhaps the main problems with tax credits are the limited capacity of tax systems to absorb and administer them and their possible lack of transparency, except where there is a detailed record of the amounts involved. Transparency is especially relevant for most developing countries, which means that using subsidies instead of tax credits may facilitate better governance of the system (Maloney and Perry 2005).

The truth is that one option is not necessarily better than the other. In short, instead of assessing the impact of an incentive in the abstract, it is preferable to analyze the system and governance of the program arrangement within which the incentive operates. For example in 1989, Australia extended a tax credit to syndicated loans for projects carried out by corporate groups. The aim was to encourage companies to assume much larger costs and risks than would be possible to take on individually (Australian Taxation Office 2004). Concerns about abuses in the syndication led to elimination of the scheme in 1996, even though much of the increase in firms' R&D expenditure was attributed to the syndicated projects. The administrative agency lacked transparency and accountability. In addition, the authorities' lack of knowledge and experience with institutions in corporate financial structures made it difficult to make decisions, limiting more and more the award of incentives.

One of the problems of incentives, irrespective of the instrument used, may be that the approach adopted is too narrow. This was the case in Australia, where a tax credit for innovation took into account only direct R&D costs, while neglecting the costs of commercializing innovation, which tend to be extremely high, especially for small and medium-size enterprises. Firms that benefited from the incentive ignored the commercialization stage, so part of the R&D did not necessarily generate value. It was therefore essential to supplement the tax credit with direct subsidy programs for commercialization.

Annex 5B Finland: Evaluation of the Electronics and Telecommunications Program

The Finnish Agency for Technology and Innovation (TEKES) funds technology programs in strategic areas identified by the agency and the business community. One of the sectors that has benefited is the electronics and telecommunications sector, with three programs funded between 1997 and 2001: Electronics for the Information Society (ETX), Telecommunications—Creating a Global Village, and the Telectronics Research Programme, the latter funded by the Academy of Finland. These programs cost a total of €300 million.

All three were subject to a mid-term evaluation. In many respects, the evaluators approved the progress of the projects. However, they questioned whether the programs were solving problems of particular technical and commercial importance for Finland. When the programs were concluded, a new evaluation was conducted by a consultant from outside the institution, two government agencies, and peer-expert panels.

This evaluation focused on four issues. The first related to the selection of the strategy and the research portfolio of the three programs and their relationship to the development needs of the economy of Finland. The second referred to the effects of the programs and projects on the ICT sector in the country (including the impact on the entire network as well as on individual participants). Third, the evaluation turned to the value added of the programs and the improvements in their administration. Last, the evaluation analyzed the way in which the two most industry-oriented programs had been able to interact with the program financed by the academy, which had been of a more scientific nature.

Seven techniques were used to provide answers to these questions:

- Analysis of networks created by the project: the TEKES database was used in mapping relations among firms and between firms and public institutions.
- Interviews with those responsible for various subject areas within projects.
- Review by panels of experts that looked at the administration of the programs and the functioning of a small group of key projects.
- Strategic interviewing of firms to test program strategies and examine any discrepancies in the expectations of senior executives of firms and corporations vis-à-vis the program's objectives.
- Interviews with project leaders about the functioning of the project and the relationship with companies and public bodies.
- Analysis of self-assessment questionnaires.
- Analysis of foreign programs, identifying and reviewing the strategies of four programs in other countries, to use as benchmark comparisons for the Finnish programs under way.

The application of the methods are outlined in table 5B.1.

Table 5B.1 Assessment Techniques

	Verification of objectives	Verification of networks	Interviews with thematic leaders	Peer Review	Strategic interviews with firms	Interviews at project level	Comparison with foreign programs
Strategy and portfolio				√	√	√	√
Impacts on ICT sector	√	√	√		√	√	
Impacts on subject areas			√	√	√	√	√
Interaction among programs	√			√		√	

This set of methods provided a fairly complete view of the program's impact in the electronics and telecommunications sector in Finland. Not only did responses suggest a significantly positive impact in industry, but a series of recommendations were delivered in relation to the actual administration of programs, interactions among projects, the need to internationalize innovation, and the need to increase cooperation between the agency promoting innovation in businesses, TEKES, and the Academy of Finland.

Annex 5B Source: Data from the Finnish Funding Agency for Technology and Information.

Notes

1. The state is also bound to comply with its agreed obligations to the multinational corporation.
2. Seth Mydans and Wayne Arnold, "Creator of Modern Singapore Is Ever Alert to Perils," *New York Times*, September 2, 2007, p. 8.
3. Until recently, multilateral development agencies did not carry out systematic and rigorous evaluations of the impact of their programs.
4. An added example is that Australia's rural R&D corporations look for a 7:1 benefit-cost return (in impact terms) for their grant program.
5. Effectiveness depends on the actual rationing system adopted (Gavazza and Lizzeri 2007).
6. See Forfás, "Code of Conduct," www.forfas.ie/about/howwedobusiness/ Forfas_Code_of_Business_Conduct_Committee_0501_webopt.pdf.
7. Not all the selected countries pay honorariums to private directors.

References

Australian Taxation Office. 2004. "Research and Development (R&D) Syndication Arrangements." http://www.ato.au/super/content.asp?doc=/content/mr2004 065.htm&pc=001/001/001/001&mnu=9861&mfp=001/007&st=&cy=1.

Benáček, Vladimír. 2010. "Is the Czech Economy a Success Story? The Case of CzechInvest: The Strategic Promotion Agency in Czech Industrial Restructuring." Serie Comercio Internacional 101, Economic Commission for Latin America and the Caribbean, International Trade and Integration Division, Santiago, Chile (March).

Cutler, Terry. 2008. "Public and Private Sector Alliances for Innovation and Export Development: The Australian Experience." Economic Commission for Latin America and the Caribbean, International Trade and Integration Division, Santiago, Chile.

Gavazza, Alessandro, and Alessandro Lizzeri. 2007. "The Transparency of Political Institutions." *American Economic Review* vol. 97, no. 2 (May).

Hughes, Alan. 2007. "Hunting the Elusive Snark of Innovation, Some Reflections on the UK Experience with Small Business Support Policy." *Proceedings of the Innovation Leadership Group Forum on Innovation and SMEs* (September).

Kotilainen, Heikki. 2008. "Establishing a National Innovation System: The Finnish Case." Economic Commission for Latin America and the Caribbean, International Trade and Integration Division, Santiago, Chile.

Levy, Gilat. 2007. "Decision Making in Committees: Transparency, Reputation and Voting Rules." *American Economic Review* 97, no. 1 (March).

Maloney, William F., and Guillermo Perry. 2005. "Towards an Efficient Innovation Policy in Latin America." *CEPAL Review* 87 (LC/G.2287-P/E), Economic Commission for Latin America and the Caribbean, Santiago, Chile (December).

Sinnamon, Julie. 2009. "Inter-American Development Bank: Short-Term Challenges, Long-Term Growth." Presentation to the Inter-American Development Bank, Washington DC, September 18.

SIRIM (Center of Strategic Enterprise Intelligence of Malaysia). 2005. *The Bedrock of Innovation. Annual Report.* Kuala Lumpur.

SMIDEC. 2006. "Policies, Incentives, Programmes and Financial Assistance for SMEs." http://www.smidec.gov.my.

Part II

Are the Operational Principles Relevant for Latin America?

6

Medium- and Long-Term Strategies Based on Public-Private Alliances

Now that we have examined principles, drawn from our success cases, on how governments should organize themselves effectively for deployment of industrial policies, in the second part of the book we explore, against this backdrop, how well Latin American governments are complying with the principles in their own efforts to support productive transformation. This chapter focuses on medium- and long term development strategies in the region and the role played by public-private alliances. But first we quickly review how Latin America got where it is today.

From a Strategic and Structural Economics Tradition to the Washington Consensus

Between the 1950s and the start of the 1980s, Latin America underwent what Ocampo (2006) terms "the age of state-led industrialization." Industrialization was a gradual process in the region, beginning in the second half of the 19th century through the independent strengths of economies exporting natural resources in response to external demand.[1] As noted in an earlier chapter, disruptive phenomena in the 20th century, such as the collapse of international markets during the Great Depression and shortages during the Second World War, had a profound impact on the industrialization process and thrust the state into a central role in the economy. This period of industrialization in Latin America was more a forced reaction to external events than a strategy as such. The 1930s and 1940s were also a period of relative success on the growth front, which gave a certain legitimacy to state action. By the 1950s one can see a clear shift from a reactive state to one that was proactive in its intervention, not only in the macroeconomy but also in microeconomic matters. Emphasis was placed on diversification of the productive structure by promoting import substitution and technological development, building basic infrastructure, fostering social development, and consolidating the state itself.

In macroeconomic matters, governments pursued active fiscal and monetary policies geared to revitalizing consumption and investment, while exchange rate policy gave priority to multiple rates to encourage the import of machinery and equipment for manufacturing, while providing some compensation for the export sector. Currencies were often allowed to appreciate to contain inflation. All of these policies were accompanied by a broadly protectionist trade policy pursued through tariffs, quotas, and nontariff barriers.[2]

In microeconomic matters, the strategy concentrated on fostering industry. The state adopted a proactive promotional stance in government procurement, subsidized credits granted by development banks, provided tax subsidies, and expanded the role of public enterprises. Over time these activities, which once sought to promote nascent industry, were beset by internal contradictions and external vulnerabilities arising from management deficiencies, political turbulence, and external sector disruptions (Thorp 1998; Ocampo 2006). Economic performance after 1950 was comparatively mediocre, as evident in the growth of output and productivity discussed in chapter 1.

The Role of Planning in the Context of State Leadership

Industrial policy after the war was broadly in the character of Evan's (1995) "demiurge," outlined in chapter 2. Formal planning played an important role in the implementation of the industrialization strategy. In the 1950s and 1960s interest in planning was largely driven by external factors, such as the region's knowledge of practices from Europe's postwar reconstruction, the construction of the Soviet bloc, advances in mathematical modeling during that period, and the predominant schools of thought on economic development.[3] In 1961 planning became widespread, encouraged by the resolutions of the Charter of Punta del Este and its main mechanism, the Alliance for Progress, which was promoted by the United States and supported by the multilateral development institutions. The planning was in a context of mixed capitalist economies—excepting revolutionary Cuba, which was excluded from the alliance and used Soviet style central planning.

Mostly indicative in nature, planning was regarded as a basic instrument for implementing national programs of economic and social development. The setting broadly favored such exercises. Because the state had a strong influence on economic activity through public enterprises, state monopolies, and widespread market regulation, the setting, in principle, allowed planning to fulfill the task of coordination. With support and encouragement from the international community, the institutions entrusted with carrying out that task were emerging, growing, and consolidating; these institutions included government ministries, offices, and secretariats as well as a number of national, regional, and sectoral planning schemes supporting investment programs, preinvestment processes, international cooperation, and the like (Lira 2006). In almost every country, planning was a formal process of constitutional rank and had three basic features: a focus on industrialization and development; a demiurge tradition of skepticism about the private sector's capacity and entrepreneurial ambition to lead investment and development; and a high degree of direct state intervention in the economy to leverage the plan (Rufián 1993).

During the 1970s most countries of the region were engaged in industrial planning (table 6.1). In line with the prevailing thinking, national development plans were geared toward increasing the absorption of new technologies and lessening perceived threats to the balance of payments arising from abrupt shifts in world demand, commodity prices, and capital flows. Although nascent industry was protected in this period, export promotion now was a widespread goal—usually more for balance of payments reasons than for any direct role exports could have in productive transformation or in strengthening a country's international integration.

Table 6.1 Selected National Development Plans in Latin America

Country	Development plan
Argentina	National Development Plan 1970–74 National Development and Security Plan 1971–75 Triennial Plan for National Reconstruction and Liberation 1974–77
Bolivia	National Economic and Social Development Plan 1976–80
Brazil	Targets for and bases of government activity 1970–72 First National Development Plan 1972–74 Second National Development Plan 1975–1979
Colombia	The Four Strategies 1970–74 To Close the Gap 1975–78 National Integration Plan 1979–82
Costa Rica	National Development Plan 1974–78 National Development Plan 1979–82
Cuba	First Five-Year Plan 1976–80
Chile	National Economic Plan 1971–76 National Indicative Plan 1979–81 Indicative National Plan 1979–84

(*continued*)

Table 6.1 Selected National Development Plans in Latin America (*continued*)

Country	Development plan
Ecuador	Comprehensive Plan for Transformation and Development 1973–77
El Salvador	National Economic and Social Development Plan 1973–77 Well-Being for All 1978–82
Guatemala	National Development Plan 1971–75 National Development Plan 1975–79 National Development Plan 1979–82
Honduras	National Development Plan 1979–82
Jamaica	Five-Year Development Plan 1978–82
Mexico	National Economic and Social Development Plan 1966–70
Nicaragua	National Plan for Reconstruction and Development 1975–79
Panama	National Development Plan 1976–80
Paraguay	National Economic and Social Development Plan 1971–75 National Economic and Social Development Plan 1977–81
Peru	National Development Plan 1971–75 National Development Plan 1975–78 National Development Plan 1979–80
Dominican Republic	First National Development Plan: Macroeconomic and Public Sector Projections 1970–74
Uruguay	National Development Plan 1973–77
Venezuela, R.B. de	Five-Year Plans 1960–88

Source: CEPAL–ILPES 1982.

The Positive Impacts of Planning on Public Policy Development.   Although the phenomenon has been submerged in the region's memory, planning had significant positive impacts on Latin America's institutional development. First, to a greater or lesser extent it fostered institutional attempts to develop a common vision of the future mediated by various social actors and a national strategy, thereby (in principle) facilitating the coordination and organization of medium- and long-term actions. Developing that link required creation of an organization to lead the process as well as the establishment of a government system of sectoral and subsectoral development promotion, headed by officials trained in several disciplines. In some countries these multidisciplinary and multisectoral teams were the pillars of transformation during the import substitution period. The very process of planning called for skills and knowledge of techniques and methodologies in the area of public administration, capacities that spread and endured beyond the planning institutions.

Brazil is probably the paradigmatic case of planning in the region. The state, under President Getulio Vargas (1930–45; 1951–54), assumed leadership of the country's economic development with the onset of the Depression in 1929, and gradually centralized the management of financial resources and the coordination of investment projects, taking on direct productive roles through the creation of large public companies. It was during this period that Brazil consolidated its strong culture of the development state, probably still the strongest in Latin America and the most successful in promoting industrialization (Castro 1994).

Apart from ad hoc initiatives, the development programs that most emphasized industrialization were the Targets Plan of the Kubitschek administration (1956–60) and the Second National Development 1975–79 (PND II), implemented by the Economic Development Council during the military dictatorship (Suzigan and Furtado 2006). The development state was motivated largely by a shared view of how to attain a significant level of self-sufficiency and economic independence, as well as by a desire for a greater role for local capital (Martinez-Díaz and Brainard 2009; Evans 1995). Throughout the postwar period, Brazil's various development plans made an uneven but cumulative contribution to the development of economic and institutional structures, some of which enjoy a very favorable legacy in Brazil to this day.[4]

Given its importance in Brazil's industrial development, PND II merits more comment. Conceived as a flexible and dynamic instrument to streamline decisions, it was designed in a period of growing uncertainty in Brazil about the direction of the world economy and sought to adapt to the high world energy prices of that time and to the new opportunities for industrial development (CEPAL-ILPES 1978).

It concentrated on the chemicals and metals industries, as well as on capital goods. In addition to industrial policies, the plan emphasized energy independence and rural development, with a focus on the export of foodstuffs, raw materials, and processed agricultural goods. To attenuate the problems associated with inequality, social initiatives promised an increase in "social wages" and an improvement in human capital.

Thus PND II was seen from the outset as a development policy document, one that avoided setting rigid targets at the general, sectoral, or regional levels. It also included perspectives based on socioeconomic indicators that were reviewed and integrated into continuous planning. The program also moved forward with detailed sectoral and regional plans, such as the Second Basic Plan of Scientific and Regional Development, and the National Postgraduate Plan. At the federal level it included financial targets in the form of multiyear budgets and spending programs, including investments by state enterprises, and entailed evaluation systems related to the budget, the programs, and the priority projects.

PND II was thus one of the hallmarks of planning in Latin America in this period. It had several features that helped ensure its relative success: first, it was an ambitious industrialization plan to which the government was strongly committed, as evident in the resources made available through-out its life. Second, it displayed more faith in the national private sector, with the government seeking the sector's support for investment in strategic areas. Finally, it was ahead of its time in its flexibility on targets and in attempts at evaluation systems.

The Limits of Planning and State Leadership.   Most of the plans devised in Latin America during this period faced serious problems for a number of reasons: political or macroeconomic instability (or both); management difficulties, including bureaucratic fragmentation and the loss of political power on the part of the institution in charge of planning; mistrust among the public and private sectors, with an attendant low level of private in-volvement and consensus; capture by special interests; and unallocated re-sources for implementation (CEPAL-ILPES 1978, 1982; García D'Acuña 1982). Additionally, more liberal economic thinking that was diametri-cally opposed to planning began to expand its influence in the region.

The strategies and plans were largely implemented from the top down. But in unstable or nonexistent democratic cultures, society had little input into the planning and its implementation and little understanding of the plans, which were often captured by special interests. The professional-ization of the state bureaucracy, including the planning apparatus, faced serious limitations. As centers of excellence were created, which happened especially in Brazil, they were too often distanced from the operations of the general public bureaucracy (Evans 1995). This approach not only hampered coordination but also impeded the planning-related authori-ties from influencing the centers of government, leading to their gradual isolation (Lira 2006). Additionally, and not unrelated to the previous point, political considerations often took primacy over the plan's technical demands. There was also a lack of transparency. Planning was conceived as a means of advancing a particular government's political and economic program, so plans were often set aside by that government's successor. Because the plans did not guide the later activities of successor govern-ments, a permanent gap opened between what was planned and what was implemented. Usually major new goals were defined and new targets proposed each time the government changed.

At the same time, most plans lacked even indicative multiyear budgets underpinned by a firm commitment to implement them. One reason for this was the absence of a shared, long-term vision within which to devise the targets and allocate the resources.

Finally, with the onset of the debt crisis in the early 1980s, the emergence of Thatcherite/Reaganite thinking on the benevolence of the free market, and a decade of structural adjustment accompanied by the withdrawal of the state under the watchful attention of the Washington-based multilateral institutions, the state-led import-substitution model withered away. Willing-ness and capacity to plan in Latin America were thus weakened further, as was the disposition to cultivate longer-term thinking and outlooks. In the face of the debt crisis, fiscal and balance of payments adjustments became the predominant objectives, while the core focus of economic policy was on managing the immediate situation. The finance minister or the president of the central bank took the lead coordinating role without any counterbalance from ministries overseeing the real economy—ministries that had become marginalized by the short time horizons of the market fundamentalism of the period. In other words, budget allocations were determined mostly by the goals of fiscal policy and external adjustment rather than by any strategic medium- or long-term objective for accelerating productive transformation. In this new mental setting, an enabling environment for market forces was all that was necessary.

Strategies after the Washington Consensus

As we observed in chapter 1, the reforms of the Washington Consensus helped bring about economic stabilization and a degree of modernization in Latin America. It is also true, however, that those reforms weakened the state's role in productive policies. The state remained active in macroeconomic management, but at the microeconomic level the notion prevailed that the liberalization of market forces would spontaneously bring about optimal resource allocation to promote growth and transformation. This policy orientation diminished the value of a vision of the future, long-term strategies, and proactive plans geared toward upgrading industry and services. The pendulum had swung and now the government authorities of Latin America mistrusted any systematic leadership by the state in the productive arena. Referring again to Evan's (1995) characterizations of the roles of government in development, Latin American governments abruptly abandoned their demiurge role in the economy to take up a custodial role.

Nonetheless, as time passed and concerns mounted over the region's lagging performance in competitiveness, innovation, export development, and growth, governments again began to devise more active policies and programs to remove certain obstacles to productive transformation. In some cases these policies were confined to specific areas, such as innovation, export promotion, and attracting foreign direct investment (FDI), while other countries took a more comprehensive approach that gave rise to new strategies and plans for major transformation and development (Muñoz 2000, 2001, Peres 1997, Peres and Primi 2009, and Melo 2001). Such plans were particularly apparent in the late 1990s and even more strongly evident in 2000–05. Table 6.2 shows nine Latin American countries where the operational principles discussed in the previous chapters have been applied to varying degrees.[5] Eight of the nine countries have explicit development strategies, almost all of which have been given shape through a development plan. The exception is Argentina, which has policies in various economic areas but no overall plan or coherent vision coordinating initiatives. The table also shows some factors related to the principles that are discussed along with others throughout this chapter.

Table 6.2 Characteristics of Contemporary Development Strategies and Plans in Latin America

Country	Documented national development strategy	Leadership	Institutional apparatus for implementation	Dedicated budgeted resources
Argentina	No national plan	None	None	None
Barbados	National Strategic Plan 2005–25	Prime minister	Creation of special organizations	Yes
Brazil	Complementary strategies: PAC, PACTI, PDP, PDE;[a] Health Plan for 2007–10	Presidency, relevant ministries	Special agencies, some of them created for the purpose	Yes
Chile	1982–95 Tacit strategy of export development in natural resources 2007 Strategy of innovation and export growth	Finance Ministry Presidency	Traditional government structure Creation of special organization	No reliable information available Resources from mining royalties and budget
Colombia	2004 Domestic Agenda	National Competitiveness Council	Traditional government structure and creation of special organizations	Yes
	National Development Plan 2007–10	Planning Ministry	Traditional government structure and creation of special organizations	Yes
	Visión Colombia 2019 Segundo Centenario	President, Planning Ministry	Creation of special organizations	Yes

Costa Rica	Since the 1980s: export diversification and investment attraction strategy,	Presidency	Traditional government structure and CINDE[b]	Yes
	National Development Plan 2006–10	Ministry of Economy, Industry and Trade	Traditional government structure	
Mexico	National Development Plan 2007–12	Presidency, Planning Ministry		
	Vision 2030: The Mexico We Want	Presidency	Traditional government structure	No
Panama	Agreements of the National Concertation for Development 2008–25	Vice presidency	Traditional government structure	Yes
Peru	National Competitiveness Plan 2005–11	Prime minister	Creation of special organizations	No reliable information available

Source: Authors, based on official documents.

[a] Growth Acceleration Plan (PAC), Science, Technology and Innovation Action Plan (PACTI), Productive Development Policy (PDP), Educational Development Plan (PDE).

[b] CINDE refers to the Costa Rican Coalition of Development Initiatives, a private agency set up to attract FDI. It collaborates closely with the government.

As noted, the mere existence of a document spelling out the development strategy does not ensure the implementation or effectiveness of that strategy. Nonetheless, making a strategy explicit by drawing up a document allows it to be disseminated, which in theory can aid the focus and coordination of state actions. And at least civil society is made aware of the key directions the government wants to take the economy in the future.

Brazil.   Brazil has had a very ambitious set of initiatives, programs, plans, and activities that cover various strategic pillars for sustained growth and that together amount to a de facto national plan.[6] The main pillars are the Growth Acceleration Plan (PAC), geared to boosting public and private investment in infrastructure; the Science, Technology and Innovation Action Plan (PACTI); the National Education Development Plan; and the Productive Development Policy (PDP), which seeks to consolidate long-term productive transformation and growth.[7] Given the PDP's importance in Brazil's efforts at productive transformation, its features merit analysis.

The backdrop to the PDP was the 2003–04 Technological Industrial and Foreign Trade Policy, which focused on only a few productive sectors but signaled that industrial policy was "back" in Brazil. The PDP took a step forward by broadening the goals, and it is now the most ambitious public industrial promotional policy program in Latin America if judged by scope and the financing available and the institutional responsibilities assigned to implement it. The scheme also has novel dimensions, such as implementation on three levels: actions designed for their systemic effects, actions designed for achieving strategic objectives, and policies aimed at structural change over the long term (figure 6.1).

Note also that Brazil's de facto national plan is an example of a well-thought-out initiative, one that was devised strategically and has adequate financing. Brazil could come to lead the revival of a Latin America that takes seriously a strategic approach to productive transformation. The main challenge will be the plan's implementation by a public apparatus that is somewhat out of practice in bringing to fruition ambitious large-scale industrial policy initiatives. Early evaluations suggest that the program has lagged behind a number of its established targets, partially attributed to the world economic crisis of 2008–09 (Zebral 2011).

Colombia.   Planning in Colombia has been a task of government since 1961, an exercise that is repeated every four years as the political cycle moves forward. The plans have been drawn up in a serious manner, but they have tended to be used to justify spending related to the political platform of the incumbent government, rather than to express strategic priorities for medium- and long-term productive transformation.

Since the 1990s Colombian governments have centered their productive development policies and plans on boosting competitiveness.[8] But the process has been somewhat discontinuous because initiatives have expired with each presidential election. In 1994, under the Samper administration,

Figure 6.1 PDP: Objectives, Challenges, Targets, and Policies

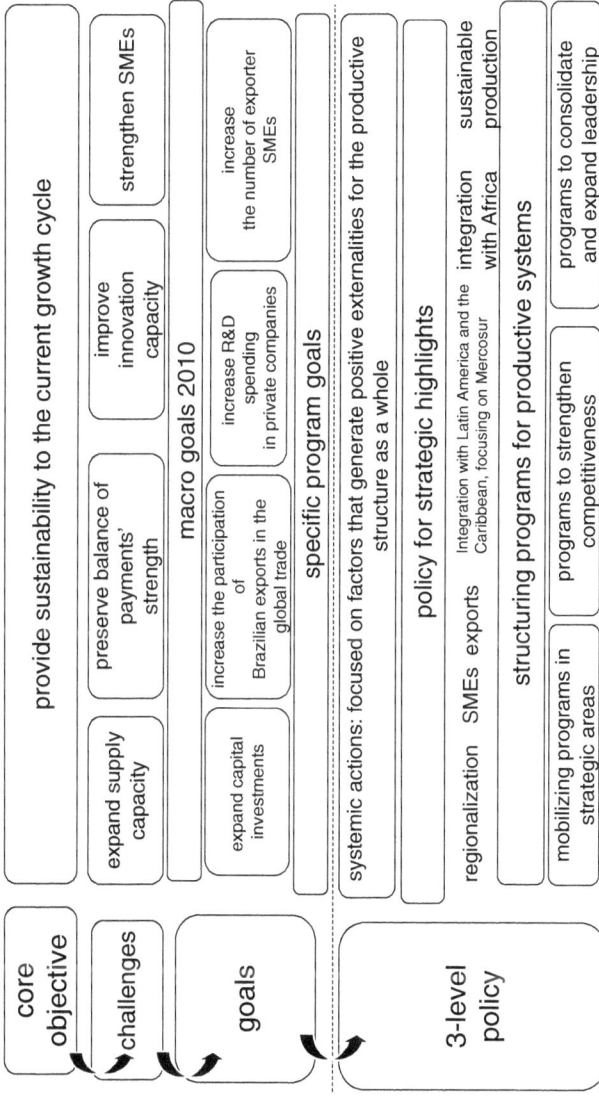

core objective	provide sustainability to the current growth cycle
challenges	expand supply capacity · preserve balance of payments' strength · improve innovation capacity · strengthen SMEs
goals	**macro goals 2010** expand capital investments · increase the participation of Brazilian exports in the global trade · increase R&D spending in private companies · increase the number of exporter SMEs
	specific program goals
3-level policy	systemic actions: focused on factors that generate positive externalities for the productive structure as a whole **policy for strategic highlights** regionalization · SMEs exports · Integration with Latin America and the Caribbean, focusing on Mercosur · integration with Africa · sustainable production **structuring programs for productive systems** mobilizing programs in strategic areas · programs to strengthen competitiveness · programs to consolidate and expand leadership

Source: Authors, based on Federal Government of Brazil 2008.

an effort was made to improve firms' productivity and enhance the business environment by means of sectoral competitiveness agreements. That initiative was redefined in the 1998–2002 National Development Plan, devised by the successor government under the leadership of the Foreign Trade Ministry, which in turn created a program known as the Colombia Competes Network (RCC). This was a crosscutting program that sought to identify, prioritize, and surmount obstacles to competitiveness.

In 2004 President Alvaro Uribe began another process led by the National Planning Department (DNP), which gave rise in 2006 to the preparation of the Domestic Agenda ("Agenda Interna") and the establishment of a National Competitiveness Commission.[9] The process of drawing up the Domestic Agenda led to a pattern of work and coordination at the national and regional levels that has continued throughout the decade and has been complemented by a foresight exercise "*Visión Colombia 2019 Segundo Centenario.*"[10] The DNP, which led the exercise, regards it as a process of consensus building on a medium- and long-term vision of Colombia, with the potential for laying the groundwork for a real national medium- and long-term development strategy.

In 2008 Colombia's National Council for Economic and Social Policy published Document 3527, which presented the strategy for competitiveness and productivity approved by the National Competitiveness Commission. That in turn gave rise to 15 plans of action that define strategic pillars, some of which have specific objectives. The competitiveness plan incorporates horizontal objectives (dealing with infrastructure and education, for example) along with programs with a more specific sectoral focus (in both traditional areas such as coffee and textiles and newer sectors such as cosmetics and medical tourism). However, no resources had been allocated for the new sectors as of the end of 2009.

Peru.   Peru's National Competitiveness Plan, prepared by the National Competitiveness Council in 2005, was spurred largely by the challenge of concluding a free trade agreement with the United States. The plan has enabled some degree of coordination among policies on productive development and competitiveness, but its first version had an unmanageable number of focal points of activity: 44 strategies, 138 policies, 431 actions, and 1,400 subactions. In 2006 the scope of the activities was reduced first to these areas (competitive production chains in cotton, textiles, clothing, cacao and chocolate, and wood and furniture); Peru Innovates, and Peru Start-Ups (*Perú Innova, Perú Emprende*); simplification of municipality-business red tape; regional competitiveness; and monitoring competitiveness).

The virtue of these initiatives in Peru, like those in Brazil and Colombia, is that they adopt concrete action plans. Nonetheless, Peru's first version of the National Competitiveness Plan also reflects the tendency, frequent in Latin America, to prepare analyses with very long "to-do" lists but without adequate priority setting. Another lesson from Peru's experience is that it is difficult to meet goals when ministries and agencies are not obligated to take action, either because of lack of a legal framework or because of dissension within the government about what should be done and who should do it. Moreover, sustained activity might be adversely affected by a lack of financing when, as in Peru, the plan depends to a large extent on mobilizing off-budget resources in the form of technical cooperation from multilateral institutions. Instability in ministerial leadership also weakened the process. Finally, in some Peruvian circles there was suspicion that President Alan Garcia was only lukewarm to Peru's National Competitiveness Plan—drawn up by the previous government.

Costa Rica. Costa Rica's national development plans are prepared every four years following changes in government. However, as President Oscar Arias stated in 2007, "The plans suffered from an exuberance of intentions, from an excess of activities and the consequent lack of priorities. The National Development Plan became such an extensive document that it was not even sent to be printed, and so complex that not a single citizen was able to understand it."[11] Hence the Planning Ministry had a vision of the future, but that vision did not take shape in actions or financing. According to Arias, the plan was dominated by government policies based on "improvisation." Moreover, because of the inability to build consensus, the plans became simply another program of the incumbent government, and in practice the country moved forward without systematic national medium- or long-term action plans. In any event, Arias committed his government to a coherent planning exercise.

Notwithstanding the aforesaid weaknesses, in parallel to the national plans, the country was able to develop a relatively tacit medium- and long-term strategy focused on diversifying and boosting exports by means of incentives and attraction of FDI.[12] Since the mid-1980s, along with trade liberalization (which has not been as drastic and swift as in other Latin American countries), the government pursued policies biased toward promotion of upgraded nontraditional exports; the export processing regime is prominent in this regard. From the outset the private sector played a crucial role, and CINDE (a private organization set up with financing from the U.S. Agency for International Development and devoted to attracting foreign investment) was a policy catalyst. What is interesting about this experience is that Costa Rica's presidents pursued (informal/tacit) public-private collaboration over the long term as the basis of the export development strategy, with a view to helping it succeed. Intel Corporation's decision in 1996 to invest in chip production in the country involved many personal interventions of Costa Rica's president at the time. This public-private collaboration has continued beyond changes in government. As internal conditions changed, however, so too did the programs and policies, as well as the associated institutional arrangements. Finally, the strategy also has involved negotiating free trade agreements such as the ones with the United States and the European Union.

Currently, the Costa Rican government's strategic vision is expressed in the National Development Plan 2006–10, which sought to avoid the *urbi et orbi* nature of previous plans. It also incorporates some of the recommendations made by the Twenty-First Century Strategy (*Estrategia Siglo XXI*), a long-term vision to make knowledge and innovation the basic engines of Costa Rican economic development.[13] This strategy was not a government project, but rather a nationwide, multisectoral initiative to devise an action plan to drive Costa Rica's overall development based on education, science and technology, and innovation, all having to be consistent with Costa Rican culture.

Chile.   Chile has had a national strategy for the past 35 years, albeit one that is not formally documented; it is geared mainly to export development based on natural resources and gaining access to external markets. This strategy began with the policies imposed by the Pinochet military regime, which evolved into an informal/tacit strategy based on economic and political consensus among the public sector, the private sector, and the leading political parties in the democratic period. It should also be noted that the prevailing thinking over recent decades has favored private sector leadership in this process and minimization of the state's scope of action.

However, Chile's export model, successful for many years, began to lose momentum in the late 1990s.[14] The country needed to move to a "new phase" of productive and export development, one focused on activities entailing greater knowledge and value added. The result was the "rediscovery" of the proactive role of the state, the clearest expression of which is the innovation strategy drawn up by the National Council on Innovation for Competitiveness. As well as pushing for improved coordination in a somewhat fragmented innovation system,[15] the council proposed concentrating resources on the development of a specific number of export clusters and creating production chains for natural resource–based goods—activities that involve greater knowledge and value added. The council had help in preparing its proposal from a foreign consulting firm and was assigned resources from mining royalties. The strategy shifted the direction of development from horizontal policies geared especially to supporting small and medium enterprises (SMEs)—policies that were justified as a means of resolving market failures, increasing firms' productivity, and updating their technology—toward an emphasis on vertical policies that focus selectively on certain sectors and clusters. Within the coalition government (*la Concertacion*) that created the program consensus on the wisdom of this approach was relatively weak, reflecting "path dependency" on the previous approach that stressed minimum and horizontal direct state interventions in support of productive transformation.[16] In 2010 a new government with unambiguous conservative economic credentials was elected; this marked a rollback of the new industrial policies and a weakening of the influence of the national innovation council.

Panama. The decision in 2006 to expand the Panama Canal and the accumulation of external debt to finance it generated political space for a national debate on the need to forge a vision of the future that would capitalize on the benefits of that initiative. This debate underpinned the creation of the Concertation National. Launched by President Martín Torrijos, the concertation had two main phases: a very extensive consultation process facilitated by the United Nations, followed in October 2007 by the conclusion of agreements on a series of key themes for national development up to 2025. Geared in particular to overcoming poverty, these general themes are related to welfare and equity, economic growth and competitiveness, institutional modernization, and education. The initiative defined objectives, targets, and development strategies, some more specific than others.

This historic effort to forge a national vision for the country's development had the virtue of being a true plan, in the sense that specific targets were set for many (though not all) the areas, medium- and long-term financing commitments were made based on projected revenue from the canal, a commission was set up to monitor and assess implementation, and it made a pledge to create a system of formal indicators to determine if the targets are being met. Nonetheless, this initiative is very broad in scope and its greatest challenge may be the government's capacity to coordinate and implement it as well as to maintain high-level political commitment over subsequent political cycles with new leaders.

Barbados. One of the most successful countries in the region, Barbados has an unbroken tradition of planning dating back to the 1940s (ECLAC 2001). Following independence from Britain, its strategy centered on export diversification,[17] the development of social services, and the promotion of tourism. To this end it promoted foreign investment, and in 1965 it passed the International Business Company Act, providing tax incentives for investment (ECLAC 2005; Artana, Auguste, and Downes 2008; Springer 2010). In this period consensus was widespread on the importance of economic opening and attracting FDI.

The governments of the 1970s focused development on light industry in an effort to increase employment. The withdrawal of Intel Corporation in the mid-1980s caused a shift in the strategy toward developing the financial sector. The strategy did not avert the serious balance of payments crisis that the country faced, and overcame, in the early 1990s. The government then shifted the strategy again to center on consolidating an international business platform, reformulating the International Business Company Act and developing complementary legislation to attract FDI.

The National Strategic Plan for Barbados (2005–25) has six general objectives: unleashing the spirit of the nation, new governance for new times, building social capital, strengthening physical infrastructure and preserving the environment, enhancing the country's prosperity and competitiveness, and branding Barbados globally. Each of these six objectives is broken down into subobjectives also made up of very general strategies and targets, although in a few cases final indicators have been proposed to verify that the targets have been met (annex 6A).

Like the Mexican plan examined below, the Barbadian strategy is a general framework within which policies are developed. In other words, the strategy expresses only relatively general aspirations about the development of a modern and competitive economy; consequently there is no operational action plan that can be effectively assessed. Since a strategy and its specific activities and actions are two indissoluble elements of the realization of the aspiration, it is unsurprising that in this case the concrete results are often limited.

Mexico.   Mexico's National Development Plan 2007–12 is another good example of a strategy that lacks the precision needed to make it operational. The plan took a comprehensive approach based on "*Visión 2030.*"[18] As in other countries, it has several strategic pillars: the rule of law and security; a competitive, job-creating economy; equal opportunities; environmental sustainability; effective democracy; and a responsible foreign policy. For each of these policy guidelines, the plan presents a series of goals and the strategies or paths to reach them. For example, the pillar on "a competitive, job-creating economy" has 13 objectives.[19] These objectives are not prioritized but, rather, represent the complete range of issues related to the pillar. One reason for the absence of priorities is confusion about the difference between a government program, which is confined to the political cycle, and a national development strategy, which addresses medium- and long-term objectives. Priorities must be set and sequenced with more than one political term as a reference point.[20]

The plan moreover does not set out in concrete terms how the goals are to be met. For example, one goal states that "the cost of opening new firms should be lowered" but offers no actions for meeting the goal.[21] One might well ask: how are the goals to be met? Who is responsible for deciding? Which agencies are involved? What resources does the government currently manage, and what resources will have to be added to meet these objectives? Nor is a timeframe given for achieving the goals, not even in the context of a program for a single presidential term.

In sum, strategies and plans like this one for Mexico are a conceptual framework of aspirations rather than an action plan. Hence it is not surprising that the programs and policies of the specific government entities are poorly coordinated with the goals of the strategy.

Contemporary Public-Private Alliances: Achievements and Limitations

Although experiences within the region have not been nearly as advanced as those outside Latin America, some dialogue between the government and the main economic and social actors has played a role in defining national economic development strategies and plans, especially in recent years. This phenomenon is evident at the national level: forums for dialogue, special commissions, and even permanent, legislation-based presidential advisory bodies. There is also public-private collaboration in sectors and regions, which in some cases is more mature than that at the national level. Finally, in some cases the private sector has gained representation in the agencies responsible for implementing public policies and programs

The types of alliances are equivalent to those discussed in chapter 3. Formal and structured alliances dominate in Barbados, Colombia, Panama, and Peru. Public-private collaboration in these countries has been legislated. This formal status can help to legitimate the alliance and its organization and may help to insulate public-private collaboration from changes in government and radically different changes in approach from one government to the next. Structured alliances need not necessarily be legislated: they can find expression in councils or commissions that sometimes, over time, acquired permanent legitimacy. There are informal/tacit alliances in Costa Rica (where the public and private sectors collaborate constantly but without formal bodies) and ad hoc forms of participation in Mexico, where the government consults the private sector on specific matters for a limited period and for limited purposes.

Several kinds of alliances coexist in some countries. Brazil, for example, has a hybrid public-private alliance. A formal, structured alliance exists in the Council on Economic and Social Development (CDES) at the highest level of government, while significant public-private collaborations have formed around specific policies and plans, such as the Productive Development Policy. In Chile, too, under the government coalition called the Concertation, the predominant form of collaboration was hybrid: a formal and structured alliance in the National Innovation Council for Competitiveness (CNIC), the regional agencies for productive development, and sectoral clusters defined for the purpose of promoting innovation. Meanwhile, ad hoc committees were also brought together for specific issues, such as the committees on education, and equity.

In understanding the development of alliances in Latin America, it is helpful to recall that antagonism has traditionally prevailed between the state and the market in Latin American countries. On one hand are the advocates of the market who continue to call for a smaller state—a process that in many cases has brought about a severe weakening of public institutions. On the other hand are those who vigorously defend the state and are mistrustful of private enterprise, calling for ever more control over the market's normal operation. These vastly differing perspectives often manifest themselves in a severe mistrust between the public and private sectors, both tied to the past in a way that hampers the formation and sustainability of alliances.

This reality leads us to reiterate an important overarching conclusion for this book: forming functional alliances is not a cakewalk. It is a highly political process that requires sustained political leadership and commitment to the idea. The alliance must be housed in an institutional arrangement that is sensitive to the idiosyncrasies of the stakeholders and local politics. The public side of the alliance must be a credible partner, which requires a steady political hand and a commitment to continuous upgrading of the capacity of the public bureaucracy. A credible alliance also needs to focus on objectives that are actionable. And while consensus is a goal, it is not an event but rather a process that can take considerable time to mature. While alliances and consensus are not easy to build, getting started now with a well-designed, governed, and financed process is important.

In any event, the public and private sectors in some Latin American countries have recently experienced a degree of rapprochement and are working together to build a joint national project that looks to the future. This trend began before the 2008–09 global financial crisis. Progressive strengthening of the alliances would be helpful, given the need to tackle the short-term impact of crisis in a manner consistent with the medium- and long-term structural changes demanded for high and sustained growth.[22]

Table 6.3 illustrates the public-private alliances in selected Latin American countries, showing their general and sectoral fields of activity, their functions, the kinds of dialogue in which they engage, and the way in which the bodies that express the public-private alliances are instituted, as well as the representation of their members. These alliances are discussed in more detail in the remainder of the chapter.

Advisory Councils to the Presidency

There are two good examples in the region of formal alliances set up using structured and participatory bodies with the aim of strengthening governments: the Council on Social and Economic Development in Brazil and the National Accord in Peru.

Brazil's council was set up in 2003 when the government recognized the importance of shared responsibility between itself and the various social actors for economic and social development. The council, which acts as a consultative and advisory body to the presidency, has more than 100 members who are formally designated by the executive for a two-year period. Members include representatives of the labor movement (unions

Table 6.3 Types of Public-Private Alliances in Latin America

Country/level	Alliance	Type of Alliance	Structure
Argentina			
National	No public-private alliance for a national strategy		
Sectoral	Public-private alliances with specific goals at the sectoral and regional levels	Formal, structured	
Agencies	Boards of agencies	Formal, structured	
Barbados			
National	Tripartite social partnership— social pact to stabilize industrial relations, raise employment, lessen inequality, and strengthen social dialogue and development	Formal, structured	High-level committee: prime minister, business representative, union representative; quarterly meetings Mid-level committee: 18 members from all sectors but with less hierarchy; monthly meetings Consultative-level committee: broad participation including members of parliament; annual meetings
Agencies	National Productivity Council (tripartite) Boards of agencies		To promote policies that raise productivity and prepare studies on issues discussed by the social partnership

(*continued*)

Table 6.3 Types of Public-Private Alliances in Latin America (*continued*)

Country/level	Alliance	Type of Alliance	Structure
Brazil			
National	Economic and Social Development Council, advisory body to the president on state reform and on medium/long-term issues	Formal, structured	Representatives of workers, businesses, social movements, and the government organized in thematic groups; 102 council members chosen by the president
Sectoral	National Industrial Development Council supervises industrial development polices	Formal, structured	14 ministers and 14 representatives of industry
Sectoral	Sectoral and state-level councils and forums for public-private alliance dialogue on the implementation of the PDP	Formal ad hoc but in the process of being structured	Sectoral and thematic business associations and representatives of sectoral and thematic public agencies
Chile			
National	National Innovation Council for Competitiveness defines the innovation strategy and advises the presidency on innovation policies	Formal, structured	Alliance operates at both the executive and grassroots levels, through the leaders of the clusters and participation in the regional productive development agencies
	Various alliance forums set up at different times on different issues	Formal ad hoc	
Sectoral	Productive Development Forum, a council for productive development (1994–99)	Formal, structured	Tripartite partnership, with representatives from government, unions, and business; 24 council members chaired by the minister of economy

Table 6.3

Country/level	Alliance	Type of alliance	Structure
Colombia			
National	National Planning Council aims to build consensus on the National Development Plan	Formal, structured	Composed of representatives of various civil society groups
National	National Competitiveness Commission oversees implementation of the Internal Agenda for productivity and competitiveness	Formal, structured	23 members chaired by the president, with members from businesses, academia and unions, public agencies, private organizations, and regional competitiveness commissions
Costa Rica			
Agencies	From the late 1990s, long-term social agreement on the need to diversify exports by attracting FDI; core of the strategy was FDI attraction, free-trade agreements for upgraded export diversification. Boards of agencies	Informal/tacit Formal, structured	
Mexico			
National	Consultations by the presidency	Formal ad hoc	Private sector participation through consultations and negotiations with business associations, unions, civil society

(continued)

Table 6.3 (continued)

Country/level	Alliance	Type of alliance	Structure
Panama			
National	National Concertation prepares and monitors national development strategy	Formal, structured	Council with representatives from business, unions, religious groups, social sectors, political parties, and the government at the central and local levels
Peru			
National	National Accord advises the government on medium- and long-term policies	Formal, structured	Representatives of national government, political parties, business associations, unions, universities, religious groups, and professional associations
National	National Competitiveness Council aims to boost competitiveness	Formal, structured	Governing Council: president of the Council of Ministers, eight ministers of state, the president of INDECOPI (an NGO that oversees competition issues), representatives of the business sector and of the labor movement
National	Permanent multisectoral commission to devise the National Export Strategic Plan	Formal, structured	Public-private body responsible for the implementation of operational export plans at the regional, sectoral, and national levels, with members from the Ministry of Trade, Industry and Tourism, exporters associations, and other private sector groups

Source: Authors, based on official data.

leaders); entrepreneurs who participate on a personal basis; and individuals from several economic sectors. Permanent members of the council, all of whom come from the government, cannot amount to more than 25 percent of the total. The business sector accounts for 45 percent.

The council's work has been organized into plenary sessions and thematic working groups whose agendas are defined by the demands of the government or the council members themselves. In 2004 and 2005 the council analyzed the importance of forging a vision for the country and addressed itself to preparing what eventually would be a series of policies gathered together as the National Development Agenda (CDES 2007). This agenda did not become a government rallying cry, but it influenced some reforms.

The council encountered some problems over time that needed to be addressed. One problem was presidential appointment of council members. In some cases the appointments did not represent the pertinent economic actors, and some complained that the president was using the appointments to reward friends and supporters—complaints that aroused mistrust in some circles about the council's role (Zebral 2011). Second, because some powerful sectors were not represented, such as the leaders of the national confederation of industry and the sectoral associations for capital goods and vehicles, those sectors communicated with the president exclusively by lobbying outside the council, thereby weakening the legitimacy of the council itself. Third, the large number of members and their diversity of interests (their organization into thematic areas notwithstanding) severely impeded the agreements and consensus needed to support operational decision making. Fourth, doubts about the real political relevance of the forum constrained high-level interest in participation. Finally, despite the efforts made, there was a need for much greater outreach to civil society regarding the council's work.

Peru is the other Latin American country with a general advisory body to the government on medium- and long-term issues. Created by the Toledo administration in 2002 and headed by the prime minister, the National Accord was set up to forge a shared vision of the future among the government, the political parties, and representatives of civil society, as a means of furthering democratic development. Up to 2009 the accord had proposed 31 state policies on democracy and the rule of law, equity and social justice, competitiveness, and state efficiency, and it has also pushed implementation of several projects. But the alliance failed to capture the full attention of senior government officials, and it lacked representatives of sufficient political importance to make itself heard. Still, the National Accord is a seed that could bear fruit over time. If, with government political leadership, the accord makes progress in linking the government's decision making with the proposals of a diverse core of important actors, be they political or professional, and if it is given proper resources and technical support, it could perhaps become a true reference point for longer-term economic policies.

Chile's Productive Development Forum no longer exists, but until it failed in 1999, it was the most important channel for social dialogue in the country. Created in 1994 to be a permanent channel for interaction among the economy's main productive development actors, the forum's chief goal was to identify and promote initiatives to facilitate dynamic and sustained economic growth in a context of stability and equity. It sought to foster a broad social dialogue that would find expression in public-private agreements, with a view to devising a shared development strategy.

The chief body of this forum was the Productive Development Council, chaired by the economy minister and with 24 members representing the government, business, and labor.[23] The council's primary function was to review the follow-up to activities springing from the agreements and recommended policies. It never gained the full support of either the government, where the economy minister had little influence, or the political parties (which were not invited to participate). Moreover, a focus on the short-term outlook among workers and entrepreneurs, as well as the government to some extent, constrained the prospects of building consensus on longer-term issues. These problems, combined with the mistrust among these groups, led to the disbanding of the council.

In 2001, during the Lagos government, a new ad hoc alliance was created between the major business group, the Confederation for Production and Trade, and the government. The Public-Private Council for Export Development, charged with implementing the confederation's progrowth agenda, organized four commissions oriented to promoting trade facilitation, productivity, international integration, investment, tourism, and exports. The alliance was effective in promoting a dialogue and agenda in the context of negotiations for free trade areas with developed northern markets. Once these negotiations were completed, however, the group lost initiative and stopped operating in the subsequent administration.

More on National Alliances

Table 6.4 shows the national public-private councils in Latin America that have won legitimacy in supporting national strategies. Those in Barbados, Colombia, and Peru are formally instituted and have been working for several years. Others are more recent, as in Chile and Panama. In Brazil there are incipient ad hoc mechanisms. Finally, there have been very effective informal or ad hoc public-private dialogues in the past in Costa Rica and Chile.

The national tripartite partnership in Barbados: progress on consensus building but with the risk of "lock in." The national tripartite alliance in Barbados has been a positive force for institutionalizing consensus building on socioeconomic issues. It was established in the 1990s as a result of economic crisis, following a history of informal and ad hoc collaboration.

Table 6.4 Participation of Alliances in Strategies and Plans

Countries	Alliance	National development strategy		Action plans in sector or specific area	
		Role in devising strategy	Role in implementing or evaluating	Devising	Implementation/ evaluation
Barbados	Tripartite Social Partnership	Yes	Follow-up and evaluation		
Brazil	PDP competitiveness forums	No	No	Makes proposals to the executive committees and secretariat of the PDP	Yes
Chile	National Innovation Council for Competitiveness	Yes[a]	Yes[a]	No	Only monitoring
Colombia	National Planning Council	Yes	Yes	Yes	Yes
	National Competitiveness Commission	Yes	Yes	Yes	Yes
Costa Rica	Private sector participation is informal	Yes via informal consultation	No	Yes but informal	
Mexico	Consultations with civil society (ad hoc)	Through consultations	No	No	No
Panama	National Concertation for Development	Yes	Yes		
Peru	National Competitiveness Council			Yes	Under way
	Export Multi-Sectoral Commission			Yes	Yes

Source: Prepared by the authors.
a. A strategy has been formulated but it has not achieved sufficient consensus, even in the government, to be considered a national development strategy.

Efforts at more formal collaboration between representatives of business, workers, and government finally took form in "protocols" that determine how industrial relations unfold and that are regarded as a tool for public policy making.[24] The three parties involved regard the protocols as a way of meeting the challenges of globalization and the demands of information-based competitiveness. The declarations in the protocols are quite general—create a modern and efficient economy, create a balance between prices and incomes by means of low inflation, attain a more inclusive society, and distribute the benefits of economic growth in a fair and equitable manner.

Although it has contributed to the national strategies for economic development,[25] the partnership's main role has been to provide a forum for dialogue to identify and address issues regarded as problematic by the members. Of course the central government is the determinant actor in public policy making, but it traditionally has considered and valued the interaction and advice that has emerged from the partnership. This tripartite collaboration has been crucial in moving the country toward a more liberalized economy at the same time that it regulates industrial relations and the labor market.

Essential parts of the partnership's success have been the general consensus among the leadership of the country's political and administrative structures, an organized and united labor movement, and a very representative private sector. These circumstances have allowed Barbados to move toward social cohesion and policy continuity that transcends changes in government.[26] Nonetheless, the most distinguishing feature of this partnership has been the relatively high level of sophistication among the unions, whose professionalism has been critical to consensus building.

Figure 6.2 shows the different levels of the dialogue in Barbados's public-private alliance, its members, and the frequency with which they meet. This structure allows the actors to participate in developing policies, as well as in the follow-up and evaluation of implementation. Another important feature is the equilibrium among the different representatives, which ensures better dialogue and the trust of the private sector—including representatives of the workers—in the institutional arrangements. The alliance receives secretarial support from a ministry.

The Barbados partnership is the most advanced in the region, but in recent years it has suffered from governance problems that have lessened its effectiveness. Its lower institutional level, which meets monthly, has had only modest decision-making capacity. Moreover, the higher level, though it has had decision-making power, is supposed to meet quarterly but has often failed to do so for lack of a quorum. Moreover the union representative at both levels has often been the same high-level person; thus, labor issues have tended to predominate in the discussions, to the detriment of sectoral economic issues and matters on the national strategic plan. And although the partnership has ad hoc secretarial support, it

Figure 6.2 Organizational Structure of the Social Pact in Barbados

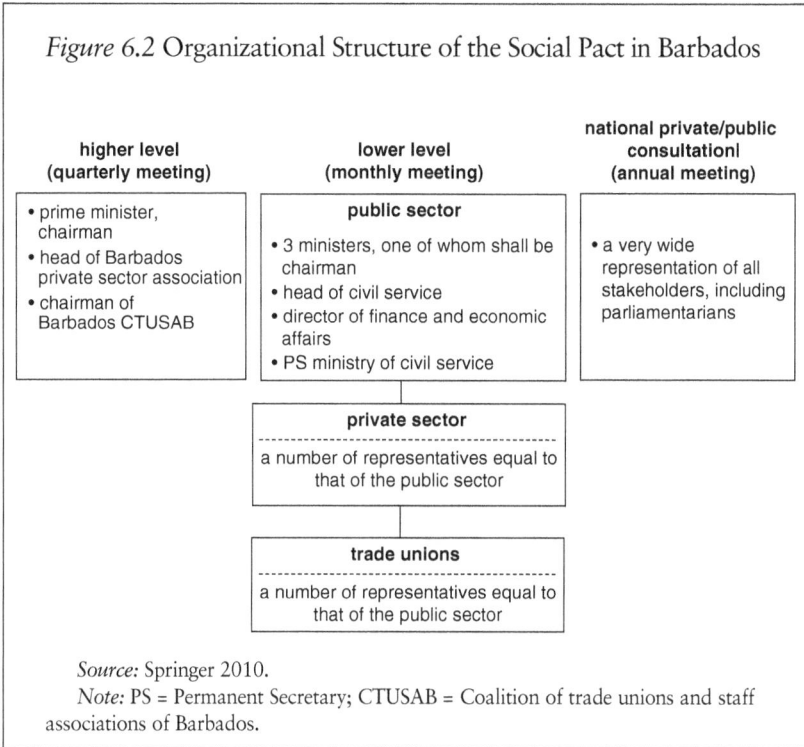

higher level (quarterly meeting)	lower level (monthly meeting)	national private/public consultationl (annual meeting)
• prime minister, chairman • head of Barbados private sector association • chairman of Barbados CTUSAB	**public sector** • 3 ministers, one of whom shall be chairman • head of civil service • director of finance and economic affairs • PS ministry of civil service	• a very wide representation of all stakeholders, including parliamentarians

private sector
----
a number of representatives equal to that of the public sector

trade unions
----
a number of representatives equal to that of the public sector

Source: Springer 2010.
Note: PS = Permanent Secretary; CTUSAB = Coalition of trade unions and staff associations of Barbados.

needs structured technical backing to underpin discussions aimed at identifying and resolving problems and at dealing with specific operational issues of the national plan. Preparing annual action plans for the national strategy, as well as formal evaluations, would have been a means of bringing the partnership's discussions on these operational matters down to earth. Finally, there has been some acknowledgment that nongovernmental organizations (NGOs) should be included in the discussions (Springer 2010). In 2008 the Democratic Labor Party displaced the long reigning Barbados Labor Party in government with some expectation that the partnership could eventually be revitalized.

Colombia has been a model of public-private collaboration for planning and implementing strategies, but its sustainability has been undermined by the political cycle. Colombia has used a participative methodology whereby economic and social actors express themselves in two central bodies: the National Planning Council and the National Competitiveness Commission. The government strengthened planning in 1991 by mandating the involvement of civil society organizations in the National Planning Council. The aim was to correct the executive's centralist and unilateral practices and to curb the clientalist conduct of the legislature and the political parties. Thus the National Planning Council was coordinated with territorial councils in 32 departments and 1,067 municipalities. The main task of these public-private councils has been to offer opinions and make proposals on the development plans prepared by the president, the departmental governors, and the mayors of the municipalities, as well as to make recommendations to actors (Forero Pineda 2000). However, with time this forum weakened, in part because of the great number of regions and the heterogeneity of the needs and capacities of the participants. Indeed, a number of the departments have ceased to participate.

Between 1998 and 2002 the Pastrana administration set up another channel for public-private partnership in the form of the Colombia Competes Network (Red Colombia Compite). This partnership was involved in raising productivity in three spheres: regional, production chains, and specialized networks. The first was involved in efforts to collaborate in regional crosscutting projects to improve productivity. The Agreements on the Competitiveness of Productive Chains were set up simultaneously. These provided an arena for dialogue and public-private coordination of activities to improve the productivity and competitiveness of firms in the chains. Finally, specialized networks were set up as a mechanism to provide national coordination of crosscutting initiatives, supporting progress in those complex activities that could not be addressed successfully solely from the perspective of sectors or chains. These networks initially had significant business participation, but their activities waned over time because of a lack of government leadership and clarity of objectives.

As noted, in 2006 the process of dialogue led to the creation of the Domestic Agenda for productivity and competitiveness and the creation of the National Competitiveness Commission to oversee implementation of it; the commission is a public-private alliance presided over by the president. The commission coordinates actors and organizations at the national and regional levels on matters of public policy related to the development plans. It offers a space for dialogue among representatives of the national government (15, mostly ministers, plus departmental delegates), two representatives named by business associations, two from the workers unions, two from universities, and three appointees of the president.

Unfortunately the civil members of the commission have not been very active. Other factors that have weakened the effectiveness of the commission and the Domestic Agenda were, according to Meléndez and Perry (2009), the persistence of clientelism and rent seeking among ministers, and Congress and organizations at the margins of the Domestic Agenda with the end result of loss of coherence and full effectiveness in public policy.

Meanwhile a group of 30 important firms (including multinationals operating in the country), along with representatives of three prestigious universities and small and medium enterprises, organized the Private Sector Competitiveness Council. Two large unions participate as observers. This council plays an important role in Colombia's public-private alliance, giving the private sector a voice in the Domestic Agenda and a leadership role in monitoring progress and sustaining a medium- to long-term national vision over political cycles. The council replicates itself at the regional level, where local councils implement and monitor complementary strategies. Figure 6.3 summarizes the structure of the council.

To assess progress on the agenda, the council publishes an annual National Competitiveness Report.[27] This document provides an updated national, sectoral, and regional analysis and highlights the obstacles and problems encountered in furthering the national strategy.

Of the countries examined here, Colombia has had the most practical experience with public-private alliances. Nonetheless, despite longstanding efforts to create synergies for expanding dialogue between the public sector, business, and academia, the process has not been easy. Perhaps the constant redefinition of the alliance with each new political cycle has most undermined joint action among the parties involved. Hence the strengthening of a body such as the Private Competitiveness Council, as Meléndez and Perry (2009) suggest, could help sustain the long-term policies of the Domestic Agenda and strengthen it with new, updated proposals.

Figure 6.3 Composition of Colombia's Private Council on Competitiveness

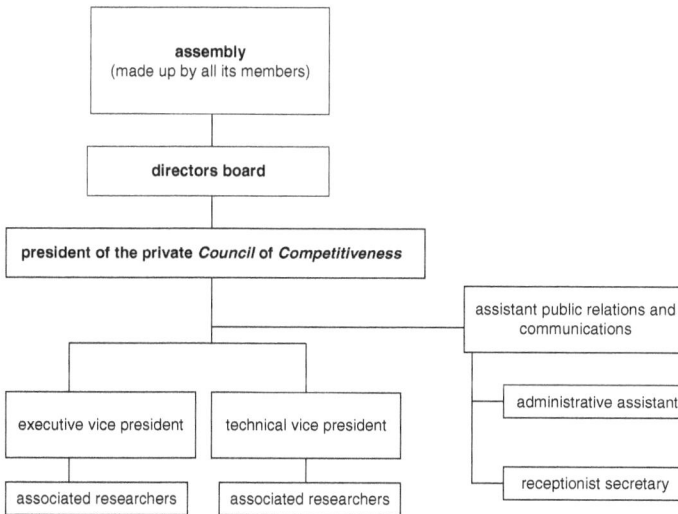

Source: Consejo Privado de Competitividad, "Esquema organizacional del CPC." http://www.compite.ws/spccompite/content/page.aspx?ID=69.

Panama's experience of public-private collaboration is recent: the challenge is to make it endure beyond changes in government and to strengthen its institutional structure. As mentioned, the Council of the National Concertation for Development was created during the Torrejos government as a public-private body of citizen participation for consultation, proposals, and approval of a development strategy. It is chaired by the vice president and initially consisted of 33 representatives of the sectors taking part in drawing up the national development plan. The representatives were drawn from three spheres: the productive sector—workers, business associations, SMEs, and associations of professionals such as lawyers and economists; the political sphere—representatives of the political parties,[28] local governments, and the provinces; and civil society—organizations working on women's issues, human rights, the environment, indigenous peoples, and education, as well as churches, youth groups, and others. The council has a technical unit and a monitoring group to oversee the implementation of the agreed strategy.

The council is relatively new; only in April 2009 did it choose its executive secretary, whose mission is to coordinate the council with a view to advancing the agreements and projects emerging from the national dialogue. The Torrejos government also promulgated a Framework Law on Citizen Participation to institutionalize the system of citizen involvement in the design and implementation of public policies at the national, provincial, regional, and local levels. The idea was to foster the shared responsibility of citizens for the management of public policies. The government that took office in 2009 will help determine whether the council consolidates its relevance in the country's development strategy.

The experience of Chile's National Innovation Council for Competitiveness is novel for that country, but approval of the draft law in Congress would strengthen its operations and civil legitimacy. The National Council on Innovation for Competitiveness, another relatively new body for public-private collaboration, was created in late 2005 by presidential decree. The council was renewed by President Michelle Bachelet in 2006 as a permanent advisory body to the presidency. Its mission was to advise the authorities in identifying, devising, and implementing policies, plans and programs, measures, and other activities related to innovation. These activities covered the fields of science, the training of specialized personnel, and the development, transfer, and dissemination of technology.

The council consisted of a president, chosen by the nation's president, 5 ministers, and 11 private sector representatives selected for their knowledge of science, business, or public policy making. These representatives were not official representatives of the sectors to which they belong, but rather took part in the council on a personal basis.

The Organisation for Economic Co-operation and Development (OECD 2009) evaluated the council, pointing out that it enjoyed several achievements in its short life but also that it exhibited some weaknesses.

Among the achievements were that it had gained credibility as an advisory body to the presidency, it had conferred greater selectivity on public policy making by focusing on certain clusters, and it had sought to strengthen the national innovation system. The weaknesses were presented as challenges and referred to the lack of clarity about its responsibilities; a certain remoteness from medium- and long-term policies, because it operated within the confines of short-term budget exercises; the excessive time taken to prepare a strategy (two years); and the weakening of its political legitimacy. In the latter regard, three factors were mentioned: the legislature's failure to approve a draft law that would have clarified the council's responsibilities; the lack of closer dialogue with the universities; and the lack of outreach to the public and to the actors in the national innovation system (OECD 2009, 5–7).

The draft law in Congress was rejected twice, weakening the council's operations for several reasons. First, in a country as legalistic as Chile, rejection of the bill weakened the council's legitimacy and power to enforce its decisions with respect to the rest of the state administration. Second, the legislation would have allowed a clearer demarcation of responsibilities between the council (an essentially advisory body) and the Committee of Ministers, the body that implements the strategy and policies.[29] This step would eliminate the overlapping activities that have plagued the national innovation system. Third, the bill proposed that the council's membership be more representative of the actors in the national innovation system. Finally, it established a formula for the distribution of resources from mining royalties, which had been at the heart of vigorous debate in Congress.

The new institutional structure also called for establishment of public-private councils and commissions at the cluster and regional levels. This undertaking has not been easy owing to a lack of coordination and links among businesses in the regions and productive sectors chosen for support in the strategy. The council's spokesperson said in an interview that great effort had been made to communicate with the business organizations linked to priority sectors; however, effectively engaging them in the strategy proved to be a difficult process given rather indifferent public-private business relations in the democratic era. Another perceived challenge was the development of a culture among entrepreneurs, academics, and government geared to new opportunities in the medium to long term. This clearly would be a learning process given past practices.[30]

In Brazil collaboration was under way between business and government for implementation of the Productive Development Policy with efforts focused on less organized sectors and on certain regions. During Luiz Inácio Lula da Silva's first government (2003–06), the National Council on Industrial Development, with 14 private sector members and several representatives of the public sector, was set up as a high-level forum for public-private debate and as a body to monitor and validate the PDP.

It was supposed to meet every six months, but because of a lack of leadership and participation, it did not play a significant role in the dialogue over the PDP.

The public sector's collaboration with business associations during the two Lula administrations took place at a lower level, through executive committees and competitiveness forums. The committees comprised officers of the public agencies involved in the PDP, who analyzed and prioritized the policies to be implemented in the sectors. The forums involved meetings of various business associations, and the participants included public officials from agencies that also operated at the level of specific sectors and thematic areas. The forums and the committees were meant to be in close communication. This collaboration was an effort to define the sectoral agenda and the programs to be implemented, as well as to collect information on the businesses' needs and strategies, which were negotiated with the public sector. An effective relationship between these two bodies was crucial for transferring information and drawing up the productive development agenda.

Several factors hampered the relationship between the committees and the forums: the technical and organizational weakness of businesses in some sectors; lack of information on the PDP itself in others. In some sectors and states, the forums did not work. According to the Federation of Industries of São Paulo State, 50 percent of the state's firms were unfamiliar with the PDP.[31] Exporters also felt they had little representation in the initiative. Members of Brazil's Association of Foreign Trade Exporters claimed that the PDP was too general and the proposed targets were less than what already had been achieved. Moreover, PDP policies were not considered in the context of decisions of multinational companies, which accounted for more than 70 percent of Brazil's exports.[32] Another factor that ran counter to public-private collaboration was the conduct of large firms, both multinational and local, which preferred to go directly to the presidency or the Ministry of Development, Industry and Commerce in an effort to gain customized benefits. This undermined the implementation of the PDP and weakened the legitimacy of those leading it. Indeed, some have characterized the PDP exercise as being partially captured by the interests of the large firms that make up Brazil's traditional "networked capitalism" (Zebral 2011). Nonetheless, the National Industrial Confederation, which brings together business associations and federations in Brazil, believes that the PDP represented a significant step forward relative to previous governments. The confederation is monitoring and evaluating the policy and has been active in trying to influence future directions.[33]

Peru's National Competitiveness Council was set up with a great deal of government support, but the absence of a common vision has weakened it over time.   In April 2002 the Peruvian government created the National Competitiveness Council (CNC) as an arena for public-private coordination; one of its missions was to develop and implement a national competitiveness plan. Some 250 experts from the public and private sectors, as well as academia, were involved in drawing up the plan. This ad hoc body lasted until the plan was produced. To prepare the plan, the CNC was especially careful in considering the policies and commitments emerging from the aforementioned National Accord.

The CNC had a governing council comprising nine ministers of state, the presidents of five business associations, a representative of the SMEs, a representative of the workers, and the president of the National Institute for the Defense of Competition and the Protection of Intellectual Property. But the CNC had only limited influence on the ministries and executing agencies, which were not obligated to comply with the national competitiveness plan. Despite their positions, moreover, the senior figures in the CNC (the president of the Council of Ministers and the Minister of Foreign Trade and Tourism) were not respected as authorities on competitiveness. Finally, the CNC's task was made harder by the lack of a common vision of the competitiveness agenda and by the absence of committed leaders from either the public or private sectors. The private sector often preferred to ignore the CNC and meet directly with the ministers, a recurring problem in Latin America when the formal channels for public-private communication lack credibility because of insufficient political and technical leadership and representativeness.

The informal public-private partnership in Costa Rica has been effective. Costa Rica's informal/tacit partnership, one that is not underpinned by institutions or legislation, has operated reasonably well in practice. To secure the arrival of Intel in the country, a series of informal public-private alliances were formed involving the president, ministries, universities, the national private sector, business associations, multinational firms in Costa Rica, the Foreign Trade Corporation, and the Coalition of Development Initiatives (CINDE). Despite the proven success of these partnerships, their significance waned once the four-year term of President José María Figueres came to an end in 1998. Chaves and Segura (2007, 41) point out that some of these activities were later undertaken by CINDE and are part of its task of promoting the country and the business agendas of firms that want to invest in Costa Rica. But the extent of the participants' involvement has not been the same as when efforts were being made to attract Intel.

Public-Private Collaboration in Sectors and Regions

In some countries forging a common national vision has been especially difficult. Where there has been mistrust between the public and private sectors, regional projects driven by public-private alliances have occasionally emerged and been successful. As Ross Schneider (2009) points out, although the policy realm might be more restrictive at the regional or sectoral levels, public-private dialogue in those areas can more easily be productive. The actors are less diverse and have a broader range of common aims, a circumstance that facilitates consensus building. In other cases the members, especially those among the elite, have links that predate the alliance. Finally, in the bigger countries with federal systems, the need to compete with other states or provinces is a unifying factor. Argentina and Mexico are examples of countries in which significant regional or local public-private alliances have developed in specific industries, such as electronics and software (both countries), coffee producers (Mexico), and the wine business and agroindustrial production chains (Argentina).

A particularly interesting case is the alliance in the high-technology industry in Jalisco, Mexico, to restore the industry's competitiveness in the face of China's penetration of its markets (Palacios 2008; Medina Gómez 2006). This joint effort by the public and private sectors centered on the electronic equipment and software industries. It began with the firms' senior executives, particularly in the affiliates of the multinationals. They were joined by local business organizations, and the collaboration fostered the emergence of a vision of the future and a cluster-based development strategy.

From the outset, the climate of cooperation allowed a range of joint projects to emerge. These centered on promoting the development of the electronics cluster, which eventually led to the expansion of the sector's export capacity, even in the face of Chinese competition. Between 1990 and 2000, the industry moved from being a mass production model—creating goods of relatively low value added and limited technological content—to one that operated on a smaller scale but produced goods with higher value added and dearer per unit transport costs, which provided Jalisco a competitive edge over China for export to the neighboring U.S. market. This shift lessened variety but heightened the sophistication of the product portfolio.

In this collaborative context, an important initiative by the state government was the launch of a consultation campaign for the preparation of the Jalisco State Development Plan, 1995–2001. The consultation involved a large number of entrepreneurs, company managers, academics, government analysts, and public officials, as well as representatives of universities and business organizations. Participants readily agreed on the need to devise a step-by-step strategy centered on the existing capacity of foreign investment, attracting new investment, and strengthening the competitive capacity of a critical mass of operations in the most dynamic sectors of the state's economy—especially electronics and information technologies. Also of note was the authorities' willingness to cooperate with foreign firms, and those companies' constructive proactive attitude to stick with their host location.[34]

In short, the experience of Jalisco's high-tech sector reveals the results of cooperation and collaboration among an already organized business sector. Jalisco had the advantage of state authorities that supported the initial private initiative. Nonetheless, with the public and private sectors joining forces and with greater government initiative and long-term commitment in terms of strategy, support programs, and resources, this process could produce an even stronger collaboration, one that is even better placed to face future challenges.

Another case of successful public-private collaboration involved winegrowers and the provincial government in Mendoza in Argentina. Between 1990 and 2000 the Argentine wine industry underwent a productive and technological transformation that allowed it to advance from being a national supplier of popular wines to an exporter of quality wines, similar to the experience of the Chilean wineries in the 1980s and early 1990s. To induce growth and competitiveness in the industry, the Argentine Viticultural Corporation was set up with the participation of several regional and local organizations. The corporation's governing body has 17 members, 12 from the private sector and 5 from the public sector. One of its main aims was the implementation of the Viticultural Strategic Plan 2002–20.[35] Representatives of the region's viticultural associations[36] and the National Viticultural Institute (an autonomous national body promoting the technological development of the sector) helped draw up the plan. It was agreed that a constant improvement in all the links in the production chain was needed to sustain growth in external markets, and to that end forums were created in which local institutions took part (Escofet 2006). The provincial government helped organize the forums, wherein dialogue between entrepreneurs and government officials opened the way to the productive, commercial, and logistical transformation of the industry; the incorporation of new technologies; and an increase in technical capacity.

The public-private alliances in Jalisco and Mendoza were successful for several reasons. First, the private sector had sufficient connections to develop a collective awareness of the benefits of organizing to tackle some grave problems foreshadowing a crisis in the sector. Second, the public sector, while not the leader, showed commitment in supporting the needs of the private sector.[37] Finally, the construction of effective alliances, as noted earlier, and as Ross Schneider (2009) points out, depends on learning through experience.

Also notable are the regional and sectoral bodies created in Colombia as a result of the Domestic Agenda. These competitiveness commissions facilitated the coordination of priorities in regional and sectoral plans for productivity and competitiveness and helped define the main crosscutting and sectoral projects analyzed in the National Competitiveness Commission. To prepare the agenda, 10 joint technical committees were set up in strategic areas.[38] Some 60 percent of the participants in these committees were public officials, 33 percent were entrepreneurs, 1 percent were from academia and research groups, 1 percent from unions, 1 percent from NGOs, and 4 percent were foreign invitees, of whom 3 percent came from multilateral organizations. The National Competitiveness Commission coordinated the regional commissions, which were tasked with preparing guidelines and coordinating activities and policies at the regional level. These commissions consisted of representatives of the public sector (35 percent), the private sector (48 percent), academia (12 percent), labor (2 percent), and others (3 percent). The regions' governor and mayors also took part, and a technical and executive secretariat staffed by the chamber of commerce and a public authority was set up.

Public-Private Alliances in the Agencies

So far we have looked at the participation of the private sector (entrepreneurs, academics, and workers) in organizations created specifically by the state to bring about effective collaboration in preparing strategies advising the executive. Private participation, however, has also been important in other public sector bodies, such as the agencies that implement the strategies, thereby allowing public-private collaboration to materialize "on the ground."

Under the traditional model used in Latin America, the executing agencies are answerable to the central government and are direct appendages of a ministry. Normally, therefore, there is no private participation in their management, and they lack relative autonomy over decisions and budgets. Nonetheless, although they have not yet been studied extensively, channels for private sector participation seem to have opened up recently in some agencies, thereby increasing the business community's influence on the implementation of the programs.

Because of its maturity, an important example is the Foreign Trade Corporation of Costa Rica, which dates from 1996.[39] Conceived as a public-private association to promote exports, its governing board consisted of four representatives from the public sector and five from the private sector. The business sector's participation was crucial in securing information on the needs of the companies and their workers, as well as in prioritizing and defining the programs. These programs were geared to gathering market intelligence, improving export capacity, creating entrepreneurs, and providing business training and advice on internationalization. In recent years the agency has promoted a series of new partnerships centered on the development of sectors that are strategic for the country's future (Chaves and Segura 2007, 31).

In Chile, following the growing interest in having the private sector engaged with executing agencies, an important initiative was the launching of the draft law on the National Council on Innovation for Competitiveness, which contemplated changing the corporate governance of the two agencies responsible for implementing the innovation strategy. The governing boards of these organizations (one consists of a large number of ministers) should gradually be transformed to include renowned experts in each agency's field of action, under the chairmanship of the responsible minister. A proposal to give the agencies consultative committees made up of experts from the public and private sectors was also offered. These committees would provide specific knowledge for selecting, prioritizing, and monitoring projects, as well as for reviewing and designing the instruments used to support them. The committees of experts was expected to include entrepreneurs, prominent scientists, and consultants. As noted, the draft law had not been enacted at the time this book was written.

Finally, in Argentina, where governments have faced difficulties in developing a public-private alliance on a national policy level, there has recently been close collaboration at the level of executing agencies to promote exports and attract foreign investment. This collaboration has been institutionalized in the agency Export.Ar, whose main goal is to make Argentine products more competitive, and Prosper.Ar, the agency responsible for promoting investment, attracting FDI, and internationalizing SMEs. Both have forms of private sector participation (for the structure of Prosper.Ar, see figure 6.4).

Prosper.Ar's private sector Consultative Council has honorary members who have been prominent in business, academia, science, and labor. Their mission is to work together to develop and implement policies and programs to foster investment, competitiveness, and innovation. The private sector Higher Council for International Assistance comprises respected international leaders whose task is to support Argentina's international commercial positioning. The initiative is relatively new and cannot be assessed until some time has passed.

Figure 6.4 Board Structure of Prosper.Ar

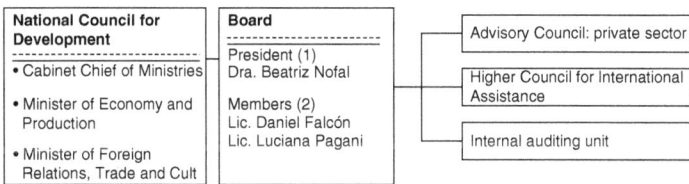

Source: Agencia Nacional de Desarrollo de Inversiones (Prosper.Ar), "Estructura organizacional," http://www.prosperar.gov.ar/home .php?page=estructura.

Annex 6A Summary of National Development Strategies

Barbados National Development Plan 2005–25

The Barbados National Development Plan (Government of Barbados 2005) has six broad targets expressed in very general terms: strengthening the national spirit; modernizing the state; building social capital; building physical infrastructure and preserving the environment; increasing the country's prosperity and competitiveness; and developing the Barbados brand internationally.

These targets involve objectives that are also somewhat vague. For example, the fifth target, "increasing the prosperity and competitiveness of Barbados," has the following objectives: to substantially increase the growth rate; to reach full employment; to ensure the strengthening of the microeconomic fundamentals; to respect food security and nutritional security; to create an entrepreneurial society; to develop an information society; to promote productivity and competitiveness; to boost exports of goods and services; to integrate Barbados into the global economy; to attain world-class excellence in services; and to fully develop the financial system and promote the private sector so that it takes economic leadership.

The indicators to be used to monitor progress are also general, such as growth of no less than 5 percent, sustained growth in market capitalization, and significant growth in savings and investment rates. For each of the six goals, there are strategic guidelines to facilitate progress toward the goals, as well as some general compliance indicators.

Brazil: Productive Development Policy (PDP)

To sustain the expansionary cycle of the period 2003–07, the Productive Development Policy (Federal Government of Brazil 2008) poses four general challenges: expand supply capacity, strengthen the balance of payments, raise innovation capacity, and strengthen SMEs.

To meet these challenges successfully, quantitative targets were established at two levels. The first level has aggregate macrotargets for 2010 that are considered feasible and that can be monitored; this level should allow the direction and scope of the PDP to be shown clearly. The macrotargets contemplate an increase in gross fixed capital formation, a rise in private spending on innovation, an increase in Brazil's share of international exports, and a higher number of exporting SMEs. The specific targets to be met in each of the PDP's programs conform to the same criteria defined by the macrotargets: feasibility and the possibility of monitoring.

The PDP's policies are arranged on three levels. First are systemic activities that go beyond the level of firms and sectors, and that affect the performance of the overall productive structure—such as tax policy, financing policy for investment and innovation, and legal security. In the second level are strategic issues of public policy purposely chosen because of their importance to the country's long-term productive development. Six areas were prioritized in this level for policies with strategic impact: the regionalization or decentralization of production; the strengthening of micro and small enterprises; increasing exports; productive integration with Latin America and the Caribbean, with an initial focus on Mercosur; integration with Africa; and environmentally sustainable production.

In the third level are structuring programs for the productive system; geared to strategic objectives, these activities take the diversity of the domestic productive structure as a reference. They include:

- Mobilizing programs in strategic areas: the industrial health complex, information and communications technologies, nuclear energy, the industrial defense complex, nanotechnology, and biotechnology.
- Programs to strengthen competitiveness in the automotive complex; capital goods; textiles and clothing; wood and furniture; personal care, perfumes, and cosmetics; civil engineering; the services complex; the naval and cabotage industry; hides, leather, and handicrafts; agroindustry; biodiesel; plastics; and others.
- Programs to consolidate and expand leadership in the aeronautical complex; oil, natural gas, and petrochemicals; bioethanol; mining; iron and steel; cellulose and paper; and meat.

Each of the favored sectors within the three programs has specific instruments to attain its goals. These can be grouped into four general spheres: incentives—tax incentives, credit, risk capital, and economic subsidies; government procurement—direct purchases by the administration and those of state firms; regulation—technical, economic, and competition-related; and technical support—certification and standards; trade promotion; intellectual property; human resource training; and business training.

Chile: National Strategy on Innovation for Competitiveness

As a central pillar of its competitiveness strategy (Consejo Nacional de Innovación para la Competitividad 2007), the Chilean government identified eight priority sectors for cluster development: aquaculture, tourism, copper mining, offshoring, food processing, fruit growing, pig raising and aviculture, and financial services. A policy was set out to underpin cluster development. It consisted of establishing public-private governing boards to coordinate each cluster; undertaking the tasks necessary to develop clusters associated with the budget recommendations for 2008; establishing criteria on selectivity and budget commitments for the instruments used to promote business innovation; using instruments that increase social capital and that also build consensus on a shared vision of the future among the actors in a cluster; building research capacity to support the development of high-potential clusters; and attracting foreign capital to the priority sectors.

Following are the primary goals outlined by the National Council on Innovation for Competitiveness for developing each cluster:

- Mining: maintain a world-leader position and develop chains among suppliers.
- Aquaculture: be a world leader in salmon production and diversify the product range.
- Tourism: make the country a leading destination for special-interest tourism in areas such as ecotourism, adventure tourism, and cruises.
- Food processing: strengthen Chile's position as a producer of processed foods with high value added.
- Fruit growing: retain global leadership in primary fruit growing.
- Offshoring: make the country a regional leader in offshoring services with high value added.
- Pig raising and aviculture: maintain high growth rates in the industry
- Financial services: increase the scope and depth of the financial sector as a domestic platform and possible regional center.

The fate of these initiatives in the new Piñera, very skeptical of government interventions in the market, remains to be seen.

Colombia: National Development Plan 2006–10

The National Development Plan 2006–10 (DNP 2007) gave priority to six objectives: democratic security; poverty reduction and fostering employment and equity; high and sustained growth; environmental and risk management that promotes sustainable development; increasing the efficiency and transparency of the state; and development of specific areas such as gender equity, youth, ethnic groups, the regional dimension, and foreign and migration policy.

The National Development Plan includes the main conclusions of the Internal Agenda for Productivity and Competitiveness. The Internal Agenda was put together by representatives of the productive sector, national and regional governments, academia, and workers. It identified the most promising productive chains in the world economy and programs and projects to foster productive transformation. The productive development strategy has two complementary substrategies: one is crosscutting and the other features high-impact sectoral programs. The first can be broken down into five lines of action: business development, innovation, and technological development; savings, investment, and financing; physical capital; human capital; and institutions for productive development.

In turn, each of these lines of action rests on different pillars. For example, the area of business development, innovation, and technological development has five pillars:

- Fostering innovation and technological development for competitiveness.
- Competitiveness associated with business productivity.
- International insertion and trade facilitation.
- Proper operation of the internal market.
- Specific productivity and competitiveness strategies for microenterprises and SMEs.

The high-impact sectoral programs consist of support for the development of products, chains, clusters, activities, or sectors that are deemed to be potential sources of employment and revenue, and that can compete successfully at the international level. The following sectors or productive chains were identified as priorities: some agroindustrial production; tourism; handicrafts; information and communications technologies and software development; transport and logistics; and professional services (starting with health care). In the traditional manufacturing sector there is a proposal to promote mid-tech chains with the potential to grow in international trade.

Costa Rica: National Development Plan 2006–10

The National Development Plan 2006–10 (Government of Costa Rica 2007) was drawn up on the basis of a program of the then current government, and thus sought to be the institutional expression of the commitments made by the president in his campaign. It follows five lines of action: social policy, productive policy, environmental policy, institutional reform, and foreign policy.

These five areas are subdivided into 16 institutional sectors that cover the structure of the government as defined by executive decrees. Some of these sectors are the social sector and the fight against poverty; the productive sector; foreign trade; infrastructure and transport; and the environment, energy, and telecommunications. Strategic actions have been developed for each of these sectors. The 135 actions were defined through a multisectoral effort in the public sector, whereby the institutions in each sector had to prioritize a set of 10 strategic activities or programs for the targets and sectoral policies of the plan.

The strategic activities are in three overall groups:

- A contract with citizens, which does not require legal reforms but does depend on the will of the government.

- The political commitment, which depends on agreements with the legislature.
- Dialogues for the "Costa Rica of the Bicentennial" initiative, which consists of activities to promote arenas for pluralist debate on the country's future.

Compliance indicators for each of these activities were devised, as were preliminary estimates of the financial requirements to carry them out, with a view to guiding the preparation of the national budget.

Mexico: National Development Plan 2007–12

The National Development Plan 2007–12 establishes a strategy centered on the search for sustainable human development. The plan was shaped largely by the project "Visión México 2030," which enabled the authorities to describe a desirable and possible Mexico, triggering an exercise in planning and forecasting that sought to broaden the country's development horizons.

The plan has five main lines of action: rule of law and security; a competitive, job-creating economy; equal opportunities; environmental sustainability; and effective democracy and a responsible foreign policy. Each of these areas entails various general objectives. Regarding "a competitive, job-creating economy," for example, there are 13 goals: tax policy for competitiveness; efficient financial system; national pensions system; fostering productivity and competitiveness; SMEs; the rural sector; tourism; comprehensive regional development; telecommunications and transport; energy, electricity, and hydrocarbons; the water sector; and construction and housing.

A specific number of strategies is to be pursued for each of the objectives. "Fostering productivity and competitiveness," for example, has six strategies:

- Devising a national competitiveness agenda involving the three branches of government, the three levels of governance, and the private sector, with a view to securing the commitment of the various political and social actors.
- Preparing agendas for competitiveness in economic sectors of high value added and high technological content, as well as in precursor sectors, and reconfiguring the traditional sectors to create better-paid jobs.
- Reforming regulations to lower the costs of opening and running a business.
- Promoting economic competition and freedom of association and fighting against monopolies.

- Furthering and facilitating scientific research, technological adaptation, and innovation to boost the productivity of the national economy.
- Taking advantage of the international context to foster the development of the Mexican economy.

Each strategy in turn has it own lines of action, which give rise to programs devised by the ministries and agencies involved.

Panama: Agreements of the National Concertation for Development (CND)

The CND (Gobierno de Panamá/Sistemas de las Naciones Unidas 2007) was based on four "tables for dialogue":

- The Well-Being and Equity Working Group centered on strengthening the social services system; increasing, focusing, evaluating, and monitoring social spending; and implementing employment and revenue-creation policies.
- The Working Group on Economic Growth and Competitiveness tackled the largest number of issues, including macroeconomic-fiscal stability, decentralization, and local development; policy on employment, labor, and minimum wages; agriculture and industry; and the financial and commercial sectors and logistical centers.
- The Education Working Group dealt with access and coverage; quality of education; education in values; and improving the quality, efficiency, effectiveness, and decentralization of the national education system.
- The Working Group on Institutional Modernization focused on citizen participation and the empowerment of the population, the judicial apparatus, accountability, access to information, modernization of the public administration, ethics, and decentralization and citizen security. Two subtables were created, one on justice, ethics, and citizen security, and the other on health.

With the change in the coalition government in 2009, there was some doubt whether the National Concertation for Development would continue as a potent force in policy making. This doubt has become a reality (Kenney and Castillo 2010; Davis 2011). The members of the new government played only a marginal role in the initiative and some officials of the administration—including the new president (a businessman)—excluded themselves. The CND made no provision for transition mechanisms that would enable the intervention of political factions that did not take part in the working groups for dialogue. The new government assumed authority to continue or interrupt the process.

Peru: National Competitiveness Plan

The National Competitiveness Plan was prepared in 2005 by the National Competitiveness Council of Peru. In 2006 priority was given to six basic strategic lines of action:

- Competitive chains. Productive chains are the main line of action because the principal efforts to increase exports of value added are made through them. Hence, the competitive chains make up the strategic area around which the others are arranged. For that reason, it was decided that the CNC's technical secretariat would initially focus on promoting productive chains, devising strategies for clusters to raise productivity, and encourage innovation in six areas: agroindustry (coffee, cacao, and chocolate, agro-export products, Andean grains); wood and furniture; fisheries and aquaculture; textiles and clothing (cotton and wool); tourism and handicrafts; and software. The cotton-textiles-fashion productive chain is currently in operation. Work is carried out in four subgroups corresponding to the bottlenecks identified in a World Bank report: supply of high-quality cotton at competitive prices; market diversification, marketing-trade intelligence, and trade facilitation; improvements in the chain's technological profile and industrial productivity (including upgrading skills and the capacities of professionals and workers); and social and environmental responsibility, labor policies, and the development of internationally competitive practices.
- "Perú Innova." This line of action promotes research, science, technology, and innovation to raise productivity and increase exports of higher value added. The projects include creation of the Science, Technology and Innovation Program Fund, which is financed by the Inter-American Development Bank; the institutionalization of the network of Centers for Technological Innovation; and strengthening of the Integrated Quality System.
- "Perú Emprende." The goal here is to identify and reward those business initiatives that involve new investment and a new supply of products and services. The program also targets initiatives related to the creation of partnerships and agreements that allow new firms to be established. Progress has been made on preparing a national public-private program to promote business capacity and the creation of new firms, as well as workshops on policies to foster entrepreneurship and new businesses.

- "Intermesa." This action line focuses on simplifying red tape to facilitate procedures to export and set up new companies. Projects that have already begun include Exporta Fácil, the Single Foreign Trade Window, and a Law of Administrative Silence.
- Regional competitiveness. Thus far there have been assessments of the potential to implement comprehensive regional competitiveness programs. The programs cover physical infrastructure, education, productive development, workplace training, administrative management, and institutional strengthening. A lack of financing has interrupted the process.
- Monitoring competitiveness. This program has allowed for the preparation of statistics to calculate competitiveness indexes. So far, progress has been made on building regional competitiveness indexes.

Notes

1. Depending on the characteristics of the product, the exploitation and export of natural resources generated (albeit limited) forward and backward links in the local economy. Domestic manufactures also developed due to transport costs and a high level of tariff protection.

2. Ocampo (2006) points out that the high tariffs of the 19th century were motivated by a desire for tax revenue and not by an explicit industrialization policy.

3. Many fashionable theories of development in the period encouraged state coordination of investment. For example, see Nurske (1953) and Rosenstein-Rodan (1943).

4. Technological capacity was created in the late 1940s with the establishment of the Brazilian Society for Scientific Progress and the National Research Council. The Aeronautical Technological Institute spawned what today is Embraer, which has been highly successful in aircraft sales. EMBRAPA, set up in the 1970s, helped with technologies that gave rise to the large agrobusiness firms of today. The renowned ethanol program was launched in this period. With PND II, Petrobras began to develop the technology that has made it a leader in offshore oil exploration (Schwartzman 2001; Martínez-Diaz and Brainard 2009).

5. As noted in the introduction, the cutoff date of the analysis of country data generally is 2007–08 with only selective updates.

6. We have been told that the strategies were prepared as programs instead of a formal, comprehensive national plan to avoid having to address political sensitivities about the word "planning," which is associated with the military dictatorship. For more detail, see the annex.

7. The policies of the PAC are grouped into five areas, notably investment in transport, energy, sanitation, housing, and water resources. The PACTI includes the expansion and consolidation of the national innovation system, implementation of technological innovation in firms, research and development in strategic areas, and science and technology for social development. This plan is linked to the PDP, as is the National Education Development Plan.

8. Meléndez and Perry (2009) and Gómez Restrepo et al. (2008) provide a summary of these policies.

9. The domestic agenda effort was motivated largely by the expectations of a free trade agreement with the United States.

10. National Planning Department, Colombia (2005), *Visión Colombia 2019 Segundo Centenario*, http://www.dnp.gov.co/PortalWeb/Pol%C3%ADticasdeEstado/Visi%C3%B3nColombia2019/tabid/92/Default.aspx.

11. Arias (2007, 2).

12. An example is the decision to upgrade the quality of FDI activities to take account of the country's higher wage level relative to its neighbors and Asia.

13. Government of Costa Rica (2007, 28).

14. For an analysis of this process, see Moguillansky (1999).

15. The system included an excessive number of support instruments, more than 130 specific and permanent funds or programs with burdensome protocols that made it hard to meet deadlines, and a multiplicity of government actors with little coordination among themselves.

16. For an analysis of these policies, see Agosin, Larrain, and Grau (2009).

17. That is, diversifying away from sugar cane, the traditional export product.

18. See the Presidency of the Government of Mexico (2007a and 2007b, respectively) for the texts of the development plan and the vision.

19. These are tax policy for competitiveness; an efficient financial system; a national pension system; promotion of employment and improved labor relations; promotion of productivity and competitiveness; comprehensive regional development; and promotion of small and medium enterprises, the rural sector, tourism, telecommunications and transport, energy, electricity and hydrocarbons; the water sector; and construction and housing.

20. The prospect of extending the plan beyond the incumbent government depends on the attainment of a degree of public consensus.

21. Barbados's plan is similarly vague.

22. As mentioned in an earlier chapter, in the successful cases, crisis has sometimes been a catalyst for formation of a public-private alliance.

23. The representatives of business and labor were elected by their own organizations.

24. The protocols are guiding principles to reach agreement between the members of the partnership; they do not become laws, although sometimes they lay the groundwork for future legislation. Five protocols have been signed since 1993 on economic stabilization and collective bargaining (1993–95); forming partnerships on wage restraint and productivity (1995–97); building a sustainable social and economic partnership (1998–2000); creating a modern economy with social inclusion (2001–04); and stressing the importance of a CARICOM common market (2005–07). The fifth protocol, which extended the previous protocols, was itself extended for two additional years, probably because of a certain stasis in the partnership.

25. To prepare the Barbados National Strategic Plan (2005–25), the government extensively consulted with the members of the partnership. Indeed, one of the issues in the plan is strengthening the partnership and giving it legal institutional expression in the constitution.

26. Continuity was also facilitated by the 14-year tenure in office of the Barbados Labor Party (1994–2008). The role of the partnership under the new government remains to be seen.

27. *National Competitiveness Report 2008–2009*, http://www.compite.ws/spccompite/content/page.aspx?ID=34.

28. The political party of the current Martinelli administration refused to participate as it did not want the appearance of supporting the Torrejos government (Kenney and Castillo 2010).

29. Future Ministerial Innovation Commission in accordance with the project, composed of the ministers of the Economy, Education, and the Treasury.

30. Interview with Hugo Arias, communications director, National Innovation Council for Competitiveness.

31. Interview with Paulo Teixeira, Department of Competitiveness and Technology, Federation of Industries of São Paulo State.

32. Interview with Lucía María Maldonado, executive vice president of Brazil's Foreign Trade Association.

33. Interview with Paulo Mol, manager of Industrial Studies and Policies, National Confederation of Industry, Brazil.

34. It was probably helpful that the managers of the branches of the foreign firms were themselves Mexican.

35. Law 25.849 and Regulatory Decree 1191/2004.

36. These were the Argentine Viticultural Union, Association of Viticultural Cooperatives of Mendoza, Bodegas de Argentina, Mendoza Winegrowers Association, and Winegrowers and Wine Producers Center of East Mendoza.

37. According to Ross Schneider (2009), the governor of Mendoza had presidential ambitions, and thought he would benefit from having supported the development of an innovative and competitive industry in his province.

38. Sustainability (millennium development goals), biofuels, biodiversity, transport logistics and infrastructure, sanitary and phytosanitary measures, air transport, construction, tourism, jewelry, and offsets (technology transfer based on defense contracts).

39. Created from the merger of the Corporación de las Zonas Francas de Exportación S.A., the Centro para la Promoción de las Exportaciones, and the Consejo Nacional de Inversiones with a view to intensifying and diversifying exports.

References

Agosin, Manuel, Christian Larraín, and Nicolás Grau. 2009. "Industrial Policy in Chile." Working Paper 294, University of Chile, Economics Department, Santiago.

Arias, Oscar. 2007. "No hay Desarrollo Sin Planificación." http://www.nación.com/ln_ee/2007/enero/25/opinion972615.html (January 27).

Artana, D., S. Auguste, and A. Downes. 2008. "Industrial Policies in Barbados." IDB Country Studies Initiative on Industrial Policies in LAC, Inter-American Development Bank, Washington, DC.

Castro, A. 1994. "Renegade Development: Rise and Demise of State-Led Development in Brazil." *Democracy, Markets and Structural Reform in Latin America: Argentina, Bolivia, Brasil, Chile and Mexico*, ed. W. C. Smith, C. H. Acuña, and E. A. Gamarra. New Jersey: Transaction Publishers.

CDES (Consejo de Desarrollo Económico y Social, Brazil). 2007. *Agenda Nacional de Desenvolvimento*. Brasilia: Presidency of the Republic (December).

CEPAL-ILPES (Economic Commission for Latin America and the Caribbean—Latin American and Caribbean Institute for Socio-Economic Planning). 1978. "Brasil II: planificación, desarrollo y política económica y social." Paper presented to the second conference of ministers and directors of planning of Latin America and the Caribbean, Lima, November 15–18.

———. 1982. "El estado actual de la planificación en América Latina y el Caribe." Cuadernos del ILPES 28 (E/CEPAL/ILPES/G.15). Santiago, Chile.

Chaves Arce, H., and J. Segura Garita. 2007. "Alianzas público-privadas, estrategias para el desarrollo exportador y la innovación. Caso de Costa Rica: la industria electrónica y de software en el Valle Central." Economic Commission for Latin America and the Caribbean, International Trade and Integration Division, Santiago, Chile.

Consejo Nacional de Innovación para la Competitividad, Chile. 2007. "Hacia una estrategia de innovación para la competitividad." http://www.consejodeinnovacion.cl/cnic/cnic/web/portada.php.

Davis, Amber. 2011. "A Critical Analysis of Panama's National Development Plan La Concertación Nacional para el Desarrollo." Johns Hopkins School of Advanced International Studies, Washington DC (May).

DNP (Departamento Nacional de Planeación de Colombia). 2009. "Sistema nacional de evaluación de resultados de la gestión pública." http://www.dnp.gov.co/PortalWeb/Programas/Sinergia/tabid/81/Default.aspx.

ECLAC (Economic Commission for Latin America and the Caribbean). 2001. *An Analysis of Economic and Social Development in Barbados: A Model for Small Island Developing States.* LC/CAR/G.652. Port of Spain, Trinidad and Tobago.

———. 2005. *Strategies of Industrialization by Invitation in the Caribbean.* LC/CAR/L.68. Port of Spain, Trinidad and Tobago.

Escofet, Horacio. 2006. "Competitividad, gobierno y organizaciones locales." *Serie Estudios económicos y sectoriales.* RE306-011. Inter-American Development Bank, Washington, DC.

Evans, Peter. 1995. *Embedded Autonomy. States and Industrial Transformation.* Princeton, NJ: Princeton University Press.

Federal Government of Brazil. 2008. "Política de desenvolvimento produtivo: innovar e investir para sustentar o crescimiento." Brasilian Agency for Industrial Development/National Bank of Economic Development (BNDES)/Ministry of Finance/Ministry of Developement, Industry and International Trade. Brasilia.

Forero Pineda, Clemente. 2000. "El sistema nacional de planeación participativa de Colombia 1994–2000." High-level seminar about basic functions of planning: Survey of successful experiences. Seminars and Conferences Series 8 (LC/ l.1544-P), Economic Commission for Latin America and the Caribbean, Santiago, Chile.

García D'Acuña, Eduardo. 1982. "Pasado y futuro de la planificación en América Latina." *Pensamiento iberoamericano* 2 (July-December).

Gómez Restrepo, H. J., A. Botiva León, and A. Guerra Forero. 2008. "Institucionalidad y estrategias para el desarrollo exportador y la innovación en Colombia: un diagnóstico inicial." Project Document 294, Economic Commission for Latin America and the Caribbean, International Trade and Integration Division, Santiago Chile (March).

Government of Barbados. 2005. "The National Strategic Plan of Barbados, 2005–2025." Ministry of Finance and Economic Affairs, St. Michael (June).

Government of Costa Rica. 2007. "Plan Nacional de Desarrollo Jorge Manuel Dengo Obregón, 2006–2010." Ministry of National Planification and Economic Policy, San Jose.

Kenney, Edward, and Andre Castillo. 2010. "Growing through the Canal." Johns Hopkins School of Advanced International Studies, Washington, DC (May).

Lira, Luis. 2006. "Revalorización de la planificación del desarrollo." Public Management Series 59 (LC/L.2568-P), Economic Commission for Latin America and the Caribbean, Santiago, Chile.

Martínez-Díaz, Leonardo, and Lael Brainard, eds. 2009. *Brazil as an Economic Superpower? Understanding Brazil's Changing Role in the Global Economy with Global Economy and Development.* Washington, DC: Brookings Institution.

Medina Gómez, Francisco. 2006. "Impacto del PROSOFT en Jalisco: el milagro mexicano en Guadalajara." Paper presented at conference sponsored by

Cámara Nacional de la Industria Electrónica, de Telecomunicaciones y Tecnologías de la Información (CANIETI), Puerto Vallarta, July 29.

Meléndez, M., and G. Perry. 2009. "Industrial Policies in Colombia." Inter-American Development Bank, Washington, DC.

Melo, Alberto, and Andrés Rodriguez-Clare. 2006. "Productive Policies and Supporting Institutions in Latin American and the Caribbean." Research Department Working Paper 1005, Inter-American Development Bank, Washington, DC.

Muñoz, Oscar. 2000. *El Estado y el sector privado*, Latin American Social Science Faculty (FLACSO). Santiago. Chile.

Nurske, Ragnar. 1953. Problems of Capital Formation in Underdeveloped Countries. Oxford, U.K.: Basil Blackwell.

Ocampo, José Antonio. 2006. "Latin America and the World Economy in the Long Twentieth Century." In *The Long Twentieth Century, The Great Divergence: Hegemony, Uneven Development and Global Inequality*, ed. K. S. Jomo. New Delhi: Oxford University Press.

OECD (Organisation for Economic Co-operation and Development). 2009. "Chile's National Innovation Council for Competitiveness. Interim Assesment and Outlook." Paris.

Palacios, Juan José. 2008. "Alianzas público-privadas y escalamiento industrial. El caso del complejo de alta tecnología de Jalisco." Studies and Perspectives Series 98, Economic Commission for Latin America and the Caribbean, Santiago, Chile (May).

Peres, Wilson, coord. 1997. *Políticas de competitividad industrial en América Latina y el Caribe en los años noventa*. México, DF: Siglo XXI Editors.

Peres, Wilson, and Annalisa Primi. 2009. "Theory and Practice of Industrial Policy: Evidence from the Latin American Experience." Productive Development Series 187 (LC/L.3013-P), Economic Commission for Latin America and the Caribbean, Santiago, Chile (February).

Presidency of the Repúblic de México. 2007a. "Plan Nacional de Desarrollo, 2007–2012." http://pnd.presidencia.gob.mx/.

———. 2007b. "Visión 2030: El México que queremos." http://www.vision2030.gob.mx/.

Rosenstein-Rodan, P. 1943. "Problems of Industrialization of Eastern and South-Eastern Europe." *Economic Journal* 53, no. 210/211 (June).

Ross Schneider, Ben. 2009. "Business-Government Interaction in Policy Councils in Latin America: Cheap Talk, Expensive Exchanges, or Collaborative Learning?" Department of Political Science, Massachusetts Institute of Technology, Cambridge, MA (March).

Rufián, Dolores. 1993. "El régimen jurídico de la planificación en América Latina." Cuadernos del ILPES 37 (LC/IP/G.64-P), Latin American and Caribbean Institute of Economic and Social Planning (ILPES), Santiago, Chile (June).

Springer, Basil. 2010. "Barbados: Private-Public Sector Partnerships." Project Document 285, Economic Commission for Latin America and the Caribbean, International Trade and Integration Division, Santiago, Chile (March).

Suzigan, W., and J. Furtado. 2006. "Politica industrial e desenvolvimento." *Revista de economia política* 26, no. 2 (April-June).

Thorp, Rosemary. 1998. Progress, Poverty and Exclusion: An Economic History of Latin America in the Twentieth Century. Washington, DC: Inter-American Development Bank.

OPERATIONAL PRINCIPLES RELEVANT FOR LATIN AMERICA?

 OPERATIONAL PRINCIPLES RELEVANT FOR LATIN AMERICA?

Zebral, Silverio. 2011. "Alianzas Publico-Privadas Efectivas para el Desarrollo: los Casos del CDES y del CNDI en el Capitalismo de Enlace Brasileño." Presentation to the seminar "Public-Private Alliances for a New Vision of Development," Government of El Salvador, Organization of American States, Economic Commission for Latin America and the Caribbean, San Salvador, January 10.

7

Implementing a Strategic Vision

We have seen that a central feature of modern industrial policy is the development of intelligent medium- to long-term strategies through construction of public-private alliances that can maximize capture of relevant information and build consensus on the future direction of the national economy and the nature of public interventions. A government can have a great strategy backed by public consensus, but all is for naught if the public sector lacks the political commitment and technical capacity to implement the strategy. This chapter focuses on aspects of Latin America's compliance with the operational principles related to implementation.

The Search for Political and Technical Leadership

High-level leadership at the political and technical levels has been crucial to the success of the development strategy in our 10 extraregional success cases, as well as of the public-private alliance that should underpin it. This same principle, which is so important in effective policy implementation, is not always taken into account in Latin America. Indeed, our study of nine countries in the region finds leadership in convening the economic and social actors to support development of strategies but an occasional lack of presidential commitment to implementing those strategies. In some cases the strategy has been used only as a partisan political platform. In 2007, for example, Oscar Arias, then the president of Costa Rica, acknowledged that politics was traditionally the driving force behind economic strategies in his country, and, as noted in the previous chapter, he promised that his government would follow through on implementing the strategy.[1]

As shown in part one, the higher the public institution responsible for overseeing the strategy and the agencies that implement it are in the political and bureaucratic hierarchy of the central government, the greater is

Table 7.1 Ministries and Agencies in Strategic Areas of Export Development

Country	Lead ministry or organization	Executing agencies
Argentina		
Export promotion	Secretariat of Industry, Trade and Small and Medium Enterprises (SMEs)	Under-Secretariat of Trade Policy and Management ExpoAr Foundation
Innovation promotion	Ministry of Science and Technology	National Agency for Scientific and Technological Development, INTA, INTI others
Promotion of foreign direct investment (FDI)	Under-Secretariat of Industry Secretariat of Agriculture Livestock, Fisheries and Food, Secretariat of Mines	Prosper.Ar
Barbados		
Tourism promotion	Ministry of Tourism and International Transport	Barbados Tourism Authority Barbados Tourism Investment Inc.
FDI promotion	Ministry of Economic Affairs and Development	Invest Barbados
SME promotion	Barbados Agency for Microenterprise Development	Fund Access
Innovation	Ministry of Trade, Industry and Commerce	National Council for Science and Technology
Brazil		
Export promotion	Ministry of Development, Industry and Foreign Trade	Development Bank of Brazil (BNDES), Bank of Brazil, regional banks, financial agents of BNDES, and the Brazilian Credit and Export Insurance Company APEX-Brazil-SEBRAE

Innovation promotion	Ministry of Science and Technology	National Research Council Embrapa, CAPEZ FIOCRUZ, FNDCT/FINEP, FAPESP (São Paulo)
Industrial promotion	Ministry of Development, Industry and Foreign Trade	Brazilian Agency for Industrial Development, BNDES, SEBRAE, FINEP, APEX, CAMEX, and others.
Chile		
Export promotion	Foreign Ministry Economy Ministry Agriculture Ministry	ProChile CORFO SAG
Innovation promotion	National Innovation Council for Competitiveness	INNOVA Chile Fundación Chile, CONYCIT
Colombia		
Export and FDI promotion	Ministry of Trade, Industry and Tourism National Planning Department	PROEXPORT Bancoldex, Fidulcodex Other regional agencies
Competitiveness promotion	National Planning Department National Competitiveness Administrative System	National Competitiveness Commission Regional competitiveness commissions
Innovation promotion	National Planning Department Ministry of Trade, Industry and Tourism	Colciencias Colombian fund for the modernization and technological development of micro, small, and medium enterprises

(*continued*)

Table 7.1 Ministries and Agencies in Strategic Areas of Export Development (*continued*)

Country	Lead ministry or organization	Executing agencies
Costa Rica		
FDI attraction	Private sector	CINDE (promotion of local investment and FDI)
	Ministry of Foreign Affairs and Worship	Costa Rica Provee
		ITCR
		PROCOMER
Export promotion	Nonstate public body	PROCOMER
Mexico		
Export and FDI promotion	Economy Secretariat	PROMEXICO
		All the programs implemented by various agencies concentrated in one organization
Industrial development promotion	Intersecretarial Commission on Industrial Policy	Nafinsa, Bancomext
		Under-Secretariat of SMEs
	Economy Secretariat	Secretariat of Labor and Social Security, and business associations
Innovation promotion	General Council on Scientific Research and Technological Development	CONACYT

Peru		
Competitiveness promotion	Presidency of the Council of Ministers	National Competitiveness Council; PeruCompite
Export promotion	Ministry of Foreign Trade and Tourism	Commission for the Promotion of Peru for Exports and Tourism (PROMPERU)
Innovation promotion	Ministry of Education	CONCYTEC Fund for Innovation, Science and Technology (FINCYT), PERUCOMPITE

Source: Authors, based on official information.

its power to coordinate and effectively manage the strategy. Shortcomings in applying this principle have been one of the problems in promoting science, technology, and innovation in Latin America, where initially the executing agencies were overseen by councils and commissions that had little funding and no real authority in the government hierarchy. These circumstances have been changing, however, and among the countries examined here, innovation is now becoming a field for a ministry of its own, improving the governance profile.

The other point to consider is the relationship between the public organizations overseeing the productive activities of the economy and the ministry of finance. In Latin America finance ministries have often assumed de facto lead on microeconomic policy as well as their traditional one in macroeconomic policy. Indeed, backed by power and technical competence finance ministries gained in the era of the Washington Consensus, sometimes this leadership, or attempt at it, was the result of a "raid" on the portfolio of another weaker ministry charged with productive activities outside the financial sector.[2] This situation is unfortunate. As noted in part one, the decision-making criteria and leadership of finance ministries are culturally oriented around issues such as stabilization plans, control of inflation and fiscal balance, financial services and the like; the microeconomic requirements of industrial policies and associated public interventions are not typically within their equalize disposition or competence. In the extraregional countries, the finance ministry typically takes part in the committee or council that draws up the development strategy and establishes the budgetary framework, but it usually does not technically lead policies in the real sector. The pertinent ministers in nonfinancial productive sectors have the decisive voice in a context of fiscal oversight by the finance ministry. The solution then is not to transfer industrial policies to the ministry of finance but rather to build up, with the urgency it merits, the institutional capacity of line ministries supporting productive transformation.

At the same time, in Latin America it is apparent that the more marginalized the territory or region in which the development agency operates, the greater the difficulty in finding motivated and capable private sector leaders to consolidate public-private collaboration and to ensure successful implementation of programs. One example is the difficulty the Chilean government has faced in creating and operating Regional Agencies for Economic Development. Promoted by President Bachelet,[3] these regional organizations sought the participation of social and economic actors in efforts to distribute more of the benefits of the country's growth to the regions. Several factors aggravated the challenge: many entrepreneurs did not have much association with each other (formal or informal) and were geographically dispersed, and many actors had only modest capacities. Some of the regional counterparts of Colombia's National Competitiveness Commission exhibit the same collaborative limitations.

Formulas to Support Leadership

There are several formulas to support the leadership of the ministries and agencies responsible for leading the strategy. One is to appoint publicly respected figures who generate respect and confidence to lead the institution. Unfortunately, in Latin America, the tendency of governments to grant insufficient attention to medium- and long-term strategies has meant that this area of government activity has not attracted the most distinguished leadership.

Just as political leadership is needed, so too is high-level technical leadership. We saw this in the case of Ireland's Forfás agency, the think tank of the Ministry of Industry, Trade and Employment that coordinates the agencies that carry out the export development strategy. The same role is played by the Economic Development Board in Singapore, and was undertaken by Finland's former Science and Technology Policy Council. Latin America generally lacks organizations of such technical leadership.

Another constraint on ministerial and agency leadership in Latin America has been the limited ability of governments to promote a professional civil service that would allow countries to develop ever more trained permanent public sector personnel at every level and to build up the institutional memory that is needed for effective strategies and deployment of industrial policies.[4] A first hurdle in this regard is the prevalence of staff without contractual arrangements consistent with development of a career of public service. In some countries the staff work under a system of "honoraria," or special location and services contracts that create a "parallel public service" vulnerable to changes in government (Echebarría 2006). As Baruj, Kosacoff, and Ramos (2009) observe in reference to Argentina, these ad hoc personnel systems have several implications. First they lend themselves to a high degree of politicization, with attendant effects on the professionalism of the staff, and this leads to a lack of knowledge and memory arising from experience because of high turnover; Argentina is not the only country to suffer from such structural weakness.[5] Moreover, the high turnover caused by changes in government is not confined to senior positions occupied by people who have the head of state's trust but extends to secretaries and under-secretaries, department heads, and even chiefs of unit and contract consultants. A result is that the new officials, lacking institutional memory, are not committed to continuing or strengthening even the successful or potentially successful programs implemented by the outgoing government; hence those initiatives often cease to be carried out and new ones are put in their place just because the status quo is associated with a previous government. This endemic "refounding syndrome" created by the political cycle plagues many of the countries in the region (Machinea 2005).

These personnel difficulties not only affect the effectiveness of policy implementation but also lead to instability in public institutions, weakening their authority. Lack of stable institutional links inhibits continuous interaction within the government and with private clients As the study of Argentina noted, in many cases these links stem from personal relationships among the individuals who are circumstantially leading each institution; they are not ground in an institutional foundation that permits continuity over time. Technical and professional links are also lacking because many agencies have only small technical teams with limited capacity to network. Moreover, lack of a long-term vision on the part of the state means there often are no operational medium-term actions plans in the policy sphere, like a business plan in the management of a company, that would foster continuity. This failing is particularly notable because it means that policies are subject to short-term and crisis-related reactions that ignore the medium-term needs of firms.

Finally, the low salaries of public officials relative to wages in the private sector is another factor that militates against the agencies' professionalism, productivity, leadership, and capacity to delegate tasks. Little information about salaries is available, but a study of the pay of senior officials in Latin America and the Caribbean, compared with senior executives in the private sector, shows significant differentials—private salaries are more than 50 percent higher on average in most of the countries studied (Argentina, Brazil, Chile, Colombia, Costa Rica, and Mexico); Chile had the biggest differential at 70 percent (Marconi, Carrillo, and Cavalieri 2003). Clearly, salaries that are not even minimally attractive impede the recruitment of talented and corruption-free personnel to the public sector. Closing or narrowing the public-private wage gap, as most of the successful extraregional countries have done, as well as creating professional public career paths that generate pride and prestige in the workforce, could foster recruitment and retention of talent and improved performance in Latin America's public sector, a key player in the deployment of industrial policies.

The study also notes the lack of effective assessment mechanisms for salaries and performance. And the salary structure is confused, lessening transparency and contributing to the breakdown of the wage hierarchy. One of the problems identified in the study is how often and how intensely the authorities resort to the aforementioned parallel indirect payment mechanisms that are not conducive to transparency in wages policy and that often have been a source of political controversy that has tarnished the image of public service.

These findings are confirmed by another study on wage differentials between workers in the public and private sectors in Chile.[6] National household surveys from 1990 and 2000 carried out by the Ministry of Planning and Cooperation (Mideplan) provide data that facilitate a comparison of public and private sector workers by gender and with similar human capital characteristics—that is, similar levels of education and experience, among other things. A notable finding is that the average salaries for public officials were well below those of private officials at both the start and end of the 1990s; the biggest gap was for workers in the municipalities. Although public sector wages have been improving in recent years, those of the senior executives have remained fairly static. As Waisbluth (2006) noted, in some cases senior private sector executives were paid between 200 percent and 500 percent more than senior public sector officials. The example he gave is telling: including the senior management allowance, the director of a public hospital earned four to five times less than the director of any private clinic. And the hospital director must work exclusively at the hospital, a demand that is not made in the private sector. Clearly all these situations make participation in public service less attractive to the "best and brightest," who are a necessary ingredient for a competent civil service capable of leading industrial policies in support of economic catch-up.

In sum, it is important to remember that the state is a major player in society and the quality of its interventions is only as good as the people involved. In this context, and in the important role of private-public alliances in policy formation, the deficient professionalization of public service in much of Latin America could be considered the Achilles' heel of public policy, especially policy supporting productive transformation. Indeed, as observed in an earlier chapter, no country has managed to converge in income with rich countries without a technically competent and highly motivated professional public civil service. Hence the professional career structures usually found in central banks and ministries of foreign affairs and finance of Latin America must be extended to those ministries and agencies that more directly oversee promotion of productive transformation.

Forecasting Exercises: A Tool to Support Leadership

Instilling a culture of medium- to long-term strategic thinking in government is important, and so-called future studies have contributed to this objective in many countries. These studies help governments foster joint undertakings between the public and private sectors and to promote a long-lasting alliance around the search for strategic definitions. This tool, which convenes many actors to deliver and analyze information, allows countries to remain alert to changing competitive conditions and opportunities to enhance social well-being and to prepare for them. To that end scenarios are devised and discussed with the different actors, and long-term conclusions are fed into policy making and strategic positioning.

The experiences of the European and Asian countries that engage in such exercises shows that they can be very useful in building capacity to look at and assess the possibilities of the future, but they are also helpful in establishing a common view among various actors with opposing interests. In Latin America multilateral organizations such as ECLAC's Latin American and Caribbean Institute for Economic and Social Planning and UNESCO, have promoted various Latin American meetings on training and prospective exercises.

Only a few countries of the region have regularly used this tool to strengthen the design of their long-term strategies. Brazil made some attempts with the project Brazil 2020, a national-level program that unfolded under the first Cardoso government (1994–98) (Popper and Medina 2008). Mexico also used the tool to help prepare parts of "Visión México 2030" under President Calderón. However, according to Popper and Medina (2008), in most cases these exercises have been sporadic, the results have not been assessed, and they have not necessarily been translated into policy decisions, because the countries of the region lack the capacity to adapt them creatively to the local context. The growing political awareness of the importance of strategies, as well as efforts to engage the future, suggests the need for a more proactive approach for prospective exercises in the region.

Leadership Also Depends on Available Financial Resources

The strategies and plans of Barbados, Brazil, Colombia, and Panama have financing for implementation; this funding obviously is extremely important for the effective execution of programs and policies. In Brazil the participation of the Ministry of Finance in the Executive Secretariat of the Productive Development Policy was a highly significant step in the government's commitment to the program, as well as in creating a long-term and shared buy-in on the part of the ministry officials. In contrast to some of the past action plans, Brazil's Action Plan on Science, Technology and Innovation had a committed budget for implementation during its four-year life.

Colombia is an interesting case, because its National Development Plan serves as the basis of budgeting.[7] The government is thus able to implement policies in line with the strategy. However, as noted earlier, at the end of 2009 resources had not yet been allocated to the promotion of the new sectoral activities targeted in the national competitiveness strategy.

In Costa Rica the Arias government made a substantial effort to ensure that the institutions quantify their financial requirements for activities and for meeting the proposed targets. The exercise provided an overall budgetary framework for the National Development Plan 2006–10, in contrast to the complete absence of budgetary allocations in previous plans. By law, Panama has committed financing equivalent to 35 percent of its canal revenue for the period 2004–14 for projects to fulfill the plans agreed to in the National Concertation for Development.

In general terms, and apart from the often weak fiscal base of the governments in the region, efforts to finance implementation of strategic policies and programs in Latin American countries face a three-fold problem. First, agency program budgets tend to cover current operating costs, leaving inadequate resources for program implementation. Second, programs may have a significant budgetary allocation for incentives, but the necessary drawdown of disbursements to carry forward implementation is subject to the uncertainties of discretionary political and budgetary allocations.[8] Third, the execution of a program and its results might receive little publicity, leaving components of the business community and civil society unaware of the program and thus unable to appraise its usefulness to their needs. (This matter is related to transparency, an issue examined in a later section.)

Chile's CORFO, an agency that has been emulated in other Latin American countries, is an example of an agency that spread too few resources over too many programs. A study by Agosin, Larrain, and Grau (2009, 13) found that this dispersion left little chance of achieving a critical mass of support for success. A similar situation prevailed in the same agency's Management Office of Financial Intermediation, preventing the agency from acting as an effective development bank. The portfolio of CORFO's Office of Investment and Development represented about 1 percent of the entire Chilean financial system in 2006, far less than similar agencies such as Nafin in Mexico (9.7 percent) and Bancoldex in Colombia (3.5 percent). Hence Agosin and his colleagues recommended concentrating the available resources on the more promising programs. In addition to the shortage of financing, there is the problem of the funding being tied to the vagaries of the budget cycle. In an environment of uncertainty about the political commitment to a medium- to long-term strategy, additional uncertainty about the budget can limit the credibility of management. For priority programs there is a need to move toward a commitment to multiyear budgets, at least in an indicative way, to extend the horizon of programs and policies to the medium and long term. Panama's financial scheme and Chile's special funding of innovation are moves in this direction.

On the Need for Coordination

Coordinating, as well as facilitating, the proper implementation of public policies, is, to a large degree, a political function inasmuch as it should be undertaken with strategic awareness and established priorities (Martín 2005). Coordination also may be one of the biggest challenges for effective pubic management of industrial policies. The presence of a lead agency that specializes by thematic area is the exception in the region, as table 7.2 indicates. Typically, several agencies coexist, often with overlapping mandates, and they often operate horizontally, leading to serious problems with coordination of policies and instruments The problems worsen if there is no explicit strategy to serve as a framework for action on the part of the ministries and agencies.

The often dysfunctional nature of relations between the agencies stems partly from the traditional way in which the institutional structure was set up. For example, Brazil's science and technology organizations date from the early 20th century. The country's innovation system was consolidated between the 1950s and the 1970s, when the state had a marked influence on the economy; in the 1990s a more competitive, open-market model was superimposed on the old structure. This asynchrony in the organizational structure has persisted to this day. As Pacheco and Corder (2009) point out, the upshot was the overlapping of legal norms and instruments, which hampered joint and coordinated action by the government.

The Lula government made a serious effort to coordinate the Productive Development Policy (PDP). Overall responsibility for coordination falls to the Ministry of Development, Industry and Commerce (MDIC), which links the PDP programs with the other ministries involved in the plan and with the Casa Civil, a part of the presidency. The Casa Civil is charged with coordinating the other medium- and long-term action plans that make up the government's development strategy. The administrative coordination within the PDP falls to the Executive Secretariat, whose activities are over-seen by two agencies and a ministry: the Brazilian Industrial Development Agency (ABDI), the National Bank for Economic and Social Development (BNDES), and the Finance Ministry. The Secretariat and the MDIC spear-headed a significant effort to coordinate a complex series of thematic and sectoral programs that are to be implemented at the national and state levels. The National Industrial Development Council (CNDI), the highest arena for dialogue and debate between the public and private sectors, was to oversee these organizations, but its participation has been weak.

The lower rectangles in figure 7.1 indicate five types of activity, each with a significant number of programs, coordinated by various agencies. Unlike in the past, the activities of the Ministry of Science, Technology and Innovation were closely related to firms. Thus there was a real effort to link the ministry's own action plan with the objectives of the PDP.

As mentioned in the previous chapter, the state's great challenge regard-ing the PDP is the capacity of the leading agencies (after almost two decades of the atrophying effects of the Washington Consensus) to play an effective role and the ability of these agencies, including BNDES, to bring about true dialogue among the agencies, coordinate their different pro-grams, and encourage them to act in consultation with the private sector in implementing a medium- and long-term agenda. All this is a relatively novel approach in Brazil, and the results remain to be seen.

In 2006 the Colombian government created the National Competitive-ness System to enhance the coordination of its policies for raising productiv-ity and competitiveness. Decree 2828 establishes this system, which incor-porates representatives of the public sector, business, and other actors in civil society that affect the country's competitiveness. The system produces rules that govern the interactions among the actors, and thus it coordinates activities related to the formulation, implementation, and monitoring of the policies needed to strengthen Colombia's competitive position.

The National Competitiveness Commission, which oversees this sys-tem, convokes meetings of the different representatives in the system, advises the government on policy, assigns responsibilities and encour-ages articulation among actors in charge of implementation of agreed

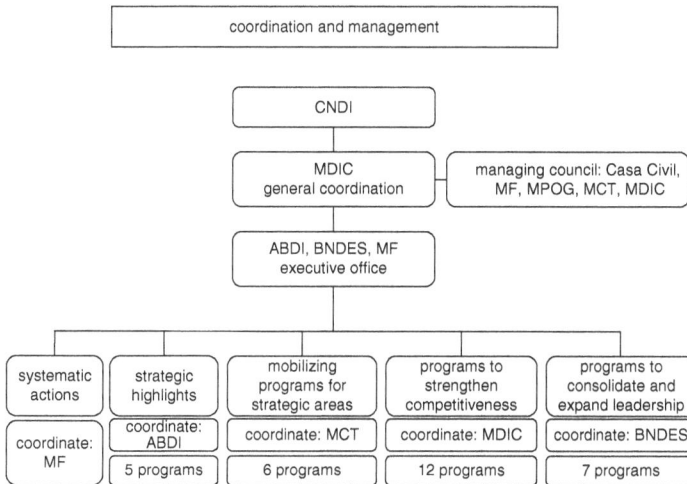

Figure 7.1 Coordination of Brazil's Productive Development Policy

Source: Government of Brazil, Productive Development Policy.
Notes: MF = Ministry of Finance, MPOG = Ministry of Planning
MCT = Ministry of Science and Technology.

actions, develops indicators for monitoring and evaluating the initiative's progress, and undertakes outreach with civil society (figure 7.2). At the same time the commission promotes creation of sister commissions in the regions with which it works to identify local counterpart issues regarding competitiveness.

To support this mission, the commission in 2007 created a mixed technical secretariat with delegates from the National Planning Department, the Ministry of Trade, Industry and Tourism, and the Private Sector Competitiveness Council. The Presidential Office for Competitiveness and Productivity oversees the secretariat's work. The secretariat meets frequently to prepare technical documents that served as proposals for the commission's discussions. Also for each strategic area or objective, the commission is supposed to develop a matrix of products and support activities, including goals and deadlines for implementation, and to designate who is to do what. This role is central to the monitoring of the competitiveness system.

Because of the institutional complexity, effective coordination is especially crucial to the system's effectiveness. In this regard, the government's own assessment was that additional efforts were needed to improve coordination between government agencies and between them and the private sector. A study prepared by Gomez Restrepo, Botiva, and Guerra (2008)

Figure 7.2 Colombia's National Competitiveness System

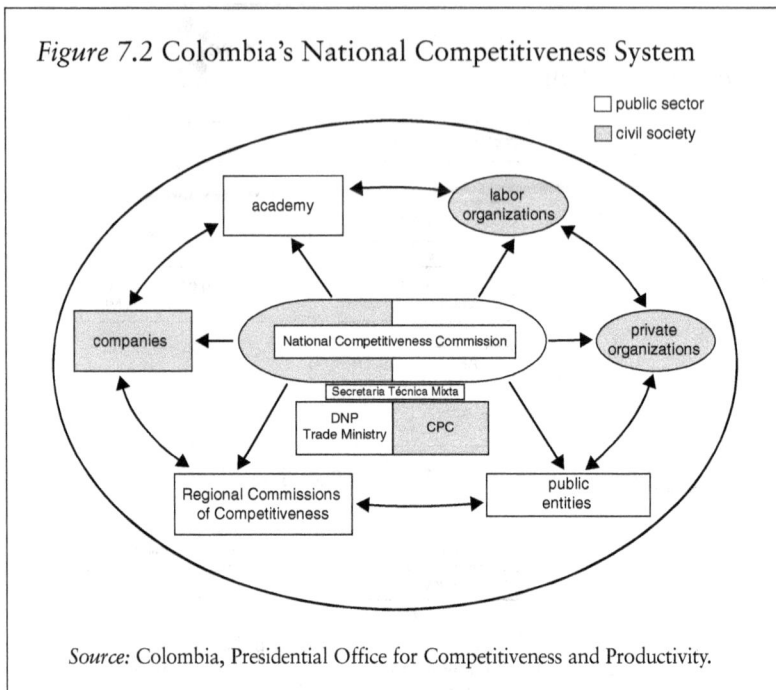

Source: Colombia, Presidential Office for Competitiveness and Productivity.

detected institutional disarticulation, which led to duplication of functions in the system. This and other diagnostics all point to a need for greater clarity in the role of the different entities participating in this initiative.

As mentioned in an earlier chapter, federalized governments present one a special challenge in coordinating public policies. The problems can arise from excessive decentralization with a consequent dilution of dialogue between national and provincial-level policies or from exaggerated centralism on the national government's part, which causes it to overlook regional requirements. As Baruj (2007) and Baruj, Kosacoff, and Ramos (2009) note, in Argentina there is a high degree of operational centralization among institutions and programs. Most of the instruments are designed and applied centrally by executing agencies within the administrative headquarters of each of the government organizations in Buenos Aires. This centralization has several negative consequences: a disconnect with regional problems and polices; mistrust among the actors and a lack of demand for the instruments; waste of resources; and a shortage of tools to deal with undetected problems. The development and consolidation of sister regional agencies with formal lines of coordination with the central government and transparent channels of communication with the relevant stakeholders in each of them would eliminate many of these barriers to the effective implementation of the strategies, programs, and policies.

Integrated Programs and Incentives to Meet the Goals of the National Development Strategy

Implementing integrated programs and incentives for meeting strategic goals is an issue not unrelated to coordination. Table 7.2 offers a highly compressed summary of the kind of incentives and instruments available in seven Latin American countries in the areas of export promotion, innovation, attraction of foreign investment, competitiveness, and industrial development.[9] In general terms, all seven countries use similar fiscal and financial incentives. Since the implementation of the economic reforms under the Washington Consensus, program and policy design has tended to be biased toward overly horizontal incentives. That being the case—and given the shortage of resources, the frequent lack of strategic guidance in the policies, and the proliferation of instruments—the programs' impact can become diluted.

In recent years countries have tended to refocus their productive development strategies by retaining horizontal incentives but focusing more attention on certain sectors and activities deemed to have particular potential for growth, technological development, and international integration. In Brazil, for example, the Ministry of Science, Technology and Innovation had funds to stimulate business innovation in strategic sectors. Notably, these resources had been approved by law, which established the amount to be devoted to the activities being promoted (CEPAL 2004, 222). In the 2000s Chile began to move to prioritize certain sectors apart from the natural resources that have traditionally been the central focus. The government had introduced selective incentives to attract investment to these sectors, such as the offshoring activities of multinational companies, using CORFO's Management of Development and Investment programs. For its part, Colombia now pays special attention to a small number of sectors in traditional and selected new activities that have been chosen because of their export potential.[10]

In our extraregional examples, successful programs for implementing strategies, plans, and policies are linked together and complement each other. In Singapore, for example, the Economic Development Board led the executing agencies, coordinating an integration of programs and incentives applied in support of industrial and export development. In Latin America few organizations have been given a similar mission of providing a holistic and comprehensive vision of the system of programs and incentives. The Executive Secretariat of the Productive Development Policy in Brazil could (or should) play such a role, as should also be the case of Colombia's National Competitiveness Commission. This integrated approach is important because a promotion instrument's effectiveness is often related less to the way it individually acts on an objective than on the way it links up with a series of other instruments, complementing them in coordinated interaction.

Table 7.2 Selective Illustration of Some Instruments Used to Promote Export Development and Innovation

Strategic pillar	Instruments
Argentina	
Export promotion	Pre- and post-export credits, financing assets and product development; financing for small and medium enterprises (SMEs), duty drawbacks, temporary admittance regimes, free zones, special sectoral regimes, and financing fairs and exhibitions
Promotion of technological capacity and innovation	Credits Subsidies and tax relief
Promotion of foreign investment	Credits Tax relief
Brazil	
Export promotion	Pre- and post-export credits, financing assets and product development, financing SMEs Credit insurance system for exports, trade promotion Duty drawbacks, exemption from value added tax (VAT)
Technology and innovation policy	Credit financing Subsidies Tax incentives Support for technology parks Fund for the development of business incubators Use of government procurement to stimulate innovative firms
Industrial development policy	Subsidies, tax credits, rapid investment depreciation, exemptions for exports and sectors that create externalities Credits and cofinancing

Chile	
Export promotion	Pre- and post-shipment credits, financing assets and product development, marketing costs
	Financing fairs and exhibitions
	Support to SMEs in management and training
Innovation promotion	Special funds to finance innovation, various instruments (CORFO), and CONYCIT
	Seed capital
	Grants and subsidies
	Tax credits
	Comprehensive incentives packages through research consortia, clusters—regions
FDI promotion	Investment attraction programs in priority areas
	Investment subsidies (CORFO)
Colombia	
Export promotion	Export financing, fiduciary services, insurance
	Tax reimbursement certificates
	Tax relief, customs and foreign trade facilitation
	Special economic export zones, special export programs
	Export competitiveness agreements
Competitiveness and innovation promotion	Cofinancing business projects, including R&D, with grants, subsidies, and credits

(continued)

Table 7.2 Selective Illustration of Some Instruments Used to Promote Export Development and Innovation

Strategic pillar	Instruments
Costa Rica	
Attracting foreign investment	Specific agreements with multinationals on investment profits
	Development of industrial parks
	Development of infrastructure
	Creation of free zones
	Tax exemptions
Foreign trade promotion	Design and coordination of programs to attract FDI for exports
	Technical and financial support to the Ministry of Foreign Trade to manage special export regimes
	"Costa Rica Provee" program: production chains with multinationals
Mexico	
Export promotion	Pre- and post-export credits; financing assets and product development; financing SMEs, insurance
	Economic Development Fund
	Duty drawbacks, exemption from VAT
	ALTEX: support to export-intensive companies (tax relief)
	IMMEX: programs for the promotion and operation of the export maquiladora industry
	PITEX: temporary import programs for export production
	Promotion of sales in foreign markets

Innovation	Mixed and sectoral funds
	Scholarships for the training of scientists and technologists
	Financing scientific research
	Grants and other subsidies for innovation and technological development
	Special programs and funds
	Tax credits to the industrial sector
Peru	
Export promotion	Tax credits, duty drawbacks, tax exemptions in free zones
	Tools for analyzing competitiveness, international fairs, training programs, special workshops
Innovation promotion	Financing technology missions, purchase of research equipment, financing for individual firms and partners for innovation

Source: Authors, based on official sources.

Brazil's Productive Development Policy seeks, among other things, to coordinate support instruments to advance the strategic area of communications and information technology. As illustrated in figure 7.3, each of the major challenges in the initiative executing agencies is assigned responsibility for implementing the program. The agencies involved are accountable to different ministries, which are committed to the strategy and are coordinated by the ABDI and the MDIC. These agencies seek to coordinate the incentives so as to provide comprehensive support to firms in the sector, improving their innovation capacity, furthering their international integration, and upgrading their export capacity. For each of the other strategic areas, the Productive Development Policy has a similar array of integrated objectives and support instruments.

This system is different from Brazil's tradition of "silos," where there were few connections, for example, between export promotion and technology and innovation policy, even though previous governments had good intentions in this regard. One author described Brazil's trade and technology policies as "completely disconnected" under the old system: "On the one hand, trade policy accords little importance to technology and concentrates on credit. On the other hand, technology policy practically ignores the needs of exports" (Tigre 2002, 277). According to Pacheco and Corder (2009), the reasons for this lay in the priorities of the policies and in the institutional arrangements. For export promotion, the priorities were financing, guarantees, tax relief, and international negotiations. Innovation promotion, meanwhile, traditionally centered on creating knowledge and training human resources, and only recently on supporting innovations in businesses. In effect, one initiative was unconnected to the other, creating unfilled gaps in the necessary chain of support.[11]

The incentives instruments in Argentina have suffered from silos that promote a lack of coordination and complementarity. Baruj (2007) cites the example of different cluster programs run by different institutions that are unconnected to each other and that proceed in parallel. Different agencies use similar financial instruments and sometimes implement programs similar to those already offered by private institutions, without capitalizing on the learning experiences of those latter entities (for example, the "SME Map" drawn up in the under-secretariat for small and medium enterprises was not articulated with the SME Observatory in the Argentine Industrial Union that had long experience in the field). Baruj points to two immediate results of this failure to connect: programs are too superficial and thus of little help to firms that already have surmounted the initial, basic hurdles; and a lack of institutional specialization undermined a sustained process of learning and self-correction.

According to Bizberg (2008), Mexico's large number of government programs to improve the competitiveness of Mexican companies (more than 130 in total) was a problem, because entrepreneurs found it hard to determine which programs were likely to be the most relevant and helpful

Figure 7.3 Brazil's Incentives in Communications and Information Technology

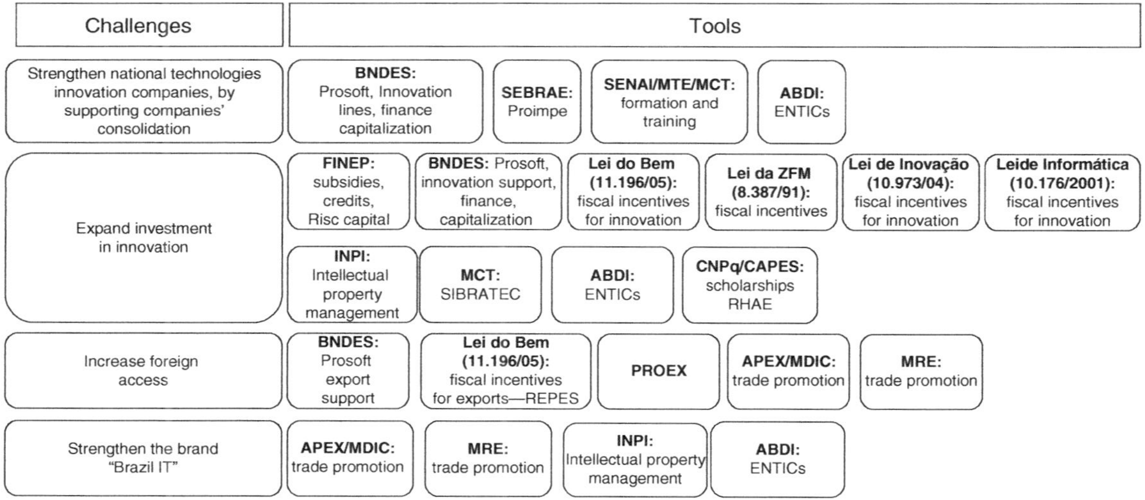

Challenges | **Tools**

Strengthen national technologies innovation companies, by supporting companies' consolidation
- **BNDES:** Prosoft, Innovation lines, finance capitalization
- **SEBRAE:** Proimpe
- **SENAI/MTE/MCT:** formation and training
- **ABDI:** ENTICs

Expand investment in innovation
- **FINEP:** subsidies, credits, Risc capital
- **BNDES:** Prosoft, innovation support, finance, capitalization
- **Lei do Bem (11.196/05):** fiscal incentives for innovation
- **Lei da ZFM (8.387/91):** fiscal incentives
- **Lei de Inovação (10.973/04):** fiscal incentives for innovation
- **Leide Informática (10.176/2001):** fiscal incentives for innovation
- **INPI:** Intellectual property management
- **MCT:** SIBRATEC
- **ABDI:** ENTICs
- **CNPq/CAPES:** scholarships RHAE

Increase foreign access
- **BNDES:** Prosoft export support
- **Lei do Bem (11.196/05):** fiscal incentives for exports—REPES
- **PROEX**
- **APEX/MDIC:** trade promotion
- **MRE:** trade promotion

Strengthen the brand "Brazil IT"
- **APEX/MDIC:** trade promotion
- **MRE:** trade promotion
- **INPI:** Intellectual property management
- **ABDI:** ENTICs

Source: Government of Brazil, Productive Development Policy 2008.

to them.[12] Since the programs were implemented by different organizations unconnected to each other, the bureaucratic requirements for using them differed from program to program, discouraging businesses from applying for them.[13] As discussed in chapter 5, businesses are unwilling to participate in programs that in their view involve too much red tape and that are too slow to produce results relative to commercial opportunities. Until 1996 no institution in Mexico was responsible for coordinating industrial promotion programs, and thus there was a duplication of effort and little follow-up. An Intersecretarial Commission on Industrial Policy was set up later to establish such coordination (Berry 2002), but it was unable to rationalize organization of support windows for each of the main problems facing Mexican industry: developing businesses; promoting suppliers; financing; and technological training, development, and research.[14]

The fragmentation of policies and their lack of effective articulation caused some agencies in countries to take steps to strengthen their joint work. In Chile, for example, the export promotion programs run by PRO-CHILE, an agency that reports to the Foreign Ministry, traditionally had little contact with CORFO, the agency responsible for promoting production and innovation, which answers to the Economy Ministry. Nonetheless, the need for a more comprehensive policy on innovation geared to export development led the two institutions to join forces; their first initiative was a program called Exploring and Researching Foreign Markets. With this new financing incentive, the agencies hoped that companies would differentiate their products and their strategy of integration into foreign marketing chains, thereby exploiting heretofore unidentified opportunities.

Finally, a common problem in the region has been the "archeological park" of incentives that grows larger each time a new government introduces its own support programs for firms without assessing and rationalizing existing initiatives. This practice creates a mass of often contradictory incentives (Baruj, Kosakoff, and Porta 2006). The cause is related to various factors such as poor coordination, lack of consensually based, proactive long-term strategies, the so-called refounding syndrome (described earlier), a dearth of evaluation of program effectiveness, and probably a dose of state capture too (capture is easier to achieve when coordination is poor and no evaluations are taking place).

Minimizing Risks of State Capture: Transparency and Evaluation

A series of factors can reduce the risk that particular interests will capture the state and unduly influence the development and implementation of strategies. Some of these have already been discussed. A true public-private dialogue in a well-structured and governed alliance, one conducted in the spirit of protecting a public good, helps to minimize capture. So too does a professionalization of the civil service, as well as reasonable pay commensurate with responsibilities. The other key ingredients are transparency and mechanisms to evaluate programs and incentives.

Transparency is measured by the extent to which an institutional system allows interested citizens or organizations to efficiently acquire enough pertinent, reliable, high-quality information about the institution's operations in the economic, social, and political spheres. When relationships are not transparent, there is a serious risk of firms being extorted by politicians, of state capture by the firms, or of other connivances that run counter to the public interest. This kind of situation spurs mistrust in the best of circumstances and corruption in the worst, undermining the prospect of effective agreements between the public and private sectors on development and of effective industrial policies. Transparency helps make policies more effective by facilitating discovery of overlapping activities among agencies and programs. In some countries little effort is made to publicize the activities of each agency (and even to do so within the agencies themselves)—in part because of fragmentation and turf struggles The upshot is the loss of an overall vision of the institution and of the possibilities for interaction and coordination with other agencies' activities. Transparency can significantly help strengthen public-private alliances, fostering more trust, confidence, and accountability among the actors.[15] Meanwhile, a well-governed alliance can be a guardian of transparency of industrial policies. From this perspective, there is indeed a growing awareness in the region of the importance of public transparency, as manifest in new laws dedicated to its promotion. Indeed, transparency laws and procedures are becoming quite widespread in the region.[16] For example, Chile has a relatively new transparency law to which all public agencies, including the development institutions, are subject.[17] In addition to the establishment of the Transparency Council, the law stipulates that state organizations must provide all the information requested by citizens within 20 days. Additionally, government departments must use their websites to provide current information on matters such as their structure, staff, the salaries of the employees, contracts signed with other institutions, transfers of funds, and the results of any audits. The public must also be informed of the design, amounts, and access criteria for subsidies and other benefits that the agency provides, as well as the beneficiaries of social programs under way. The Transparency Council is tasked with overseeing compliance with the new legislation and with protecting the right to obtain information from state institutions.[18] Citizens who do not receive the information they have requested can appeal to the council, which will determine if the information sought is legally in the public domain. Although the Transparency Law has not yet been fully implemented (it calls for people to be trained, as well as the effective use of technology in all public offices, including those in the regions and municipalities), its enactment is a major achievement demonstrating a broad political will to tackle the issue.[19]

Evaluations are also important because, in addition to revealing information on the effectiveness of policies and programs, they are fundamental tools for transparency and good governance. Evaluation were not used much in the 1970s and 1980s, but in the 1990s some countries began using them in their strategies, programs, and policies. Where the practice does exist, however, it is often not carried out systematically and often focuses on compliance with programmatic outputs rather than on assessing whether the program had the desired impact vis-à-vis a specified objective.

Chile and Colombia are good examples of the evolution of evaluation in the region. Evaluation of public policies in Chile dates back to 1990 when democracy was restored (Marcel 1998). The first efforts at evaluation involved ministerial objectives, which were extended to the regional governments in 1995. But this initiative was brought to an end because of its excessive bureaucratization. The reform and modernization policy pursued by President Eduardo Frei (1994–2000) provided a new incentive for the government to pursue evaluation schemes, namely, the Strategic Plan for the Modernization of Public Management (1997–2000), in which one of its basic principles was efficiency and effectiveness in government activities.

According to Olavarría (2008), the plan gave a great deal of authority to the Finance Ministry's budget department (DIPRES). Under the Lagos administration (2000–06), DIPRES devised a form of evaluation known as the Comprehensive Spending Assessment. The aim was to identify the extent to which there is consistency between the Treasury's institutional mission, its strategic goals, its structure and functional set-up, and the goods and services that it produces; appraise its capacity to implement the public policies with which it is entrusted; and assess the results in terms of effectiveness, efficiency, quality, and the level of resources used in achieving those results (DIPRES 2003).

Chile's Mideplan also evaluates public investment projects, but the power rests with DIPRES, which biases the criteria of the evaluations toward those that are relevant to the Finance Ministry's objectives. As Waisbluth (2000) notes, and as we saw earlier regarding successful practices in countries like Finland, evaluation is not simply an activity carried out when an initiative is completed; it is an ongoing, permanent process that should be part of a management style based on objectives and results. In Chile project evaluation was undertaken only at the level of investment projects. The aim should be to extend evaluation to all public interventions from their inception, something that Waisbluth imagines would be politically difficult to implement. According to Olavarría (2008, 12),

Analysis of the situation reveals the need for more coordinated, institutionalized and stabilized evaluations of public policies, programs and projects in Chile. The country constantly exhibits concern about the proper use of public resources and the effectiveness of state interventions, and much progress has been made in the evaluation field since 1990. But the next challenge is to devise an evaluation system that has a stability conferred by regulations and that formalizes the roles of the different public institutions. This would avert institutional tensions and the duplication of functions. Coverage should be increased—both the number of interventions and the stages of the public policies assessed—and the methods used in the evaluations should be improved.

Finally, in Colombia, emphasis has been placed on creating a National System of Management Evaluation (SINERGIA). Resolution 063 is intended to strengthen management capacity in public investment; analyze the efficiency and effectiveness of formulating and implementing policies, programs, and projects; determine compliance with targets; consider quality, defects, coverage, and impacts; and generate appropriate information for decision making and resource allocation. The system covers the institutions and agencies of the public administration under the coordination of the National Planning Department.

The designers of Colombia's evaluation system also emphasized that evaluation of management is the best possible tool to bring about a change in the culture of public administration, because it allows for public assessment and accountability. According to Ospina Bozzi (2001), while the system had been well thought-out and had met several of its goals, there were still problems of implementation, caused partly by a lack of coordination between administrative levels, and partly by the political context within which the system was created and implemented. Ospina Bozzi argued that because of the high level of deficient governance and uncertainty, senior management did not dare to risk imposing accountability on their teams, and instead focused on other, less important priorities. Finally, evaluations tended to focus more on whether agreed programs were completed than on whether they effectively met their stated objectives for enhancing competitiveness.

Notes

1. Speech by President Oscar Arias Sánchez, January 27, 2007. http://www.nacion.com/ln_ee/2007/enero/25/opinion972615.html.
2. This usually occurred in emerging high profile priority initiatives in trade, competitiveness, and innovation.
3. See Seminario Agencias Regionales de Desarrollo, CorpAraucanía, and Friedrich Ebert Stiftung, September 14, 2006.
4. Almost all Latin American countries have laws in place calling for a professional civil service, but few have fully implemented the laws (Grindle 2010).
5. See Echebarría (2006) for a study of 18 countries.
6. Bustos Muñoz (2003).

7. Preparation of the budget entails a discussion in the National Council on Economic Policy, and the joint work (albeit not very well coordinated) of the Treasury and the National Planning Department.

8. Or they depend on international technical cooperation that often ties the country to the bureaucracy and agenda of donor organizations.

9. It should be noted that all the countries have pursued free trade agreements and consider them as a tool to promote exports and attract FDI.

10. As mentioned, it remains to be seen if resources will be allocated to promoting the consolidation of the "new" sectors highlighted in the national competitiveness strategy.

11. It has been illegal in Brazil to grant incentives for innovation to businesses, a factor that widened the gap between universities, centers of excellence, and businesses. The new legislation and the Action Plan for Science, Technology and Innovation seek to tackle this problem.

12. Six different institutions are involved in business promotion policy at the federal level.

13. Bizberg (2008) has detected conflict between the different agencies. For example, the Law on Innovation being promoted by Concamin and the Economy Secretariat passed through the Chamber of Deputies but was blocked in the Senate by CONACYT itself, because the latter had not been given the central role.

14. Bizberg (2008); interview with Yeidckol Povlensky, ex-president of the National Chamber of Transformative Industries (CANACINTRA), June 26, 2007.

15. As our successful cases have shown, this transparency still allows certain aspects of partnership processes to remain confidential.

16. See the Organization of American States Country Guide on transparency rules in the Americas. www.oas.org/es/sap/dgpe/guia_mecanismos.asp.

17. Transparency Law 20285, promulgated August 11, 2008.

18. The Transparency Council was to have four members proposed by the presidency and ratified by the Senate. It was to be instituted within 60 days of the date of promulgation.

19. Another example is the creation of the Ministry of Transparency and Anti-Corruption in Bolivia. Under the Marcelo Quiroga Santa Cruz Law of Transparency and Anti-Corruption, approved by Congress in 2010, the ministry was given broad powers to pursue these two major objectives, which are also priority areas in the Plurinational State of Bolivia's National Development Plan 2006–10. The Correa government in Ecuador also has a new comprehensive framework for transparency in government (Apaza 2011).

20. The components of the National System for the Evaluation of the Results of Public Administration are: *Follow-up of results*—constant verification of compliance with the targets and priority goals set by the ministries and administrative departments, so as to devise the guidelines for the National Development Plan and the government's plans and programs; *Focused evaluations*—exhaustive analyses of the operation, impact, and development of the government's main policies and programs; and *Dissemination of results*—providing the public and interested stakeholders with the results of evaluation and follow-up, to provide feedback to the government, ensure accountability, and activate social control.

References

Agosin, Manuel, Christian Larraín, and Nicolás Grau. 2009. "Industrial Policy in Chile." Working Paper 294, University of Chile, Economics Department, Santiago.

Apaza, Carmen. 2011. "Estudio Comparativo de Reformas Estructurales en Países Seleccionados," Department for Effective Public Management, Organization of American States, Washington, DC.

Baruj, Gustavo. 2007. "Las políticas de la promoción de la competividad en la Argentina." Economic Commission for Latin America and the Caribbean, International Trade and Integration Division, Santiago, Chile.

Baruj, Gustavo, Bernardo Kosacoff, and Fernando Porta. 2006. "Políticas nacionales y la profundización del Mercosur: el impacto de las políticas de competitividad." Project Paper 74 (LC/W.74), Economic Commission for Latin America and the Caribbean, Santiago, Chile.

Baruj, Gustavo, Bernardo Kosacoff, and Adrián Ramos. 2009. "Las políticas de promoción de la competitividad en la Argentina. Principales instituciones e instrumentos de apoyo y mecanismos de articulación público-privada." Project Paper 257 (LC/W.257), Economic Commission for Latin America and the Caribbean, Buenos Aires.

Berry, A. 2002. *Valoración de políticas de apoyo a la pequeña empresa.* Washington, DC: Inter-American Development Bank.

Bizberg, Ilan. 2008. *Alianzas público privadas, estrategias para el desarrollo exportador y la innovación: el caso de México* (LC/MEX/L.866), Economic Commission for Latin America and the Caribbean, Mexico City (June).

Bustos Muñoz, Daniela. 2003. "Diferencias salariales entre empleados del sector público y privado de Chile en los años 1990 y 2000," Estudio de caso No. 71, Masters in Management and Public Policies, University of Chile, Santiago.

CEPAL (Economic Commision for Latin America and the Caribbean). 2004. Desarrollo Productivo en Economias Abiertas (LC.G. 2234 [SES.30/3]), table 6.4, Principales Fondos Sectoriales de Brasil, Santiago, Chile.

DIPRES (Dirección de Presupuestos). 2003 "Evaluación comprehensiva del gasto," Ministry of Finance, Santiago, Chile. http://www.dipres.cl/574/propertyvalue-15154.html.

Echebarría, Koldo. 2006. *Informe sobre la situación del servicio civil en América Latina.* Washington, DC: Inter-American Development Bank (May).

Gómez Restrepo, H. J., A. Botiva León, and A. Guerra Forero. 2008. "Institucionalidad y estrategias para el desarrollo exportador y la innovación en Colombia: un diagnóstico inicial." Project Document 294, Economic Commission for Latin America and the Caribbean, International Trade and Integration Division, Santiago, Chile (March).

Grindle, Merilee. 2010. "Constructing, Deconstructing, Reconstructing Career Civil Service Systems in Latin America." CID Working Paper 204, Center for International Development, Harvard University, Cambridge, MA (October).

Machinea, José Luis. 2005. "Competitividad y bienestar: balanceando el corto y largo plazo." *Las visiones de país importan. Lecciones de experiencias.* Washington, DC: International Institute for Democracy and Electoral Assistance/ World Bank/Economic Commission for Latin America and the Caribbean.

Marcel, Mario. 1998. "Lessons from Chile." Public Sector Performance: The Critical Role of Evaluation, ed. Keith Mackey. Washington DC, World Bank.

Marconi, Nelson, Laura Carrillo, and Claudia Helena Cavalieri. 2003. "La remuneración de los altos dirigentes del sector público, un análisis sobre los países de América Latina y el Caribe." http://unpan1.un.org/intradoc/groups/public/documents/CLAD/clad0050802.pdf.

Martín, Juan. 2005. "Funciones básicas de la planificación económica y social." Public Management Series 51 (LC/L.2363-P), Economic Commission for Latin America and the Caribbean, Santiago, Chile.

Olavarría Gambi, Mauricio. 2008. "La evaluación de políticas públicas en Chile." Paper presented to the 13th International Congress of CLAD on state reform and public management, Buenos Aires, November 4–7.

Ospina Bozzi, Sonia. 2001. "Evaluación de la gestión pública: conceptos y aplicaciones en el caso latinoamericano." Revista del CLAD reforma y democracia, Caracas.

Pacheco, C. A., and S. Corder. 2009. "Mapeamento institucional e de medidas de política com impacto sobre a inovação produtiva e a diversificação das exportações." Project Document 293, Economic Commission for Latin America and the Caribbean, International Trade and Integration Division, Santiago, Chile (November).

Popper, Rafael, and Javier Medina. 2008. "Foresight in Latin America." *International Handbook on Foresight and Science Policy: Theory and Practice*. Cheltenham, U.K.: Edward Elgar.

Tigre, Paolo. 2002. "O papel da política tecnológica na promoção das exportações," *O desafio das exportações*, ed. A. Castelar, R. Markwald, and L. V. Pereira. Economic and Social Development National Bank, Río de Janeiro.

Waisbluth, Mario. 2000. "La modernización pública: cuatro asignaturas pendientes." *Revista mensaje*, Santiago, Chile (April).

———. 2006. "Presente y futuro del sistema de alta dirección pública de Chile." http://www.mariowaissbluth.com/secciones/articulos/pdf/sistemadealtadireccion.pdf.

8

Conclusions: The Three Main Pillars of Our Operational Principles

In part one, we reviewed 11 operational principles on how to conceptualize, develop, and execute industrial policies for economic transformation and catch-up, using strategies of support for export development as the organizing objective to illustrate the points. These 11 principles were inductively generated from detailed case studies on "how" public sectors in 10 extraregional countries—most of which are models of successful postwar catch-up with rich countries, and all of which have performed better than Latin America—organized themselves to formulate and implement strategies for economic transformation and development. While each of these countries differs from the others in many ways, observing the "how" (in addition to the "what") of their public policy organization, when reduced to its bare substance, allowed us to identify these quite generic operational principles. We then selectively illustrated the concrete forms in which the principles uniquely manifested themselves in our extraregional success cases.

Latin America has not succeeded in sustaining a postwar process of catch-up, and generally has slipped even further behind the richer countries. Indeed, the region has been a laggard for most of its history. Chile narrowed the income gap for more than a decade beginning in the late 1980s, but even before the great world recession of 2008–09 its growth had slipped back to lackluster levels. Although many other South American countries experienced record levels of growth in the early 2000s, much of it was induced by unusually high commodity prices and easy international finance conditions that few expect to be fully repeated even in a recovered world economy. As the world economy showed some signs of a recovery in 2010, many commodity prices were still buoyant, in no small part owing to China's remarkably sustained hyper-growth rates. Aside from the question of the sustainability of China's voracious demand for commodities, reliance on commodity prices for growth entails historically proven risks and serious vulnerabilities that only economic diversification and upgrading in the world's hierarchy of production can reduce. Moreover, the recovery is expected to lead to a "new normal" world economy, with new opportunities, but even bigger competitive challenges, for the region.

An X-ray of Latin America suggests that notwithstanding pockets of excellence—such as aeronautics or deep sea hydrocarbon exploration in Brazil and the auto complex in Mexico—systemically speaking, the region's productive sectors and entrepreneurial spirit have not been "pumped up" enough to reach beyond obvious static comparative advantage, whether by preparing to occupy openings for upgraded activities created by countries moving out of higher-level industries where they are losing competitiveness (Lin and Monga 2010), by a riskier strategy of developing learning and capacities to pursue the unexpected, or by a combination of both. In any event, the region's static comparative advantage is not enough to produce the very high rates of growth that the region needs to sustain for decades if its income levels are to converge with those of rich countries.

Moreover, productivity in the region lags its competitors in many areas of existing comparative advantage. With few exceptions, the region's competitiveness indicators are poor. Even those countries that fare better in the aggregate, such as Chile, seriously underperform in many subindicators of dynamic competitiveness, including education, research and development, and innovation. Many of the countries of the region have been slow to diversify their economies and export products. When significant diversification has taken place, it has been either horizontally in natural resources, a pattern which *on its own* historically has been an unreliable means of successful catch-up, or in manufactures with low value added and knowledge content and often dependent on trade preferences. Nevertheless, each of these types of export activity has much untapped potential as a base for bigger and better economic performances.[1]

The depressive effects of the world economic recession of 2008–09 also present challenges. On the one hand, countries have to deal with adjustments, economic stimulus in the short term, and correction of potential macroeconomic imbalances in the medium term. But these adjustments must be consistent with promotion of medium- to long-term economic transformation. As we observed in chapter 1, many of the adjustments of the 1980s, and even the 1990s, were inconsistent with this objective. Successful national economies—Singapore is one example—made necessary short-term adjustments during the crisis but integrated them with proactive strategic longer-term thinking, coupled with related retooling and investments, to fully exploit new opportunities that will emerge as the world economy recovers.

The First Pillar: A Proactive Medium- to Long-Term National Strategic Vision Is Essential

The first of the 11 principles is that a country needs to look ahead to the medium and long term to determine not only how it will compete today but also how it will progressively upgrade itself to close in on the technological frontier where high incomes are located. The critical component for achieving this vision is a strategy that projects itself ambitiously, but realistically, toward climbing up the world's production hierarchy. Lagging economies need to foster emulation of productive activities in richer countries through continuous capacity building, knowledge accumulation, learning, and innovation. We have pointed out that market failures, institutional obstacles, and attitudinal barriers, such as a preference for the status quo, make it unlikely that, on a systemic basis, free market forces alone will drive a process of catch-up; indeed, market forces may even risk locking countries into low-level comparative advantage. As Adelman (2000) has observed, new and better comparative advantages are not a gift of markets but are the result of "man-made" policy and programs that enable market forces to deliver structural transformation and accelerated growth.

Although industrial policy has been a subject of a heated, unresolved debate since the beginnings of capitalism, we and others find that historically few countries have been able to catch up to richer countries without intelligent industrial policies deployed in medium- to long-term strategies for economic transformation. These strategies, characterized by focused objectives and selectivity in either horizontal or vertical applications, have been gradually built up explicitly or tacitly in most historical processes of catch-up.[2] In our group of success cases, the best performers have deployed strategies based on industrial policies, some expressed in formal national plans. In all of them proactive integration with the world economy has been a goal, but with the timing, speed, and modalities differing from country to country and based more on pragmatism than on any conventional economics textbook formula.

Rigorous empirical analysis has been inconclusive about the impact of industrial policies (IPs) in successful East Asian cases of catch-up. This is not surprising, given the many technical difficulties in evaluating the impact of a single, precise industrial policy incentive at the ground level, not to mention IP in higher degrees of aggregation and across counties, as is often the methodological perspective. But industrial policy is unquestionably associated with successful economic transformation, as documented by several pioneering and comprehensive case studies discussed in chapter 2. Moreover, when countries with industrial policies have failed in their transformation efforts, as many have, the cause has usually been identifiable flaws in design or execution rather than the industrial policy approach itself. Meanwhile, attempts to demonstrate that successful East Asian economies were fundamentally based on neoclassical market principles is, with the exception of Hong Kong SAR, China, a stretch, to say the least.

We (and others) contend that few of the arguments against industrial policy are cogent. The one valid argument is that IP requires a state capacity that many governments may not initially have. However, the Washington Consensus has advocated selective policies in many complex social areas and encouraged governments to build necessary state capacity for that purpose, often with the assistance of multilateral agencies. We think that experience and logic are sufficiently compelling to suggest that Latin America should risk a "bet" on industrial policies subject to certain conditions we lay out in this concluding chapter. The bottom line, however, is that, in our opinion, the question is not *whether* Latin America should do IP, but rather *how* to do IP right.

Latin America was an earnest student of the Washington Consensus. The consensus made positive contributions in some areas, most notably in underscoring the importance of macroeconomic stability and engagement with the world economy. However, as the region attempted to convert to the market fundamentalism required by the Washington Consensus, it found itself lagging or flagging in the convergence race, while countries elsewhere, less observant of the consensus orthodoxy, achieved catch-up. This result has contributed to the growing interest in Latin America in government promotion of medium- to long-term strategies for economic transformation supported by IP. Indeed, industrial policy is rapidly returning to the center of the Latin America development agenda after being demonized during the era of the Washington Consensus. In reality, IP never disappeared from the region, but under the weight of the dominant neoliberal ideology, it was for the most part without strategic focus and hence sporadic and incoherent.[3] The new IP has often manifested itself as a response to the emergence of competitiveness strategies, often motivated by the challenge of signing onto North-South free trade areas. Some countries, like many in Central America, focus on improving existing competitiveness and clusters—IP "in the small," in the words of Hausmann, Rodrik, and Sabel (2008).[4] Other countries, either modestly (Colombia, Chile) or expansively (Brazil), combine IP in the small with strategies to create new comparative advantages (IP "in the large").

The new strategies in the region are not always operational, however. In some cases they are only generic aspirational statements with little guidance on exactly what is to be done, how it is to be done, and who will do it. Some strategies have so many priorities that in the end there is no strategic prioritization at all, or even any hint of the sequencing of desirable actions. In other cases there are uncertainties about the allocation of resources—will they arrive to strategically pinpointed areas or activities, and will they be enough? Will the strategy be, as often has been the case, just a piece of paper used for short-term political motives? Then there is uncertainty about continuity and commitment between political cycles.[5] Among the cases we reviewed, in recent years Brazil and Colombia would seem to have the most sophisticated strategies for productive transformation in the region—and, while not without their flaws, to be the least plagued by these and other problems outlined in chapter 6 concerning emerging medium- to long-term strategies.

National plans, once common in Latin America, fell into disuse with the debt crisis and the political delegitimization of the strategy of import substitution industrialization in the 1980s and 1990s. A few countries such as Colombia and Costa Rica, even though plagued by some of the problems mentioned above, did keep a planning exercise in place. We believe that for countries well behind the technological frontier, such as those in Latin America, reinstituting or seriously committing to formal and truly operational multiyear national plans would be a valuable tool for productive transformation. Serious planning would force forward-looking thinking, serve as a coordinating tool for government, and provide accountability in the allocation of resources. Plans could be indicative in their overall goals, but operationally specific and adjusted annually to new realities. Or they might focus on broad guidelines, as in Finland where executing agencies are authorized to execute strategic policies and programs as they see fit but are held accountable by responsible ministries and the overarching council that prepares the three-year guidelines for policies and financing of programs for productive transformation. And, of course, an annual budget for the plan would have to be committed. Plans would have sectoral or cluster development as an objective, along with strategic horizontal initiatives to respond to the emerging world industrial organization where broad networking endogenously drives innovation—an "open industrial policy," in the words of Sabel (2009). The bottom line requirement, however, is a real political commitment to the plan and its implementation. We saw in chapter 6 that in 2007 Costa Rica's then-president Oscar Arias committed to transforming the country's national planning exercise from words to deeds. Intelligent national plans with the Arias imperative would serve the region well.

The Second Pillar: The Support Role Played by Public-Private Alliances Is Critical to Success

Looking forward with specific strategic goals is only one part of the equation—and not the lead variable. Successful catch-up countries deploy public-private alliances as inputs to the development and implementation of industrial strategies. In the era of globalization the private sector dominates in markets and has a clear competitive advantage over governments in gathering specific contextual information about market behavior. It also can identify government failures, being victim of some of them. However, the private sector has limits too, stemming from uncertainty, myopia, and a tendency to favor the status quo. Fear of not being able to fully appropriate the returns to innovation, coordination problems, and constraints on access to information beyond a familiar market context can also restrict private sector activity. Meanwhile, governments have advantages in dealing with the aggregates of the big picture, providing national leadership and coordinating and producing public goods. Governments can also strategically engage with multinationals that can serve as ports of entry to new knowledge and international links. Working together constructively through a public-private alliance, and thus maximizing the input of national talent and capabilities, the public and private sectors are more likely to develop an intelligent strategy than either party can working alone. Buy-in from economically and politically relevant stakeholders outside both government and the business sector can multiply the prospect of gaining agreements that will survive changes of government.

Although the state must collaborate intimately with the private sector in an alliance, it must be careful not to be captured by special interests, or achieving what Evans (1995) called "embedded autonomy." This admonition is easy to voice but harder to follow. The government must implement process and institutional designs that reduce the always present risk of capture by special interests. Moreover these requirements are not static but must constantly evolve, like the development strategy itself, in response to changing internal and external circumstances. Meanwhile, in developing countries mistrust between business, academia, and government is often historical, creating serious challenges to alliance formation. These challenges can be overcome only by effective political leadership, coupled with a technically credible and engaged public sector. There are no formulas; each country must find its own way of creating local conditions for public good–like alliances and maintaining them over time. It can be done because countries have done it—to the benefit of formulating and sustaining effective medium- to long-term strategies for economic catch-up.

The most successful of our extraregional examples have had stable, nationally focused alliances, most of them formally structured with functional input from the main economic forces in the country. The configuration and governance of the alliances have been tailored to accommodate the political, cultural, and economic realities of each specific country. Nevertheless, key elements of some of the most effective alliances have been real political support at the highest level of government, relevant high-level social representation without an unmanageable number of participants, and closed-door deliberative, problem-solving exercises (with neutral technical support) that periodically produce public policy recommendations. Moreover, these alliances combine a focus on growth and competitiveness with social cohesion as a way to encourage consensus around a true national vision with maximum commitment, financial and otherwise, to a strategy. The best alliances also penetrate deeply into the public bureaucracy through participation on boards of directors and advisory councils. As a general proposition, the autonomy of the state is not in question. The autonomy is achieved by the institutional design of the alliance and its governance procedures as well as by the availability of a professionally driven and motivated state bureaucracy.[6] But even well-designed alliances can fail. We showed how long-successful alliances in Ireland and Spain devolved into dysfunctional relationships and were captured (by the construction and finance sectors) in part because of the complacency bred by previous success and the failure of the institutional design to evolve appropriately.

Most Latin American countries have traditionally had uncomfortable private-public relationships, including with multinationals, which, when strategically engaged, can serve as ports of entry to new knowledge and international linkages. This situation has to change. And indeed, as part 2 illustrated, the situation is slowly changing in some countries. Barbados has a long tradition of a tripartite alliance inscribed in law. Other countries have emerging alliances, many of them also mandated legislatively.

But these alliances also face problems. Internal governance of the alliance can be dysfunctional, unable to solve problems or reach consensus, as appears to have been the case in Barbados in the 2000s. The highest levels of government in almost all Latin American alliances have declared formal support for them but then often have failed to back the declaration with action, making the alliances somewhat toothless. The low political legitimacy of the alliances turns them into shops of "cheap talk" and discourages dedicated private representation at the high level required for public credibility and influence. The alliances tend to have an excessively large number of participants, moreover, which can be unwieldy for governance and consensus building. Adequate resources for administrative support and, especially for objective, high-caliber technical support for true problem-solving deliberation, are the exception rather than the rule. Penetration of the alliance in the public bureaucracy generally is still limited, and the ministries or agencies in charge of productive sectors and the resources at their disposal are often not credible for the private sector clients. Procedures to avoid capture by special interests are generally inadequate. A vacuum of real political leadership and poor governance often leads the players to make "end runs" around the alliance to push their own bilateral agendas. These weaknesses in the governance of alliances are critical, because, in the modern interpretation of IP, it is out of the social and institutional processes of an appropriately organized alliance that effective public polices, support programs, and their effective implementation emerge.

Creating an effective alliance is itself a process of trial and error. Multilateral agencies—such as the Economic Commission for Latin America and the Caribbean (ECLAC), the Organization of American States, and the Inter-American Development Bank, and regional development banks, such as the Central American Bank for Economic Integration, the Caribbean Development Bank, and the Andean Development Corporation—could support locally based diagnostics of the governance of existing public-private alliances and studies of options for creating alliances where they do not exist, to exploit the growing recognition of the functional importance of alliances for the emergence of intelligent industrial as well as other policies.

The Third Pillar: Execution

This leads us to the third critical ingredient for support of economic transformation: state capacity.

Part 1 showed that the most successful extraregional cases have a professional and motivated state bureaucracy that can act as a credible partner in a functionally designed public-private alliance, can formulate a strategy with associated policies and support programs that draw on the insights and capabilities of the alliance, and can effectively implement the strategy. Indeed, the big secret of success in our extraregional cases—and in the history of economic catch-up—is effective execution of strategy and programs by a well-organized and capable government. The bottom line is that execution is often the difference between success and failure.

In short, a highly professional, capable, and motivated state bureaucracy that can strategize with the private sector and can implement the strategy at different levels within government without capture by special interests is the sine qua non for successful industrial policies. Moreover, a professional management corps creates an institutional memory that fosters learning and a degree of continuity between governments. In Latin America few state bureaucracies meet these criteria. Indeed, the lack of a highly qualified professional civil service may be the Achilles' heel of the region's efforts to catch up with rich countries. This is even more of a handicap in an era of global networking where horizontal cooperation and delegation of decision making becomes of increasing importance for effective management. Under the Washington Consensus, government service became an inferior good. Low pay, low morale, hiring based on who you know rather than what you know, limited career paths with management posts filled by ad hoc contracts, and high turnover at top levels of management, especially when one government succeeds another, have been the norm.

Central banks and finance ministries, the ports of entry for the Washington Consensus, have tended, along with ministries of foreign affairs, to be exceptions to the norm. The quality and esprit de corps of these pockets of excellence in government need to be extended to government as a whole and expressed in the development of a highly professional, technically capable civil service based on decent pay, meritorious recruitment of the best and brightest, training opportunities at home and abroad, career paths for line and top management positions, and explicitly sanctionable codes of conduct. This same goal has to be extended to local levels, especially in federal political systems.

Multilateral development agencies have increasingly been concerned about being catalytic agents of the private sector. Perhaps the best catalytic role they could play for the private sector would be to support more intensively the development of excellence in civil service systems and the efficacy of public sector organization for executing industrial and other policies. In effect, government is only is good as the people in it and the organizational setting in which they work.

Another important factor in our success cases is the delegation of strategic leadership to ministries and agencies charged with overseeing the real economic sectors of industry, trade, technology, and innovation. Finance ministries in these countries focus on ensuring that the strategy is consistent with overall fiscal balance, and they provide inputs to strategies, especially in financial services. But the ministry of finance is not the dominant voice on the direction of strategy or the modalities of implementation. In Latin America finance ministries led the adjustments that have allowed the region to manage crisis and consolidate a culture of macroeconomic stability. This important achievement has made them a powerful voice in government that has often extended to areas of policy where they have little competency, or cultural disposition, especially in areas that need support of industrial policy. This overreach has been made easier by the marginalization of ministries and agencies overseeing real productive activities in government decision making during the era of the Washington Consensus. The competence, power, and influence of these public entities must be strengthened if Latin American countries are to catch up with the richer countries. This strengthening will require policies that permit these entities to recruit and retain "the best and brightest" to help plan and execute the development strategy as well as support from the highest levels of government and the private and civil society stakeholders involved.

State bureaucracies also must be encouraged to think strategically and long term after 25 years of policy driven by mainstream macroeconomics with short-term policy horizons based on faith in the benign forces of the market. The real-sector complex needs a powerful, highly trained, and respected technical "brain," similar to agencies and councils in Ireland, Singapore, Finland, and Korea highlighted in part 1. Many Latin American countries have not yet established a focal point in government devoted to thinking about medium- to long-term strategies; in those countries where such a focal point does exist, its capacity for strategic thinking and influence atrophied during the ideological age of structural reforms or has been captured by the dynamics of the political cycle. Here again multilateral institutions can provide assistance in developing, or strengthening, a "neurological" center in Latin American governments to support strategic thinking, the development of pragmatic strategies, and their execution using sound modern industrial policies.

State bureaucracies in Latin America also probably should create additional space for long-term thinking by embedding complementary or specialized sister units in individual ministries and executing agencies; promoting a culture of longer-term thinking for economic policy and programs within these entities would help to override any remaining "path dependency" on the short termism of the market era fundamentalism. Periodic "future studies" exercises would be another way, in addition to structured alliance forums, for the public sector as a whole to engage with civil society in strategic thinking.

A critical factor in our extraregional success cases is government leadership in the area of productive transformation—both the active political leadership of the top level of government (president, prime minister, vice president, or deputy prime minister) and the leadership of a dedicated ministry or executing agency with appropriate technical manpower, strong top management, and the financial resources to implement agreed priority mandates. Neither of these types of leadership is common in Latin America. The presence of political leadership in priority areas tends to be a formality, transitory, or nonexistent. And designated ministries and their agencies tend to be politically or technically weak, face diffuse or competing mandates, and are unable to mobilize adequate resources from the general budget.

Coordination is as important as leadership in implementing a strategy. Most of our success cases use multiple instruments to achieve coordination in priority areas of the strategy. Coordination in the central government is another big shortcoming of execution in Latin America. Mandates among ministries and executing agencies often are unclear, creating duplication and excessive turf wars, even including the bureaucratic drama of stronger ministries unilaterally carrying out wholesale "raids" on established mandates of weaker ministries.[7] Where they exist, assigned coordinating agencies may have insufficient power to coordinate, because of either shortages of technically qualified staff and top management or an inferior position in the bureaucracy's hierarchy. In federated states, the task of coordinating actions of the central government and the states can be extremely difficult. Some type of formal or tacit division of labor might overcome those difficulties. Alternatively, state modules of the overall national program could be developed and monitored, as Brazil is trying to do with its Productive Development Policy.

Another dimension of execution is effective management of incentives. This is a vast area where Latin America can learn much from many of our success cases. Some, but far from all, of the major points of attention would be:

- Incentive programs should have clear ex ante quantifiable objectives; assessment of risks, including private sector firms' "gaming" the incentives; and procedures to manage those risks using administrative procedures that balance rigor with timeliness and the need to avoid an undue burden on beneficiary firms.
- In the framework of coordination, it is important to integrate the application of programs and incentives. When programs and incentives are designed in discrete compartments, as is often the case in Latin America, there is the risk of "gaps" in coverage of critically interrelated activities that undermine the synergies needed to achieve strategic objectives. This lack of attention to more integrated programs design not only leads to gaps but also dulls awareness of the need to upgrade support programs to meet more complex objectives as firms progressively overcome obstacles and are ready to master new capabilities.
- At the same time priorities need to be established in the set of integrated programs to avoid the common flaw in the region of having too few resources chasing too many objectives, eroding the legitimacy and effectiveness of any single program.
- In Latin America an incentive program often becomes an entitlement. Hence, incentive programs should be a consistent response to the agreed strategy for productive transformation and not an ad hoc response to special lobbies. Sunset clauses can help ensure that incentive programs are automatically evaluated and withdrawn when the support is no longer needed or when objectives are not being met.
- Rigorous evaluation of support programs must occur on a regular basis and be explicitly incorporated in the cost of administration. Moreover, the evaluation must focus on the impact of the program in meeting ex ante indicators of the objectives for productive transformation, such as productivity, quality, innovative products and processes, and new market penetration. This kind of evaluation is technically very challenging and a new area for governments to undertake, but an inevitable one for effective strategies and the embedded autonomy of the public sector.
- As industrial policy matures, incentive programs will increasingly focus on supporting innovation for a "leap" to new and upgraded activities or products. Support will naturally have a higher risk of failure than incrementalism. Hence, there is a need for some tolerance of losses, which can be nevertheless mitigated by good strategy

and program design aided by rigorous evaluation. In activities such as discovery of new cost-feasible activities and innovation, where experimentation is a key objective, a support program with a very high rate of success is probably a flawed program. Nevertheless, as we saw in Finland and Ireland, if program design gets it mostly right (and commitment to rigorous evaluation is a critical support tool), the subsidies contained in incentives can actually be an investment in growth that generates a fiscal return.

• Latin America needs to build the five basic instruments deployed by our success cases to avoid state capture: development of a highly motivated and professional civil service; a representative public-private alliance; transparency; regular and rigorous evaluation of the strategy, executing agencies, and support programs; and codes of conduct and prudential procedures for public and private players of the alliance.

Where to Begin?

Latin American countries are in very different states of development and have different state capacities, none of which mirror those observed in most of our success cases. Nevertheless, almost all Latin American countries have experience in horizontal state interventions, and many have moved toward more focused IP "in the small" (strengthening existing comparative advantage or already emerging new activities with clear signs of success). As mentioned, some like Brazil, and to a lesser extent Colombia and Chile, have embarked on IP in the large too (promotion of basically new activities, products, and sectors).[8] Governments should work on incremental improvements in their current setting.

First, where possible, more political and technical capital has to be invested in diagnosing and strengthening the institutional design and governance of public-private alliances along the lines discussed here and in chapter 3. Where political and technical capital is not available, consideration should be given to launching experimental pilot programs at the national (or at sectoral or regional levels where interests are more homogeneous). In designing pilot alliances, aside from some of the governance issues raised in this book, special care should be taken in assessing the traditional nature of the interaction of the relevant parties, their interests, relationships with the government, and disposition to consensus building, because these factors will help tailor realistic objectives and the composition of representation. Deepening the alliances' interaction with the public bureaucracy by securing their participation on executing agencies' boards of directors and advisory panels should also be on the agenda. We would also council less trepidation about internationalizing the alliance through encouraging representation of cooperative multinationals with economically important operations in the country of strategic interest and about creating international advisory panels in strategic areas to support IP formulation as well as to have more "antennas" in international networks.[9]

Second, parallel to strengthening the design and governance of alliances, there should be major investment in strengthening state capacity in the areas discussed above. Improving capacity should be treated with the urgency of a "national emergency." It will require political leadership and consensus building because existing public resources will have to be reallocated and new resources mobilized through a more solid tax base than is found in most Latin American countries.

Third, and closely linked to the two previous points, governments must tighten the design and management of interventions to enhance their effectiveness for support of private sector upgrading and in a prudent manner that minimizes risk of state capture.

Finally, multilateral development agencies in Washington should rethink their traditional skepticism about industrial policy and embrace the concept as an historically valid, pragmatic tool for supporting catchup. This will not be easy given their path dependency on the Washington Consensus era. However, in recent years thinking about industrial policies has strongly evolved, and a modern school of thought has much to offer the region. Moreover, countries in Latin America are moving ahead to explore the IP tool on their own anyway. We hope the multilateral agencies will catch up in their own thinking and accompany Latin America in doing it right this time.[10]

With political awareness and leadership at home, deliberation and nationally oriented problem solving by high-level representatives of civil society in public-private policy alliances, a state organized to build a professional civil service with the capacity to technically lead and effectively implement the right industrial policies, and a little pragmatic help and encouragement from their multilateral friends, the region's countries will be better positioned to generate the strategic directions for productive transformation that are needed "to make" Latin American economies tigers too.

Notes

1. Many countries, such as Finland and Sweden in our group of success cases, have experienced catch-up starting with a base of natural resources. However, they proactively pursued policies that supported the progressive adding of value and encouraged migration to new, upgraded, and more knowledge-based activities in manufacturing. Natural resources per se are not a "curse," as some have argued, but catch-up depends on exploiting these resources in a way that makes them a platform for adopting ever more sophisticated activities with endogenous processes of learning, capacity building, absorption of technology, and innovation (Stijns 2001). Meanwhile, although the Caribbean Basin, stimulated by U.S. trade preferences, has significantly diversified its exports, only limited progress has

been made in using these preferences as a platform for more than just low-wage employment.

2. The closer a country comes to the technological frontier, the more diffuse and subtle industrial policies become. They rarely disappear altogether, however, as happens in most developed countries (Lin and Monga, 2010).

3. The policy often has been a response to some interest group. Moreover, as we observed in chapter 7, layers of IP were superimposed on each other through inertia as government succeeded government, creating an "archeological park" of incentives, often inconsistent with each other or with economic transformation.

4. Kurtz and Brooks (2008) call these state-mediated supply-side interventions a less orthodox type of "embedded neoliberalism."

5. There unfortunately is a "refounding syndrome" in Latin America that seems to make new governments abandon the microeconomic objectives (when they exist) of the previous government and start at "zero kilometer." This tendency in part reflects a lack of consensus about the long-term objectives of the country.

6. In Malaysia the alliance by law must give preferences to the native Malay population, a mandate originally perhaps useful for social cohesion but increasingly recognized to be in need of adjustment. The Irish Alliance, once considered by some to be the gold standard, has fallen into difficulty for several reasons, some of which are related to a progressive and excessive institutional dispersion of its governance.

7. Raids have occurred frequently in conjunction with negotiation of trade agreements, especially when these were hot topics in the 1990s. This same phenomenon of raids is reoccurring in the new hot topic: national competitiveness and innovation.

8. IP also can be used for an organized "death" of uncompetitive industries that minimizes destruction of skills and knowledge that are useful for new activities.

9. Many of the old battles with foreign corporations were in natural resource extraction where there were large rents to be distributed. This is much less an issue in competitive manufacturing and services.

10. A recent working paper coauthored by the World Bank's chief economist is an encouraging sign (Lin and Monga, 2010).

References

Adelman, Irma. 2000. "Fifty Years of Economic Development: What Have We Learned?" Paper presented at the World Bank ABC Conference, Washington, DC (June).

Evans, Peter. 1995. *Embedded Autonomy. States and Industrial Transformation.* Princeton, NJ: Princeton University Press.

Hausmann, Ricardo, Dani Rodrik, and Charles Sabel. 2008. "Reconfiguring Industrial Policy: A Framework with an Application to South Africa." CID Working Paper 168, Center for International Development, Harvard University, Cambridge, MA (May).

Kurtz, Marcus, and Sarah Brooks. 2008. "Embedding Neoliberal Reform in Latin America." *World Politics* (January).

Lin, Justin Yifu, and Célestin Monga. 2010. "Growth Identification and Facilitation: The Role of the State in the Dynamics of Structural Change." Policy Working Paper 5313, World Bank, Washington, DC (May).

Sabel, Charles. 2009. "What Industrial Policy Is Becoming: Taiwan, Ireland and Finland as Guides to the Future of Industrial Policy." Columbia Law School. http://idbdocs.iadb.org/wsdocs/getDocument.aspx?DOCNUM=1843147.

Stijns, Jean Philippe. 2001. "Natural Resource Abundance and Economic Growth Revisited." University of California, Berkeley (March).

Index

coordination of policy
implementation, 217-18,
218, 219*f*7.1
export development
instruments to promote,
222*t*7.2, 226, 227*f*7.3,
232*n*11
ministries and agencies
involved in, 208-9*t*7.1
and financial resources link to
leadership in, 216
ICT in, 226, 227*f*7.3
incentives to promote
development goals, 221
innovation promotion,
222*t*7.2, 226, 227*f*7.3,
232*n*11
national development plans
and strategies, 159*t*6.1,
161-62, 194-95
post-Washington Consensus,
166, 167*f*6.1, 201*nn*6-7
public-private alliances, 176*t*6.3,
187-88
role of planning in, 161-62,
201*n*4
and use of forecasting
exercises, 216
Brazilian Industrial Development
Agency (ABDI), 218,
219*f*7.1
Brown, Gordon, 15
budgets, 239
for agencies, 216-17, 232*nn*7-8
Chile, 230-31
for development plans, 162
and policy implementation, 216
bureaucratization, 230
business promotion policies,
Mexico, 226, 232*nn*12-13
business sector, and public-private
alliances, 189-92

C

Calderon, President FIRST
NAME, 216

capacity building, 247
education as element of, 53,
73*n*28
and forecasting exercises,
215-16
and industrial policies, 42
in SMEs, 137
capitalism, 38, 71*n*5
capital-to-output ratios, 17
capture
minimizing risk of private sector
capture of government,
148-50, 153*n*7
see also state capture
Casa Civil, Brazil, 218, 219*f*7.1
centralization, 220
Chile, 173, 212
agencies in, 209*t*7.1, 228
budget department, 230-31
characteristics of strategies and
plans in, 164*t*6.2
evaluation of public policies in,
231, 232*n*20
export development, 118,
209*t*7.1, 223*t*7.2
finance ministry, 230-31
and financial resources link to
leadership, 217
incentives to promote
development goals, 221
income in, 13, 235
innovation promotion, 118,
223*t*7.2
national development plans,
159*t*6.1, 195-96
public-private alliances, 176*t*6.3,
181*t*6.4, 186-87, 192-93
salary comparisons, 214-15
transparency law, 229, 232*n*18
and Washington Consensus,
29*nn*17-18
post-Washington Consensus,
170-71, 202*n*15
China, 41, 71*n*9, 190, 236
CINDE. *see* Coalition of
Development Initiatives
(CINDE), Costa Rica

www.ingramcontent.com/pod-product-compliance
Lightning Source LLC
Chambersburg PA
CBHW050704280326
41926CB00088B/2449